Retired Not Dead:
Thoughts Plastic Surgical and Otherwise

First published in
Great Britain in 2008
by Artnik Books

Artnik Books is an imprint of A Jot Publishing
UK address:
Suite 774, 28 Old Brompton Rd
London SW7 3SS, UK

© Robert M. Goldwyn
All rights reserved. No part
of this publication may be
reproduced, stored in or
introduced into a retrieval
system, or transmitted in any
form or by any means (electronic,
mechanical, photocopying, recording
or otherwise) without the prior
written permission of both the
copyright owner and the
publisher of this book.

ISBN: 978-1-905904-42-6
Design: Jay Huggins

Retired Not Dead:
Thoughts Plastic Surgical and Otherwise

Robert M. Goldwyn

artnik books

Dedication

**With love to my wife Tanya,
our children and our grandchildren**

PREFACE

To those who may have thought that my retirement as Editor of *Plastic and Reconstructive Surgery* would stop my pen (I have yet to learn how to use the computer), this volume should end that speculation. It may be welcomed or not, depending upon opinions for or against me, personal or literary or both.

When someone asked H.L. Mencken, the Baltimore editor and critic, why he wrote, he answered, 'For the same reason a hen lays eggs.' The obvious difference is that for the hen the urge is inborn; for me, it was acquired.

The title of this book reflects the defiance of this 77-year-old, like others of similar vintage or older: the desire to be counted and not counted out while still viable and 'taking nourishment,' as a medical colleague in his fifties used to reply when asked how he was. I hope that I am doing more than merely eating and drinking. To prove that to myself, I have written this book. Anyone who attempts to record his or her thoughts about life and about his or her work has to be self-revealing, engaged in not only something autobiographical but, particularly someone of my age, in a kind of 'summing-up,' a phrase of Somerset Maugham with regard to his life's story.

The young generally look ahead because there is more ahead; oldsters have more behind them than in front. And so it is with some parts of this book.

As the title states, I am a plastic surgeon or was for half my life. I chose my career and lived it with no regrets. This does not mean, however, that I could not have done things better or more wisely.

PREFACE

Retirement, as I began to realize and finally have learned to accept, is an inevitable phase for most, not necessarily all, who have worked within a technologically based society which demands skills and energy. When one is a young surgeon and doing what one likes, one enjoys what would seem to outsiders to be days that are excessively long with too much stress, the prospect of retiring – of laying down the knife if one is a surgeon – is depressing, so much so that I remember repressing the thought of it and vowed that I would deal with it in the future. Yet, retirement comes to us or, perhaps more correctly, we come to it and surprisingly it is not as fearsome as we had once imagined. For a doctor whose life and labors have made a positive difference in the lives of others, retirement is a harrowing specter. I was afraid that I would no longer be important or worse, that I would no longer truly matter, except to family and friends.

When much younger, I confess that I looked upon the majority of retirees as being good consumers, self indulgent even though I recognize that they had deserved to be able to play golf, dine out, attend musical events and exhibitions, whenever they wished. They had earned their leisure and had the savings to pay for it. Nevertheless, I thought that they were passing time until the next stage, the final one. Now being among them, my views have softened, undoubtedly as a means of self-protection. Those who have retired are called in French *retraites*, which connotes retreating; the Italians are more realistic when they call retirees *pensionati* – pensioners. The startling percentage of American citizens who no longer work depend for survival only on social security – without even a trace of pension fund or any kind of IRA. I am fortunate that I am not in that category although that I realize that except for accidents of birth and different circumstances, I could well have been.

Since I do not need to generate an income by taking another job, I have unscheduled time but there is a difference between that and 'free time.' I will talk about later in this book the curious phenomenon of those who might have secretly yearned to be unfettered and then when the opportunity has arisen, flee from it. To my credit I was able to thwart that compulsive drive in myself even though this book is proof that I had to do something but at least it was on my own terms with respect to time. Gone were those days over those many years when I was a slave to the

PREFACE

system even though I may not have realized it; when I was a prisoner of my own rigidity and that of fixed time allotments in the operating room and in my office. From an existential sense we may have free will but it is less than we think when we must confront the exigencies of life.

Now it is different for me and can be for anyone else who has the desire or capacity for reflection. Every day is longer than what it used to be. If one is so inclined, one can follow the sun, observe that gradations of light as our earth moves around it (maybe Copernicus was wrong).

A lot happens in a day and a bewildering amount in a lifetime, even a short one but certainly in someone who has lived 77 years. No diary, no continuous audiovisual recording could capture and reproduce even in a half day what transpires in an individual's life, outer and inner. True activities can be noted and recorded in an appointment book or a diary but even Samuel Pepys could not encompass everything. Consider also James Joyce's magnificent attempt in **Ulysses.** If that literary miracle had been much longer or the author, excruciatingly more obsessive, Leopold Bloom in its entirety would yet remain beyond the pale of being fully revealed. The obituary pages of a daily newspaper record in skeletal fashion the lives of those whom society or the editors consider important. It is the lives of those whose deaths have been simply listed into which I would like to delve. I believe that every person's existence is significant. Nothing illustrates my point better than Jules Romains' short masterpiece, **The Death of a Nobody.** The message is that everybody is a somebody and for me, while I am not the generic everyman (is there such?) I am also not an extraterrestrial alien. My thoughts may be idiosyncratic (or worse, idiotic) but they still have, I hope, sufficient universality to be meaningful to readers.

Robert M. Goldwyn

Acknowledgments

I am grateful beyond expression to Frank S. Sivacek, who shepherded this book from dictation on tape to hard copy and finally to its electronic form. Without his talent and support and that of his wife Jane and their friendship, this book would never have appeared.

My publisher, Countess Valentina Joulebina, deserves special recognition and thanks. From the outset, she understood why I wanted to write this book. Her encouragement, counsel and insight have been remarkable. Her staff also have been invaluable supporters. I am deeply appreciative.

CONTENTS

Preface	9
Everyone Likes to Advise a Retiree	13
The Delights of Deceleration	16
Operating at Night – Sort of	18
So You Were a Plastic Surgeon	21
What Did You Do Before You Retired?	24
Plastic Surgeons Age Too	28
Work	30
Dear Lord, Where Did I Go Wrong?	32
The Lady With The Dog	34
When Two Retired Doctors Meet	37
Why I Part My Hair On The Right	40
Life Is A Supermarket	50
You Can Retire But You Can't Hang Out	52
The Importance Of Pat Boone	54
'There Is Still Good Water In The Well'	57
Little Acts Of Random Surgery	59
Am I an Original Or A Copy?	60
Retrograde	63
W & W	65
'Plastic Surgery is Moving More and More in the Direction of Aesthetic Surgery'	67
Overhearing	69
Virtual Medical School	71
Length of Life	73
Is Truth Always A Virtue?	74
A Counterproposal to Looking Younger	76
Polaroid and I	79
Hospital Politics: A Nosocomial Disease	81
Ethics – The Non-abstract Kind	83
Progress Is Not For Everyone	86
Community Service – Medical Style	87
Take My Identity – Please!	88
Can I Age Without Becoming Cynical or More So?	92
Compensation and the Computer	94
'Burglarious'	95
The Holding-on Generation	97
Horror of Horrors: A Sick Doctor Among Us!	99
Cosmetic Surgery with Spirituality	100
The Charity Conundrum	105
A World of One's Own	107
'Live Richly' !or?	108
Saving Money During Retirement	110
When Residents Graduate – Finally	112
Brevities	114
It's the Mission, not the Money	119
No Hope, No Medicine	122
Who Will Remember Us	125
Memory: Don't Leave Home Without it	127
'Getting to Know You'	129
Willing Regression	130
Jean-Paul, Simone, Albert and I	132
The Art of Getting it Right	137
Why Be A Doctor	
When You Can Be An Endorser	136
Wanting More	137
Staying Power	139
I Laugh Now But I Didn't Then	140
The Age of Nefarious	142
'Something Old, Something New, Something Borrowed, Something Blue'	145
Advice To The Lifeworn: Do Less, Live More	146
The Sameness of it All	149
Primum Nocere, Secundum?	150
Retirement: Time for Savoring Tidbits	152
Let Them Take Steroids	155
Driven Crazy	157
For Some Another Obstacle on the Road to Cosmetic Surgery	160
'But Their Appearance Was Overrepresented'	161
My Shoes were too Big for My Feet	163
Names	164
Vestigial Activity	167
The Joy of Being Unscheduled	169
A Self-Made Self-Inventor	172
Shredding	174
The Little King	178

CONTENTS

The Portrait	179
Achieving The Impossible: Making Sex Boring	181
Helping and Teaching Children and Residents	183
Hurricane Katrina: Some Lessons Learned, More Forgotten	185
Be Exclusive, Buy a Maybach	187
'Besame Mucho' ('Kiss Me A Lot')	188
What Remains? Not Much	190
Excellence Is Where You Find It	193
'Sauve Qui Peut'	194
Another Triumph for Trial Attorneys	197
You Are As Old As You Are – Even To A Real Estate Agent	199
Three Cheers (silently of course) for the Library	201
An Ode to Jell-o	203
Seven Pins: Learning from a Shirt	204
The Ultimate Smart Car	205
Das Kar-pital	208
Be Careful Whom You Call Fat	209
Benign and Malignant - Uninvited Guests Within Us	212
Going Public	214
Languages	215
Death of a Flap	217
Jack Armstrong, Where Are You Now That We Need You?	218
Self-Destruction as a Sport	220
'Brush Like A Dentist'	222
Inconsistency	223
Operating Room Talk	225
Now for Some Questions	227
The Folly of Extreme Behavior	228
Long Talks, Long Walks	229
'Doctor, Can You Give Me an Idea of What I Will Look Like After My Facelift'	231
Irrationality: The Inexhaustible Fuel	235
Enjoying the Tidbits	236
William T. Bovie and His Theory of Social Behavior	238
Compromises Along the Way	241
From Pediatrician to Gerontologist	242
Planning For the Future: Some Cool Thoughts	244
Seeing Without Feeling	245
Memory: the Miraculous Attic or Basement	247
How to be More Than You Are	248
How Scientific Am I? Not as Much as I Should Be	250
Life Smarts	252
Ratio	253
Are You Happy?	256
'Nuanced Decision'	257
The Olympics and Plastic Surgery	260
Pes Anserinus	262
The Curse of Alzheimer's in Reverse	264
The Worst Battle to Lose	265
Perspective for Self-preservation	266
Fenway Park 60 Years Later	267
'He Is At That Time In His Life'	268
Looking at Your Looks	269
Blackberries in Winter	271
There's Agony and There's Agony	273
Aesthetic Surgery and Beyond, Inc.	274
The Photograph	277
Spas for Kids: Just What Our Society Needs	278
PSA 6	280
How to Make Relaxation Into Work	281
'Listening with the Third Ear' – Even One Will Do	282
Learning Along the Way	285
Advertising and Marketing in Plastic Surgery: Uncomfortable Realities	286
Viagra®: a Symbol of Our Times	288
Not Hearing a Complaint Doesn't Mean There Isn't One	290
Fragments	292
Epilogue	295

Fear no more the heat o' th' sun,
Nor the furious winter's rages.
Thou thy worldly task hast done,
Home art gone and ta'en thy wages.
        [Shakespeare: Cymbeline, act 4, sc. 2]

Everyone Likes to Advise a Retiree

Before I retired and even now I have been the recipient, not necessarily a beneficiary, of advice about what to do at this time in my life. I did not solicit these suggestions but I confess I was more grateful than resentful that others, such as family, friends, and even strangers made an effort to be helpful. Some of my unofficial advisors were retirees, a number of them, physicians. One of them told me that he had never been happier than when he retired and he used the word 'ecstatic' but he had never been successful and always struggled to grow a meager surgical practice.

Many were correct in their intuition that while I might not disintegrate in the throes of excessive free time, I could become depressed if I were left unstructured. This thought occurred to me frequently and I did experience a let-down for a week or two after my official retirement. I am thankful that its duration was brief.

Here are some of the recommendations.

'Join the Elks; my brother-in-law did and he loves it.' From the security guard in my office building. I have nothing against Elks either in the wild or as a group. However, the thought of committing myself to scheduled meetings and parties with those whom I would likely not know was forbidding. The once over scheduled part of me rebelled at the prospect of more 'must-shows.' In the 37½ years of surgical practice and in my continuing the editorship of *Plastic and Reconstructive Surgery*, every day was crammed with things to do, with start times in the operating room and office hours and with respect to the Journal, unrelenting correspondence and submissions which I could not in good conscience allow to go unattended for more than 24 hours unless I was away. Maybe I had a mild case of Post Traumatic Stress Syndrome!

'Do volunteer work at the hospital.' A frequent suggestion. But what would I actually do? Would I man a desk? If so at the same hospital where I had been Chief of Plastic Surgery? I am ashamed to admit that it would be, to use an old fashioned phrase, 'a come down' – not so much with regard to my previous role or status but to what I would now be doing for patients and their families compared to what I had done for them in the past. Somerset Maugham, whom I quoted previously, observed correctly that the problem with old age is not so much getting older but having been younger. For some reason peculiar to me, I remembered having gone with my wife to visit Alcatraz and having met someone who had been a prisoner 'on the rock' for ten years. He was promoting his book and did so in a friendly and charming way, so much so that I could not reconcile what I saw before me to what he must have been to have warranted confinement to Alcatraz for a decade. In short, the present edition did not jibe with the past. Would I appear this way to others? But, of more consequence, would I have that sentiment about myself?

'Do volunteer work with Interplast or similar organizations.' Obvious excellent advice but after brutal self-appraisal, I reasoned that my current surgical skills would not meet the needs of those whom I would be asked to treat. The emphasis in my practice was on problems of the breast not cleft lip – palate or microsurgery or hand surgery. I would certainly be capable of skin grafting acute burns and their sequelae. How many of those patients would I likely see? I did not want to do aesthetic surgery in a technologically lagging country. I would not want to travel a great distance and be the responsibility of not just the group who was sponsoring the trip but of my hosts unless I could contribute significantly – in a role far more than being an onlooker.

Many years ago when I was an intern at the then Peter Bent Brigham Hospital in Boston, I wrote to Doctor Albert Schweitzer in Lambarene to offer my services. He wisely replied exhorting me to become a fully trained surgeon so I could 'be of more use.' Incidentally my chance came four years later when I became his general surgeon for a couple of months at the end of my general surgical training. Admittedly I was not even then a seasoned surgeon.

In brief the underserved should not be subjected to the undertrained. It is not only the young who fit that category.

'Teach medical students.' This was certainly a possibility and I would be able to complement what I do now with respect to medical students who rotate through the Plastic Surgical Service at the Beth Israel Deaconess Medical Center whose weekly conferences I try to attend and have done so almost regularly. In that setting I believe I can contribute and my colleagues, Dr. Sumner Slavin and his staff, have welcomed me warmly. Yet I do not believe that I would be the best teacher of medical students for something more basic, such as physical diagnosis. Would I be able to pick up easily the murmur of mitral stenosis, something I prided myself doing when I was early in practice? I could serve as a mentor but I am reaching the point where I would be out of touch with what is new and exciting in areas not my specialty. The reader by now must think that I am simply offering excuses not to get properly involved. Perhaps, but I doubt it. I did want to make a choice to do something I truly desired and this book is its fruition (perhaps there will be others).

'Take extension courses at a university – such as Harvard.' While I am not against knowledge and certainly not when offered by my alma mater (college and medical school), I realize that I like to read and study what I want when I want – again not within the strictures and pace similar to what I experienced in my work.

Oscar Wilde once remarked 'Why kill love with marriage,' something I do not believe but what occurred to me was why kill learning and the pleasure from it with assignments? I remember thinking that when I was an undergraduate at Harvard that it would be a wonderful place to study if I had no exams. How often did I feel when I was overly busy that medicine would be wonderful if we did not have to see patients. This is obviously a ridiculous oxymoron to those who are practitioners but, as I was recently told by my doctor, the 'cool thing now is to go into something other than taking care of patients – such as working as a dean or for industry.' That was the aim, he said, of many who are in their late 40s. This to someone my age was extraordinary to hear.

'Become a consultant.' This suggestion from friends who thought that an independent opinion 'from a plastic surgeon who was not operating but was knowledgeable' would be valuable to patients. While I believe that theoretically there is a need for this, I am not sure that practically it or I would be viable. Patients go for second or multiple opinions to surgeons who they believe might operate on them or provide non-operative treatment, such as dermabrasion, laser, injection of fillers both synthetic and autologous such as fat. I believe also that for me at my age to build a practice as that kind of consultant would take more time than I have to spare or the Lord has allotted me!

'Learn Chinese – don't have free time.' That I found in a fortune cookie. I have decided to limit my acquaintance with Chinese to going to restaurants and revisiting China and Taiwan.

The Delights of Deceleration

If we are truthful, we are more likely to believe that everyone is different when we think about ourselves than when we think about others. Some with poor self-esteem may not perceive their own individuality. This has never been a problem for me undoubtedly due in large measure to my having been an only child. I never lacked attention from my parents who, however, though fostering self-confidence in me, disallowed any show of arrogance or conceit. Through the years my father's saying has reverberated: 'Never toot your own horn. If you are any good, others will recognize it.' He coupled that frequently with another unforgettable maxim: 'The empty barrel makes the most noise.'

My faith in my own abilities never led me to think that the laws of Nature did not apply to me. Maybe I was an unrecognized neurotic in my childhood but I recognized that I was not exempt from the malevolence of chance, accidents, aging, disease and ultimately death. The fact that my father was a physician, a neuropsychiatrist, exposed me to the human condition as seen from the viewpoint of a doctor.

The laws of Newton and Einstein I neither wish nor am I able to dodge and least able to understand. Now I am more conscious of another law that I do comprehend: the one that C. Northcote Parkinson enunciated (***The Economist***, November 19, 1955):

'Work expands so as to fill the time available for its completion.'

Goldwyn's Law, which few know and fewer will remember, is: 'The retiree will always find something to do.' The corollary is that 'The retiree is more likely to convert non-work into work than the reverse.'

Consider that it has taken 77 years to perfect – imperfect myself (the latter more the reality)- almost fourscore years to create a potpourri of inconsistencies but I now discover that Parkinson's Law defines me, lays me bare, not letting me hide among my idiosyncrasies. In short, I am like almost everyone else at this stage in life.

Einstein's Theory of Relativity applies to me also in my ignorant interpretation: 'Time seems to have slowed and I, with it.' While I have not become, so I think, lethargic or listless, I am no longer revved up, a chronic speed for most physicians. Compared to pre-retirement, whatever I do, requiring physical exertion, is in slow motion, except for my self-imposed two mile a morning walk at what is objectively a semi-brisk pace. For everything else, leisure has replaced haste; minutes subtly elongate. And miracle of miracles, there are enough hours in the day ('Yes, Virginia, there is a Santa Claus').

For example, going to the post office or bank becomes not just something to get out of the way but a relaxed expedition.

For most days of the week I begin the day when I want not when I must. I take more time to lather my face, to select from among three razors the one I wish to use that morning – all this I do enjoyably. I am also more closely shaved than ever since I can pass and re-pass the razor(s) as many times as I want without anxiously consulting a clock.

Since I do not need to huff and pant to be at the hospital for rounds and then in the operating room by 7:30 a.m., I let time go by me, no longer hurtling through it. The title of Kundera's book ***The Unbearable Lightness of Being*** describes the new me. I can well empathize with how Javier De Cuellar, the Peruvian Secretary General of the United Nations, said after he retired: 'I am a free man. I feel as light as feather.' It would take several months, perhaps years, with Weight Watchers for me to reach that stage but there is a freedom in shedding tasks. Maybe it is that I never ran the UN and had to confront the excruciating problems that besieged the Secretary General but I do not want to feel totally unfettered. The paradox is that the joy of the proper retirement for me lies in the latitude of being able to choose the what, the when and the how of spending one's time. I would not like to be free of everything and everyone. Even though I tell myself and my wife, who now laughs at me when I say that I am a recluse, I realize that I am not. I need connections, personal and social. Writing this book is testimony to my need not to remain an island. Yet I do not wish to replicate my previous life by compulsively rushing around to keep busy. I have come to admire even more the butterfly who flies around, gracefully, unhurriedly but then alights at a pleasant place from time to time.

In our society and for most people during most of their lives they become slaves to quantity rather than quality. In retirement the opposite is true, perhaps due to the realization that depth and breadth of each day is more important than the number, which is not as large as we would like. Although Kafka was right when he said 'The thing about life is that it stops.' I would add that this being so, the thing about life is to make the best use of each moment we have, but few do.

Operating at Night... Sort of

Plastic Surgeons operate: that is our identity and, in fact, the logo of the American Society of Plastic Surgeons is a knife carrying Venus Di Milo.

When I was a general surgical resident at the then Peter Bent Brigham Hospital in Boston, Dr. John Brooks, on the attending staff, used to say: 'Whenever you operate, you get a good feeling in the pit of your stomach.' He was referring to the satisfaction that comes when a surgeon is doing what he or she is supposed to do.

I recall when unexpectedly a patient had to have an operation canceled, usually because of a respiratory infection, I experienced a letdown although I welcomed the free time. Though lacking data, I believe that for male surgeons the act of operating is a act of masculinity. A psychoanalyst might say (although I had never heard one say it) that putting the knife into someone else symbolically represents a phallic thrust.

Several retired surgeons have told me that they longed to go into the operating room whenever they enter a hospital – any hospital – perhaps to attend a lecture or rounds or visiting a sick friend. I see that same look in the eye when retired baseball players are interviewed on television and gaze wistfully at the playing field and at those who are still active.

While we surgeons may not miss the long hours, the emergencies, the complications and the emotionally difficult patient, most have nostalgia for the importance and the excitement of their work and the gratification we got from captaining a surgical team or teaching and directing residents and students. More than all that was the pleasure of getting an idea in the operating room of what hopefully the anatomical result would be and foreseeing, again hopefully, the improvement that we would make in a patient's life.

While it is true that some older surgeons who have stopped operating continue in office practice, I sense that for them it is the second best thing but they are grateful, nevertheless, for still being able to be an active, useful wage-earner.

A surprising statistic is that the average age of general surgeons who retire is about 60. Dr. Frances D. Moore, the Moseley Professor of Surgery at Harvard Medical School and my Chief of Surgery at the Peter Bent Brigham Hospital, once said that 'Someone 70 shouldn't be sticking a knife into anybody else.' He said this without any attempt at a psychoanalytic interpretation.

Under the Americans with Disability Act no surgeon healthy and competent can be told when to retire because of age. Astonishing now to me is realizing that Joe Di Maggio left the New York Yankees at 35 at his volition. In contrast I worked until my seventies and thought it not unusual, perhaps because my father, a neuropsychiatrist, was seeing patients until he was 84, a few months before his death.

Robert M. Goldwyn

During these five years since I stopped operating, I have pleasant daydreams about being in the operating room but more often, I have nightmares in my sleep when I am thinking about surgery, I am almost always in trouble. Just the other night, for example, I dreamed I was doing a facelift on the wife of the Chairman of the Board of Trustees and encountered profuse, uncontrollable bleeding. I was desperately packing the wound to no avail when mercifully, I awakened and was ecstatic to know that I did not have to deal with that horror.

I thought that I was having these nocturnal tortures because a great deal of my career was devoted to recording unfavorable results in plastic surgery. I hasten to add that these were not all mine! But other retired once very competent plastic surgeons have told me that they also have had operating room nightmares. For one of my friends it was nicking the intercostal artery during reconstructing the breast with an implant; for another surgeon it was a pneumothorax during breast reduction.

These nightmares peculiar to surgical retirees are probably no different from those that I and my classmates had and subsequently discussed during our college and medical school reunions. Many of my classmates at college recalled their nocturnal anxiety when they were rushing to submit a paper but failed to do so on time. In the lenient era of today, that probably would not have been a problem. Now teachers are more likely to be punished than students.

The common denominator of all these nightmares is botching the job, failing to meet a responsibility. A psychiatrist friend said that these nocturnal phantoms were more likely to happen to good students or those successful in later life.

Many years ago I visited a church in Seville and was told about a well-known priest who on his deathbed said he regretted that he had not prepared and delivered his sermons to his satisfaction and that of others.

I confess to another side of this phenomenon of my surgical nightmares. They take me back to the operating room and although the experience is unpleasant, I am still operating.

'So You Were A Plastic Surgeon'

A few years before I closed my practice, I wrote an editorial 'So You're a Plastic Surgeon,' which read in part: 'The sequence is too familiar, you go to a party and someone, usually a woman, accosts you because she has found out that you are a plastic surgeon. She puts her hands to her face, pulls the skin back and asks: "Would a facelift help?"

'How do you respond? You can feign deafness or tell her that she has mistaken you, a stratagem successful only if nobody else recognizes you. You could say that you never give consultations except at the office or the hospital, or you could tell her that the present lack of privacy and the poor lighting prevents proper examination. Even if the room is brilliantly illuminated, you can indict the lighting as being inadequate.

'The best reply for you and her is that she does not need a facelift – if this is true, but you have likely rendered an opinion without careful appraisal. But what if you believe that a facelift would benefit her significantly? To tell her may be the reality, but few like to hear it. If you are entrepreneurial, you could hand her your card.'

Now that I am retired, the situation is different. The opener, usually still likely from a women, is: 'So you were a plastic surgeon.' The inquiry is not from a perspective patient for you. You are off one hook but on another. You will probably be asked your opinion of another plastic surgeon whom she has already seen and with whom she may have scheduled an operation.

As before when I was in practice, the procedure concerns most probably a facelift – a part of the body visible under cocktail conditions. You might have used inadequate lighting as a way of having dodged the query when you were in practice but you are more relaxed about the situation.

If you know the surgeon she has named and his or her work and it is good, your reply is simple and can be supportive both to the patient and the surgeon. If you have no knowledge of the plastic surgeon, your response is also simple: you enter a plea of ignorance.

Robert M. Goldwyn

The problem arises when you have had numerous unpleasant experiences with that surgeon or perhaps have heard reports about his or her character, judgment and skill. Under those circumstances, I behave like a physician, who though not having been consulted officially still maintains a license although no practice. Some might justifiably dispute my decision but I believe my primary obligation is to the patient although she is not mine. In short, I will suggest that he or she seek another opinion and, if pressed, provide a name.

In my retirement I have had to field complaints from people whom I have first met socially about the results of their surgery. You are lucky if was done where the sun rarely shines. It would be a rare person, even a friend, who would ask another doctor, especially one retired, to examine him or her – a happening even more unlikely with someone of the opposite sex. But even if you can see and theoretically examine the area – face, eyelids, or ears or nose superficially, your recommendation to the patient should be to advise return to the surgeon for more discussion.

Occasionally the aggrieved (and grieving) patient has severed contact with that doctor and requests a name of somebody else. I have no compunction in obliging.

Now for a confession, which seems to get more frequent with age. Unfortunately I remember what de La Rochefoucauld, the 17th century writer and moralist, said: 'We confess only our little faults to persuade people that we have no big ones.'

In that spirit, I confess that despite my protestations about getting involved in some of these 'So you were a plastic surgeon' ersatz consultations, I get some satisfaction from being remembered for what I did and for being asked my opinion. Fleetingly I wish I were still seeing and caring for patients, back in my operating room clothes, still in the game, not on the sidelines or in the bleachers. The longer one is retired, the further one is from the playing field.

Friends, acquaintances and absolute strangers make an interesting and valid distinction when they comment 'So you were a plastic surgeon.' They seldom say 'So you were a doctor.' They assume that although you are retired, you continue to be a doctor because although you lack your office, you retain your degree.

Retired Not Dead

When I was in medical school, my Uncle Harris, then aged and a retired attorney, told me that he was upset the previous week when someone asked him: 'Are you still a lawyer?' He told me his reply: 'I will be a lawyer until I die.' In those days, and even now, continuing certification is not required of lawyers.

This highly specialized society assigns people according to their special skills. Therefore, 'So you were a plastic surgeon' emphasizes the species and not the genus – doctor.

For most of us death ends our earthly designations unless we are very famous, e.g., Justice Brandeis, President Roosevelt (any of the two). But there are a noble few who have made it to the Pantheon and because of their universal recognition, need no titles or first names: Aristotle, Socrates, Plato, Napoleon, Einstein, Lincoln, Freud, Marx, Hitler... the last occupying a different Pantheon.

Death ends one's earthly role but tombs may perpetuate it. The tombstone of the Athenian physician Jason, second century BC, shows him palpating a patient's abdomen and in the foreground also in relief, is a large cupping glass.

Said frequently in mockery and despair is the phrase 'Born a man, died a gastroenterologist.' This is an obvious warning about what can happen if you let your work replace your soul and it is also an exhortation to do more with your identity as a human being. What would our reaction be if we had the epitaph 'Born a man (woman), died a plastic surgeon or a liposuctionist?' The obvious answer is that we would have no response since we would have been interred. At least those who are cremated do not run the risk of being diminished by what is placed on their tombstone.

If I were to learn new techniques and to find myself in an afterlife where I had the opportunity to continue as a plastic surgeon, would I do so? In heaven, yes but not in hell, were there would be a herd of attorneys looking for dissatisfied patients.

Robert M. Goldwyn

'What Did You Do Before You Retired?'

This is obviously a companion piece to the preceding 'So You Were a Plastic Surgeon.' In the former, what you did for a living is already known. But what do you say in response to the person who asks 'What did you do before you retired?' Depending upon your mood or motive, you have available a few stratagems:

1: Deny you have retired as a plastic surgeon.

Perhaps you would say this just to be perverse; maybe in a crowd of people who have not retired, you wish to display an importance that you no longer feel as you did when you were an active surgeon.

Unfortunately saying that you are still a plastic surgeon is not just a dodge but a lie.

> O, what a tangled web we weave
> When first we practice to deceive
> [Walter Scott, **Marmion**, 1808]

Like most lies, it will catch its spinner. The person who is eager for information from you might then try to make an appointment at your non-existent office. Extricating yourself is now more difficult but you could say:

'I am renovating my office and everything is in a mess.'

But don't think you have successfully bailed out; you may have verbally decamped until she (usually a she), never one to surrender, suggests: 'I would be very happy to see you at home anytime at your convenience and, of course, I would be very happy to pay. I can speak to your secretary when I get there so she can bill me.'

Now what do you do?

You can say with finality: 'That really would be impossible.'

However, that women has aroused you – not sexually but professionally. You have been moping around the house and your wife, busy with her volunteer work, is frankly sick of your attitude and tired of you. You have become to youy wife what the joke says: 'Twice the husband and half the income.' You haven't been retired for that long – just about six years and you retained your license – God knows why but perhaps God did know all along that you might get back into the game once more.

Your devious mind begins to think creatively. You will see that patient at your home but not for another few weeks. This will give you time to establish an ersatz office and will also lead her to think that you are hopelessly scheduled.

You think more about your house and even more about your wife who will never permit you to establish an office within her four walls. Your ingenuity knows no bounds. You will hire a trailer and park it to the side in your driveway, whose length you have never liked particularly in winter when you have had to shovel it clear. You will call the local colleges – the personnel office. There must be some undergraduate or graduate student who will come for the day that you will see as your 'first' patient in this new era of your life. You get her telephone number and tell her that you will call her (heaven forbid that she should call you and speak to your wife before you have had a chance).

Your wife finds you at the cocktail party and asks whom you were talking to. You do not want to reveal your plans and you say simply, 'Oh, just someone who came up to me.' The fact that the 'someone' was 50-ish and attractive (and your wife is 65 and 'still – despite everything – attractive') is not a sufficient answer for her. She replies: 'I bet.'

Things are tense as you drive home and finally, before you go to bed, you tell her what transpired. Your wife, who has previously let you know that you are straining her sanity, says (shouts): 'This is the craziest thing that I have ever heard. You're too old to see patients and to operate. You're too tired to go to a play at night so what are you going to be like after an operation – even if it were just one a week?'

'Nonsense,' you say with the hollow sound of lack of conviction.

Your wife continues: 'If you think that I'm going to have a trailer parked around my house, you are mistaken. Our whole street will look like a trailer park (you think but do not say that a trailer park requires more than one trailer). Frankly I believe you are not well and should be checked by our internist. In fact, I'll call him myself to be sure that you go there. I will tell him what I think: that you have somehow lost it.'

Robert M. Goldwyn

Her choice of words is disturbing because you think that now you have found it – a real purpose in your life, just like the old days when people respected and needed you and you could do something for them.

You who were a surgeon will not capitulate to your wife. You even invoke and tell her that part of the home could be considered the office, with good tax benefits, enough to take that Pacific cruise that she has hounded you about for more than a decade.

'Well, I never thought about that but I still think you should see Dr. Kvetchhelfer.'

You agree because it so happens that he is chairman of the staff at your hospital. You will need his help to get back your operating room privileges. Your status is Honorary Surgeon, a title given to you in the hope that you would never admit and operate on patients again, the shortage of beds and O.R. time being what it is.

The next few weeks are the busiest you have ever spent but you are home and because your grandson, age seven, has taught you the computer, you can reach anybody at any time. The trailer arrives; so does your secretary who used to be an interior decorator and offers to 'make a real office out of it.' She calls the woman whom you encountered at the party, Mrs. Matty Batty, who sees you in due course and on whom you operate successfully -so much so that she sends you her friends and now you are busier than ever.

Needless to say, when you re-appeared at the hospital and in the operating room, disbelief soared:

'Can you imagine, he's back; I thought he had died.'

'He may be back but I'm not going to scrub with him. He might still throw instruments.'

'He is a real dear. I love hearing stories about this hospital before I was even born.'

Soon your colleagues who are active begin referring you patients. Your peers, most of whom have retired, are now considering active practice once more. True that many of them have medical problems but so what if they have a pacemaker or a catheter. After all, the Americans with Disabilities Act is still on the books and they are prepared to sue the hospital and anyone else who tries to impede their professional resurrection.

One day, however, you get in the mail a notice from the city that you are violating an ordinance that does not permit commercial enterprises in a residential area. Naturally you will call your attorney, I. Will Phyttem. As far as you know, he has never lost a case because he wears everyone out, including the judge. However, should the unthinkable happen and you lose, you will simply hire a truck and hitch it to the trailer and go somewhere else.

2: Admit you were a plastic surgeon.
This is the simplest thing to do but only if you are prepared to answer questions and to give advice.
If you are not, you can feign deafness. Your would-be interrogator who had hoped for a quiet consultation will flee the scene when you bellow: 'Did you ask me if you'd benefit from a facelift?' (if she did) or 'Did you want my opinion about your sagging belly?' something to say even to the person who inquired about having a younger face.
The only danger with this approach is to the waiter carrying drinks and hors d'oeuvres, who is likely to be flattened by your fleeing questioner who curses fate for having brought you and her together.

3: Divulge nothing.
Do not admit you were a plastic surgeon. A simple reply will be your escape: 'I wish I were allowed to say,' as you look furtively behind you.
The person who asks will immediately conclude that you are in highest echelons of the CIA. He or she may even step back in awe or more likely fear with fantasies of your being involved in John Le Carré or James Bond espionage. That person will think 'He doesn't look old enough to have been in Berlin in the 1950s but he might have had plastic surgery to look younger. Who knows maybe even a sex change. Perhaps "they" are still looking for him, to settle a long standing debt. He did glance over his shoulder a few times and stared at the entrance. Come to think of it, he stood with his back against the wall. That bulge in his pocket – that I thought was probably due to his glasses – could be a gun.' I'm out of here, he or she thinks and rapidly moves away – features blanched, hands sweaty.

As mentioned earlier I offer these possibilities. You may use any or all of them. Patents are pending, however. With a little initiative, these answers can be modified to help plastic surgeons still in practice but who in a social situation might wish a different identity.

Plastic Surgeons Age Too

Like everyone else, plastic surgeons age, show it and, worse, know it. Although I lack data, my impression is that those who do primarily cosmetic surgery mind this more than those who do mostly reconstructive. It is not surprising that for people who devote their careers to the surgery of appearance, their looks get their attention.

My practice was divided between aesthetic (40%) and reconstructive (60%). That may be the reason for my not spending a disproportionate (by whose criteria) amount of time in front of the mirror, although in retirement I have more time to do so. Perhaps it is not so much that I am unconcerned as I am cowardly, afraid of literally confronting reality. Tallulah Bankhead, the actress was correct: 'They aren't making mirrors the way they used to.' Unlike some of my colleagues, I am not motivated to have done to me what for years I did to others. In this instance to modify the saying 'what is surgery for the goose, is not surgery for the gander.'

Some plastic surgeons have become devotees of their own trade. Usually the procedures, which may be repeated, are eyelidplasty, facelift, hair restoration, liposuction, abdominoplasty, and Botox injections.

For a plastic surgeon to have plastic surgery is not as common as a psychotherapist having psychotherapy. The plastic surgeons I have known have struggled with the decision: Do I really need it now? When can I schedule it? Who is going to do it? And where? Whom will I tell, if anyone?

One of my friends had his facelift done by an associate in his own surgical suite. He said it was easier for him but I am sure it was more difficult for his partner and his staff who were dubiously honored to have been chosen and feared what might happen should a complication occur.

I have had a few friends who have gone to another part of the country and abroad. The concern is what would happen in the event of a complication. Can one stay far from home for a long time? If one returns, it would be awkward if you had to go to a plastic surgeon whom you had not chosen initially.

An advantage of being retired is the time one has to become sick and recover. One can schedule an elective procedure without the anxiety of having to meet a deadline, having to sandwich the operation between commitments, personal and professional.

Concerning the visible signs of aging, I have noted myself that as the years go by I look more like my father. When I tell this somewhat incredulously to my wife, her retort is: 'Why is that surprising?'

I suppose my source of wonderment is that I am getting as old as my father was. Since he died at 84 and I am 77, I do the uncomfortable arithmetic. Oscar Wilde's observation was apt: 'All women become like their mothers. That is their tragedy. No man does. That's his.'

Another phenomenon I have observed is that the older some people become, the more they resemble their ethnic origins. From unscientifically collected findings, I have concocted a law: 'Aging reveals ethnicity.' Obviously I was inspired by Heckel's pronouncement: 'Phylogeny recapitulates ontogeny.'

The other day while shopping I met a friend, now in his seventies, who, though born into an Orthodox Jewish family, has spent a great deal of his life's energy denying and hiding that part of his identity. Years ago he was able to join an exclusive country club after changing his name and becoming a Christian Scientist. I doubt that he would have been accepted then if he had then exhibited his present atavistic features revealed through his aging.

Many years ago I had a patient, a 58-year-old lady of Armenian background, on whom I did a facelift but a decade later, she returned to have another one saying: 'You made me look younger and now I need you to make me look less like an Armenian.'

The thought of 'ethnic cleansing' is abhorrent but the concept of ethnic remodeling or ethnic hiding is not.

In my fantasy I have compiled a wish list of plastic surgical procedures I would want if they could be accomplished at night while I am asleep in my bed at home, and they were completely without risk:
> lower eyelidplasty,
> lower facelift,
> ventral herniorrhaphy with component separation.

But I would not stop there. I would ask my urologist to find me a pristine prostate, cancer-free.

In short, I would be requesting a modest resurrection! I am beyond 'an extreme makeover.'

Work

Most retirees think about the work they did: its duration and intensity. Work fills much of our lives or we fill our lives with much work. In talking to doctors who have retired I have met only two who bemoan their choice of career and neither had been a plastic surgeon. In regard to work, people vary enormously in the what, the when, the how, and the why. They certainly differ in recalling its joys and stresses.

Despite the protestations of our young, this society is much less regimented than others, such as China or North Korea (DPRK). We have more latitude and consequently more pleasure but more anxiety since we are largely responsible for the direction of our lives. No commissar forced me to become a doctor, then a plastic surgeon. After residency I set my expectations of myself and my work but it was not in a vacuum.

Harvard Medical School as a teaching hospital has an environment that implicitly and explicitly has rules and presumptions of which I was not ignorant since I went to medical school and did my general surgical training there. All of us belong to a time: although ahead of his time, even Einstein was still attached to his era. For us residents, it was 140 hours a week not 80 as the law now mandates. Then we were expected and required not by law to work 36 hours on and 12 hours off with alternate weekends on duty. After completing our residency (or more than one), former trainees had more choice in how they wish to work, at what pace and for how long.

The parameters vary according to country, as a BBC radio broadcast this morning (February 9, 2005) discussed. According to the information I heard and has been reported elsewhere, Americans have the longest work week and the shortest vacation compared to other westernized countries. The Brits work on the average of 39 hours a week but have six weeks of paid vacation. The French work less than that – 35 hours a week – and have two months of paid leave. The Englishman who provided these statistics said that his countryman would never trade their schedule with that of America and 'Why should we if we can still enjoy a good economy with less work?' An excellent question indeed.

I am not an economist and certainly would not attempt to discuss the reasons for and the consequences of various patterns of work throughout the world. Economics, I confess, never failed to baffle me. I am confused and amused that Nobelists in economics differ mightily among themselves on many issues. One need not be an economist to deal with money to earn it. Most of us eventually made decisions about what we wanted to do for a living, where and how long – under what conditions.

J. M. Barrie (1860-1937), the British playwright, said: 'It is not real work unless you would rather be doing something else.'

One can still enjoy one's work, as I certainly did, and look forward to weekends and vacations. I believe that the hours or days or weeks, if one is fortunate, become more delicious because of the contrast with the work-a-day world from which we extricate ourselves periodically,

What one chooses for a vocation and how much time one spends with it depend upon relative expectations, personal and societal. What did our parents do and what did they want for us? These, however, are not the only influences. Consider a few others: relatives, teachers, friends, lovers, books, articles... and all the media.

In academia I met more people who lived to work rather than

worked to live – an admitted cliché but a pertinent one. In fact I thought that many colleagues looked for things to buy in order to motivate and sanction their working harder: e.g. a second or third home, collecting art and books, constantly redoing their home(s), purchasing the most expensive cars, filling their wardrobes with clothes they might wear not even once, always traveling like royalty, with accoutrements and jewelry to suit their self-assigned status.

When I used to discuss these matters with doctor friends who are still active, some would say: 'I want to make enough money so that I can retire and live well.' More pertinent, however, was what one surgeon said to me in the dressing room: 'If I only knew when I was going to die, I would know how long I had to work.' He was referring to money for retirement. Jackie Mason said it best: 'I have enough money for retirement if I don't buy anything.' Whatever else work is, it is a filler, occupying most of the time for most of us between adolescence and death. If we did not have our work, what would we do? I certainly would not have wanted to spend the 40 years I did working in living as I do now, a retiree. That thought has to be only conjecture since I cannot run the experiment and no one ever could. Even string theorists cannot lead parallel lives and compare the process and the outcome. Joseph Brodsky, the Russian born poet and critic, remarked cryptically: 'After all, it is hard to master both life and work equally well. So if you are bound to fake one of them, it had better be life.'

'Dear Lord, Where did I go Wrong'

Anyone familiar with Henny Youngman will recognize the title from his signature joke: 'I've been married to the same women for 50 years. Dear Lord, where did I go wrong?'

I recalled that line when I was viewing a television show whose host was presenting an array of quintessential victims:

A 33-year-old woman whose step-father had raped her when she was five until she was thirteen.

A man, 40, who had been a choir boy and illicitly more. When he complained to his parents, they punished him for 'slandering the clergy.'

A 32-year-old prostitute, recently rehabilitated, whose mother had initiated her at fifteen into the same trade, which she pursued until her mother die of alcoholism.

To their credit each of them reversed their circumstances, thus displaying what some but not all human beings can achieve.

Oscar Wilde might have remarked but did not: 'The hardest obstacle to overcome is no obstacle.' Maybe that is what most of us – the great washed as opposed to the unwashed – can point with pride to what we have done with our lives. Like most who are reading these pages, my life has been remarkable for what I did not have to surmount:

I was born normal physically and mentally into a stable bourgeois home. My parents had good values. I was an only child, loved, and not beaten or cast away. Neither my father nor my mother broke society's laws, except for an occasional traffic violation. Being upper middle class, our household had enough money (my father was a neuropsychiatrist) for us to live well, not opulently, and for me to go through college and medical school without incurring debt. My father was my first role model and because of him I chose to be a doctor.

The longer I have lived, the more I value my secure childhood. I should emphasize that my parents wisely encouraged originality if it reflected creativity.

I did not have to contend with parents who were separated or divorced. I married happily and had two healthy daughters who have their own families and are doing well in life.

I experienced no unexpected tragedy until I was 63 when my first wife Roberta died in an auto accident. I was fortunate later to remarry and find happiness again.

My career as a plastic surgeon and editor I enjoyed and according to my standards and those of others, my professional life in both capacities was successful.

I could add more facts but you get the idea: 'Dear Lord, where did I go wrong by not going wrong in this age that seeks and extols victims?' And,

I should add, victims who have not had the strength or fortune to shed their misfortune. The media voraciously forage for perfect victims. TV anchors who make 20 million dollars or more a year, scour the country through their staffs to find candidates for 'can you top this?' in the misery category. Who wants to be bored by hearing about the average Joe or Joan. A 100,000 normal lives is not worth noting except as a statistic cited to draw attention to the incredibly unfortunate among us. Our society is a paradox: we love winners, certainly in sports but in other areas – people who win elections, become billionaires, and receive Nobel prizes but we also pay homage to the magnificent losers among us, especially if they have turned their values to become more like what we usually honor.

Having served on various admissions committees, I know that the achiever from disadvantaged circumstances has the edge on the same caliber of the candidate who is born if not with a silver spoon in his or her mouth but at least a spoon. That is probably how it should be because it is not only ideally good for society but practically so. We treasure the belief that 'anyone can make it' and, indeed, we easily can find many examples of this phenomenon. This social sentiment discourages the growth of communism since what Karl Marx called 'the masses' are more likely to act from hope than resentment and less likely to rebel. Certainly in medicine someone who is hard working, intellectually curious, mentally stable, physically well and has good judgment and can learn from mistakes will find rewards, tangible and intangible. To its credit, our society increasingly allows for diversity of circumstances in its quest for excellence.

The Lady with the Dog

Some readers undoubtedly will associate the title, as did I, with the short story of the same name by Chekhov. There the similarity ends.

Man is a classifying animal who himself or herself is also classified.

I am not referring to the trained taxonomist among us – few could equal the prowess of the 18th century botanist Linnaeus – but I am talking about what most of us do as am I now: we group and stereotype individuals into categories rightly or wrongly. For example, we comment on the young, the middle-aged, the elderly and the millions more as groups in a small attempt to bring order in our minds to cope with the almost six and a half billion other humans on the planet. The public can talk about doctors and we, patients. I am writing about the retired. The well developed egos of most doctors do not diminish appreciably when they close their office doors. The reality, however, is that every doctor is as different as is every patient but not necessarily in the same ways. We should recall that Homo sapiens is the species name from Homo, the genus plus sapiens, specific epithet. We should remember that sapiens is from the Latin for wise, intelligent. Keep that in mind when you read the morning newspaper.

When we treat (or have treated) patients we are surprised when someone does not behave as we had expected. For example, let us suppose a nurse has ushered a patient into our waiting room when we are elsewhere in the office. Upon return we find that the patient is sitting in our chair, the M.D. side of the desk, not in front where 'patients belong.' I could cite infinite situations. We certainly have our ideas about how children should comport themselves. They should act 'like children,' according to the rules and precedents of our society, rational or irrational they may be. The ten year old who meets the principal of his school for the first time and calls him Herb and does a somersault in front of him is definitely aberrant in real life although he might earn guffaws on TV.

When I was in my twenties I ascribed homogeneity to those of my grandparents' generation. How simplistic and foolish that was I now realize being a grandparent myself. We elderly and retired are as varied and individualistic in terms of our personalities as we were when we were younger and working. That we have lost part of our identity associated with a previous vocation does not mean that we have lost our personal identity. Furthermore, not everyone who has retired is elderly. Some have given up the workplace not because they are young or middle aged but because they are very rich or very ill, mentally or physically.

Robert M. Goldwyn

On an extremely cold February morning, as most are in Massachusetts, I was walking around the neighborhood. A lady who looked in her mid-fifties was with her dog (I discovered it was a seven-year-old female), which was strong enough to pull at her leash and drag her mistress precipitously into a snow bank. I made the predicable comment, 'Your dog is taking you for a walk.' She told me that she was visiting her brother and sister-in-law in a nearby house but that she lived in central Massachusetts. Her reason for coming to Brookline (a suburb of Boston) was to see her oncologist because of her cancer. I told her that I was a doctor and asked what she was dealing with.

'A malignant brain tumor,' a glioma, she later specified. She had undergone removal of part of her frontal lobe, radiation, and several trials of chemotherapy. I would not have deduced such a saga because she appeared and acted normally during our encounter.

Though not poor, her life, apart from her illness, was not easy. She was divorced and friends as well as family where not plentiful. She had to support herself and a son in college.

As we walked together for about twenty minutes, she told me that she had severe headaches, requiring many medications, including cortisone. She also complained that one of her biggest problems was that her 'thinking was not always what it should be' and sometimes she 'made the wrong decisions.' Without being flippant, I pointed out to her that many people without her medical history did not always think logically. That brought a smile.

I said I lived in the neighborhood, something that she had already assumed. The relative anonymity of our meeting gave us both the freedom to divulge personal information, something one might have expected her to do with me, a retired doctor (I had told her I was retired) but not for me to have done with her if she had been a patient or an acquaintance. I talked about my prostatic cancer and that it was at the moment 'behaving itself.' I was aware that because we were strangers and older and even though we were of the opposite sex, we had reached the stage of life where we had a better grasp of the human condition. Without articulating the reality that we once thought we would with our diagnoses, we revealed ourselves with an ease that was more pleasant than surprising. Sharing with another human being the vulnerabilities and vicissitudes of life, although for less than a half hour, made that day, at least for me, memorable and comforting.

I realize that had I not been retired I would not have been able to take a leisurely walk and to take or make the time to get to know a stranger who, though not a friend, was no longer a stranger. Chance brought us together and chance or destiny, God, or a Superior Being or Force determined not just the cancers that each of us has but everything else about us – from our age and gender to almost every other facet and event in our lives.

'The lady with the dog' became much more to me than a lady with a dog, just as a patient becomes an individual if we take the time and make the effort to allow it to happen.

When Two Retired Doctors Meet

As I advance in age (and I hope I will advance further but not as did Napoleon into Russia), I meet more doctors who are also retired. If we know each other, we begin with the usual: hi, hello, shaking hands. In that regard, I have one friend, once a very active orthopedic surgeon, whose aim, I am convinced, is to crush my metacarpals, thereby demonstrating his enduring hardiness. The instinct to survive is strong and I have learned to bear-hug him first, even though I am half his size and one hundredth his brawn. He reacts flustered; maybe he is a secret homophobe.

During the preliminaries, both doctors usually eye one another – really inspect each other, each hoping the other looks older. This phenomenon is similar to what happens at alumni reunions; I can only conjecture what it must be like for alumnae.

The serious conversation begins with predictable inquiries about spouses, children, grandchildren: their health and activities. To your surprise and sadness, you might find out that his wife is ill or has died or something else cataclysmic has happened in the family.

Bad news is almost inevitable the older you are.

Then the question: 'Are you still living at the same place?' At this time in our lives, the probability is that one or both of us has moved into something smaller but it may be one of two residences, the winter hideout probably in a snow-free zone, such as Florida or Arizona.

Almost without exception, what follows is discussion about the hospitals in which we practiced back in the Jurassic age and what they are today: residents – they have it easier than we did. Imagine working only 80 hours a week! Too few hours to learn anything, especially surgery. Too much technology and not enough bedside medicine. Each of you expresses the hope that should you get ill, your physician or surgeon or the residents will have 'old fashion values.'

Somewhere in the discussion one of you will say 'We got out just in time', referring not only to the utopia of not having emergencies, especially nocturnal, but 'the good old days' when patients respected you more and sued you less. Now you have more time to do what you want (each of you really doesn't because there are still obligations in life).

One of you might remark that when the phone rings at three in the morning, you are relieved that it is not a patient but now you have the terrible anxiety that it might be a tragedy in the family. Wherever you are now standing, you convert into a consultation room, with each asking or subtly probing (not so subtle that the other does not notice) medical histories. If the doctor you have met used to treat an affliction that you now have, you unburden yourself, seeking not just knowledge but assurance and confirmation that what your doctors are doing is right.

You are no longer a detached Olympian, looking down from your high perch onto patients and their maladies. You are now one of them. Most likely the other doctor will take the opportunity to tell you something in exchange for what you have revealed to him.

The other day, for example, I met a physician and said to him: 'Well, Bill, when you ask me how I am, I wish I could say that I was terrific. Although I feel really good, as you know or may not know (I hope he does know) I had cancer of the prostate and went through the prostatectomy, followed by irradiation but the damn thing recurred and now I am on hormones.'

I felt better that I had gotten it out of my system – the telling but unfortunately not the cancer.

He says, 'You look wonderful but we are all going to get something and it is how we deal with it. Right now in my life it is angina – nothing really serious (of course, he knows that it is serious because he is an internist) but my cardiologist, Jim Wallace, is taking good care of me. He is a terrific doctor.'

Here, he is behaving as we all do, as did our patients, putting faith in the power of the doctor, just as those do from other parts of the world when they see and invoke the wisdom and fame of the shaman. We did the same thing when we were kids, when we said: 'My father is stronger than yours and can beat him in a fist fight.' The battle unfortunately now is for survival and the opponent is faceless.

When someone who knows about my prostate cancer asks me directly what my PSA is now, it may be not just for his curiosity or his hope that I am doing well but because his urologist has found that his PSA is rising and he is facing a biopsy or he is actually had his prostate malignancy treated.

In a peculiar way, this kind of exchange between physicians is a way of continuing to be a doctor even though not officially. Each obtains a history from the other, partial, indirect but still we are exercising some of our previous skills in maintaining a role as a physician, much reduced, yet important emotionally. Each of us remembers how important that aspect when we could do nothing more for a patient or a friend. General Douglas MacArthur said that 'Old soldiers never die, they just fade away.' From my observations, I would say that doctors whose minds are intact do not relinquish their doctoring until they die.

Robert M. Goldwyn

Why I Part My Hair on the Right

The reader might well ask: Why would he write on such an absurdity or worse, why should I read it? Strong questions demand feeble answers (paradox intended). I wrote this to amuse myself and hopefully others.

I admit that I had not considered this question for many decades until I retired and had the time to think about trivia. The Spanish essayist, Ortega Y Gasset (1883-1955) said: 'For the person for whom small things do not exist, the great is not great.' Trivia nicely fills the days and sometimes parts of the night.

I part my hair on the right because of my Uncle Al, one of my mother's five brothers. She was the next to the youngest in a family of nine and my Uncle Al was next to the oldest. He was born in the late 1890s in Clinton, Massachusetts, where my grandparents had immigrated from the then Austrian-Hungarian Empire. My grandfather, Samuel, opened a secondhand store which, I assure you, even though his last name was Altman, did not resemble in the slightest B. Altman & Co., although within our family there was a rumor, most likely spurious, that the families were somehow related. If so, they were certainly not joined in a bank account. My grandfather and grandmother, Molly (Matilda), labored mightily to raise their increasing family, to give the boys, not the girls, college educations if they had wished, as two of my uncles, but not Al, did.

My grandfather had a horse and buggy that he used in his work and for pleasure. My mother used to tell me wonderful and wondrous tales of going on Sunday rides in the horse drawn carriage.

My Uncle Al not only liked horses, he loved them and became an expert in training them. When he was just ten years old, neighbors asked him to break-in their horses and he did so with avidity. He went to Dean Academy and I believe he graduated. Proudly he always wore that school's emblem on a gold chain from his vest. It looked very much like a Phi Beta Kappa key, a misconception my Uncle Al slyly perpetuated. When I became Phi Beta Kappa at Harvard, his reaction was not so enthusiastic as I thought it would be until I realized that he wanted to be the only member in the family to dangle a key – any key would do. Probably as a reaction to his behavior, I never wore mine.

After Dean Academy, Uncle Al sought his fortune in New York and the family story, whether truthful or not, was that within the first few days of his arrival, he saw a milk delivery man whipping his horse. My uncle crossed the street and quickly calmed and directed the poor animal. The owner of the milk company happened to view this scene from across the street and hired my uncle. By the time he was 22, he had become an owner and had expanded the company. A few years later, he was named director of a Manhattan bank.

To his family, my uncle's success was a miracle. He became their royalty, especially when they saw pictures of him with Mayor Jimmy Walker. My uncle complained to him that he was awakened at night by the screeching of cars at the stop light in front of his hotel. The Mayor obliged him by removing it. Imagine, the family back home would say, 'All this happened in New York City – all this to a Jewish kid from this small town.'

While my Uncle Al never denied his Jewishness, he never broadcast it. His name was Israel Alfred Altman but soon 'Israel' disappeared.

From time to time Uncle Al would invite my mother to New York City not only to entertain her but to introduce her to those whom Uncle Al considered 'right people.' They had money, status, and education. Even before her teens, my mother had enviable social graces which, when combined with her beauty, made Uncle Al proud to introduce her as his sister.

He had excellent business acumen and became a millionaire – in those days a real millionaire before he was 30. Not surprisingly whatever his opinion in any matter the family considered gospel.

My father, more dispassionate in his appraisal of his brother-in-law, thought him a bit of a phony – an assessment that did not endear my father to the rest of the family. The passage of years, however, proved my father right.

When I was about six years old, Uncle Al's presence and even mention of his name had a magical affect on me. One reason was that wherever he went, and he traveled extensively, he would send me a postcard. When I knew that he was on a trip, I eagerly assaulted the mailman in the hope of hearing from him. The foreign scenes and the stamps gave impetus to the hobby of philately, to which my father had introduced me and which I excitedly embraced.

And, as it is written in the Bible, it came to pass that one day when I was five, Uncle Al visited us in Worcester, Massachusetts, about 50 miles west of Boston. He observed my mother brushing my hair. I suppose she was training the part to be on the left when, I recall distinctly, my uncle saying: 'No, Polly. So many people part their hair on the left. Bobby should have his on the right.' That was the way that my uncle did it but he alluded to the fact that a member of the English nobility, whom Uncle Al claimed to know, parted his hair on the right. Since my mother did not feel strongly about the matter, why argue with my Uncle Al on this point, especially if it would make me even more eminent should I become eminent! Later I realized that my Uncle Al took a fatherly interest in me and since he was unmarried and had no children, I would fulfill a role as his progeny.

Now as I am older, what used to be bountiful dark brown hair is much less in quantity and strikingly white. When I comb it, I occasionally think of my Uncle Al and his continuing influence on me.

My reminiscences of him are many. I would occasionally visit him at the Sulgrave Hotel, where he had a large apartment that included an enormous Elizabethan bed and scores of antiques. He associated each object with someone whom he had visited or who had visited him, a person who usually was known throughout the world, at least, according to him. In particular, I recall a tiger rug given to him by some raja with a name longer than the rug itself. What fascinated me especially was its mouth with all its teeth present.

My uncle also had a dog, an English Labrador, who was trained to the point that it merited pity. It would stand at attention, holding the mail in its mouth, and deliver it along with the daily **New York Times** to my uncle whenever he commanded and wherever he was. One night I heard the dog screech in obvious pain. I leaped out of bed and ran into the living room to find the dog's snout caught in the mouth of the tiger or what was left of the tiger, now a uni-dimensional rug. My uncle seemed very calm about the situation and he said: 'Bob, there is only one way to handle the problem. Please call Dr. Cohen.'

'Uncle Al, who's he?'

'He is my dentist and quickly do as I say. Here is the number and tell him to come right over and bring his equipment.'

I knew that my uncle was a world class eccentric and I was proud of him for that. I thought also that his sense of reality was sometimes deficient and this was undoubtedly one of those moments. What dentist in New York City would make a call in the middle of the night for this kind of problem? But when I called Dr. Cohen and told him who I was, proud of my connection to such a great uncle, and described the emergency, he enthusiastically agreed to come and arrived 20 minutes later. With his instruments he extricated the dog from the jaws of the tiger without damaging the tiger's teeth or any part of the dog's nose. His fee must have been commensurate with his a Houdini-like triumph at 3 a.m. in a wealthy man's pad.

But something else happened during my visit to my Uncle Al. He wanted me to meet one of his 'friends', a beautiful girl who, I now realize, was about 30 years younger than he and was his mistress. I should add that although my uncle was older, of slight build, he dressed elegantly and could be seductively charming. We dined at a place where the head waiter almost eviscerated himself to please him, obviously a regular patron. I was never sure what that woman did for a living. Although I had read extensively, I was woefully innocent. At the conclusion of the dinner, we parted, my uncle and I returning to the hotel and she, to wherever she lived.

The next day, as I was walking alone down Madison Avenue, with a list of errands that my uncle wanted me to do – he had to amuse me somehow – I met his friend of the previous evening. She invited me to her apartment and told me that she was writing a novel. She had deduced from the previous evening that I was interested in books and asked me whether I would like to read what she had written.

I sat in her modestly furnished apartment which, I realized later, was probably rented by my uncle, and I began reading. I remember that two pages concerned a white sweater that fit very tightly to a young woman. In my remarkable naiveté, I asked why she went to such lengths to describe this detail. She looked at me as if I were an alien, an emasculated one: 'Well, a lot of people would find that sexy.' That word I knew but that it could make fools of mere mortals and heads of state I would later learn.

In my puerile attempt to vaunt my non-existent knowledge and sophistication, I said: 'I do find it boring.' She smiled indulgently at me. Whatever her reasons for having invited me to her apartment I will never know but she ended the visit by saying that she had many things to do and I probably had to meet my uncle early. That was the first heave-ho, but not the last, by someone of the opposite gender.

Later in the evening when my uncle returned, he asked me what I had done that day. I told him about the errands I had done and whom I had met. At the time, I thought he took the news with an incredulity that I could not explain but increased when I told him that she had invited me back to her apartment. He then questioned me obliquely about had happened there. In essence, I told him that she gave me milk and cookies and asked me to read the beginning of her novel.

His response I have never forgotten; its significance became more obvious when I was older:

'Bob, I am glad you had the opportunity to see her again but I would not tell this to your mother because you spent some time inside at her place and your mother would be very upset with me if she knew that you were not getting enough fresh air while you were in New York.'

You have a good idea of where I was in life mentally and physically and certainly hormonally when I say that this seemed perfectly reasonable. I never mentioned the incident at home and never again to my uncle.

Talking about home, when my Uncle Al would visit and stay, I would hear thumping downstairs after I went to bed. In the morning I would find out that my uncle, who thought that he could improve the appearance of anything, especially where we lived, directed my father to move furniture back and forth so that the house would be more pleasing, at least to Uncle Al's eye. I am amazed that my father never objected probably because he wanted my mother to get happiness from the illusion that my uncle was a connoisseur in such matters. After a few weeks, the furniture would somehow find their place to their pre-Uncle Al status. When he visited again, the same thing happened.

In the heart of New York City, Uncle Al rode horses with the best of them at the Columbia Riding School. Somewhere in my files, although I have tried unsuccessfully to locate it, is a well-worn photograph of my uncle riding with one of the elder Rockefellers. I have also (or had) a picture of him on a horse in the company of Queen Elizabeth's family when she was very little.

A minor but distinguishing feature of my Uncle Al was his gold toothpick which he would extricate from his vest at the end of a meal and use it vigorously. To others it was disgusting; to me, intriguing – to the point that I asked my mother and father whether they could get me a small toothpick: 'It doesn't have to be gold; brass will do,' I said unselfishly. Not surprisingly it never arrived.

When my Uncle Al was working away at his teeth, I remembered that he wore a bridge as a result of his beloved horse, Gaiety, kicking out a few front teeth when, as Uncle Al said, 'I approached him the wrong way in his stall. I should have known better.' I always thought that the horse should have known better but the way my uncle twisted this incident is proof of his love for his horse.

In one of his closets he had a remarkable array of riding boots and riding clothes, all custom made, as he said, by the boot maker and the tailor to the King of England – true or not I do not know.

He was punitively punctual. Once when he was to meet me, I was four minutes late because I had gone to the wrong floor. He had already prepared to leave and lectured me on the sins (there are many) of tardiness. He liked to assign a rendezvous for a precise time and favored doing so in London where there are a number churches. He would meet the unfortunate person at the final ring of the bell. Sometimes he made these arrangements months in advance.

I acquired my desire to travel and my enjoyment of it largely because of him. He loved things foreign and took pleasure in having them near him. For example, he had beaver hair brushes from England, 4711 cologne from Germany, malted candy from Sweden should he awake at night, hats from Ireland, shirts from France, canes from Italy, fur coats from Russia, pipes (not of the bag variety) from Scotland and tobacco from all over the world.

Robert M. Goldwyn

Desirous to prove his superior pedigree, he embarked on a summer expedition to Austria and Hungary. He hired in Vienna an expert in genealogy who accompanied him throughout Austria and Hungary in his search for a crest (and I am not referring to the toothpaste). At fifteen I was precocious in cynicism and realized that if my uncle could pay for a desirable lineage, he would doubtlessly receive one. Indeed, my uncle returned with what was supposed to be the family moral insignia. It depicted a man either sitting or remarkably short with a black helmet and a black beard holding an implement in each hand. These were a septre and a staff, according to my uncle. They were intended to be emblems of authority but somehow the person entrusted with them looked as if he were about to stoke a furnace. To me it was laughable but not at all when my uncle talked about it. I have never tried to probe my ancestry because I am not sure whether I would be disappointed more because I might find out that what my uncle had uncovered was true than if it were false. The fact that my mother's family was called von Wiesenbach was intended, I assumed, to give a false status to a middle-class Jewish family of teachers in Vienna. Although I had strong doubts about where the 'von' came from, I had the decency not to confront him on this matter.

As I mentioned, my uncle would relentlessly travel throughout the world on the Orient Express and even on the Normandie, the latter on its maiden voyage. When the Normandie was sabotaged in New York harbor and burned into nothingness, my uncle was so distraught that for two months he wore a black armband.

When I graduated from Harvard College and was preparing to go to Harvard Medical School, my uncle, who I thought would be pleased with my achievements and plans, said to my father: 'I think Bobby would do well to put off going to medical school. I suggest that he go to West Point.' Neither my father nor I could believe what I had heard and when I asked him why, he replied that 'it is good for discipline'. I thought I was always well disciplined and nobody until then had ever said the contrary. In retrospect, I wish I had been less disciplined but my uncle's response truly amazed me. In discussing it with my mother and father, both gave the same reply, 'Well, you know how Uncle Al is.' I did not and I realized that neither did they.

Retired Not Dead

My uncle was so mindful of time, as I mentioned earlier, that when he was ready to return to New York by train from Worcester, he would have me dial the phone twenty-four hours before to get the precise time of the train's departure. This was not a simple task in Worcester because it was almost impossible to get anyone to answer the phone. He seemed always to be on an important mission and, as a matter of fact, and I gather it was true, he did know President Roosevelt and when he was in Berlin, he met for a brief time with Adolph Hitler. He said that when he met with Hitler, he carried nothing in his pockets and thought that Hitler was 'a very dangerous man,' an observation that he supposedly reported to President Roosevelt. I would like to think that all this happened but frankly I am not sure.

During World War II, my uncle, then President of the American Dairymen's Association, sold powdered milk, something he had pioneered in its manufacture in Cuba and Latin America. CARE included it in packages sent to service personnel and to our allies and to nutritionally deprived areas of the world. He was doing very well financially and seemed very happy. His life, however, taught me another lesson and probably the most important, that no one is invulnerable and no amount of money can insulate anyone from adversity. I am not referring to health. Uncle Al lost his money and I am not sure why but I do know that it was said by the family that he was too proud to ask those whom he had known for help.

He had to relinquish his residence and moved to run-down quarters. From time to time he called to ask for money and I readily gave it to him. He dropped out of sight, became demented, and was sent to a hospital when he was found wandering on a Manhattan street while he was dressed in a tuxedo and, not surprisingly, carrying a clock. All this we discovered after his death. He is buried in a pauper's grave and at this writing, I am trying locate his tomb so that he can be moved back to the family plot in Clinton.

When I finished medical school, Uncle Al told me that he hoped that I could achieve the greatness of 'the late, great Kapetsky.' I did not know who he was but have since learned that he was an outstanding, world famous otolaryngologist. My uncle expressed his never ending gratitude because he helped him with his 'chronic catarrh.' From the time I was seven or eight, I heard about my uncle's catarrh, an affliction that caused him to blow his nose with what looked like the most expensive handkerchiefs in the world. I believe he bought them in London but they made whatever Hermes could offer look like Kleenex. For some reason, by some marvelous medication, my uncle improved to the point in his final years that he no longer had to battle catarrh. Either one of them had to go and catarrh went before he did.

Another uncle, Harris, laughingly remarked, 'What has happened to all those people who had catarrh.' It is a term that one does not use often but in my uncle's day, it was in vogue and certainly was within our family. I remember telling a fellow fifth-grader that my uncle 'suffered from catarrh.' My friend went home and told his parents that he had heard that I had an uncle who 'suffered from a guitar,' which prompted a call from his mother to mine.

Before my uncle came under the care of Dr. Kapetsky, he found a 'Russian specialist,' who was, in my uncle's words, 'not really a doctor but a genius – he knows more than any doctor.' That winter when my Uncle Al's cough became worse, he called his Russian consultant who advised him to sit bundled in a fur coat, with the window open. It was in that condition, in fact, that I found him one snowy day in December and convinced him to go to the hospital, where he stayed for about a week.

My Uncle Al could be depended on for an opinion on everything. With regard to my Harvard undergraduate education, he thought it was unnecessary that I should have majored in Social Relations, a peculiar term even then but one that applied to the field fusing clinical psychology, social psychology, sociology, anthropology, and God knows what else.

'I learned psychology in the jungle,' he would say talking about the times when he was in Latin America and in the wilds dealing with animals and riding his horse. Contrary to what I had learned at Harvard, my uncle believed that genes determined everything and that nothing one could do could change that fact. My horror at his thought simply amused him. I did my best to make him think otherwise especially when he said that 'people born in Africa will remain primitive and they make things worse by playing primitive music.' Not surprisingly he used to enjoy Viennese waltzes and he danced them in his riding boots. He had the Jewish Viennese malady of identifying with those in power, those who would eventually destroy that culture and six million Jews and others in their zeal for racial purification.

Paradoxically, my uncle might have inherited some of his thinking from his father, a seemingly gentle man from whom emanated a Prussian bearing and quasi-Prussian thinking. His wife, my mother's mother, was extremely competent and somewhat dictatorial. She imposed her way of thinking on my grandfather and together it was passed down to my Uncle Al.

My uncle had certain rituals, beyond parting his hair on the right that I learned being with him. At his insistence, shoes had to be shined every night before one went to bed. I developed such a habit that I remember a girlfriend who saw me in the morning being amazed, really hurt, that I immediately shined my shoes because I forgot to do so in the passion of the previous night.

My uncle believed in manners with regard to women – at least publicly. At a restaurant in New York, when a waitress dropped some dishes, he made me get up to help her. 'The fact', he said, 'that she is a waitress does not relieve you of the responsibility of being gallant to women.' I thought that I was an egalitarian but, as I was assisting her, I felt myself blushing. I believe that throughout my life I treated most people more fairly than did my uncle but I realized then and still that I can do better.

One day when I saw Uncle Al in his office on Madison Avenue, he was obviously tired; the heavy curtains had been drawn and he looked at me in what was left of the day and said, 'The problem with New York is that there are too many people too close together.'

My uncle had a secretary, a midget. I am not sure whether he hired him to show his lack of discrimination or whether he did so to make himself feel more powerful. My uncle, about 5' 5", was not tall but the midget was certainly shorter. Most people who entered the office and saw Albert were taken aback but naturally they never said anything. My uncle (remember his name was Alfred) was once trying to find something and he leaped from his desk and shouted: 'Albert, Albert, where is that G-Dammed Albert.' This made me realize that my uncle treated Albert the same as he probably would anybody else although I am not sure whether he would raise his voice to a secretary, male or female, who happened to be 6' tall.

My uncle since he was a child had known the family living in the house where 'Mary' of 'Mary Had a Little Lamb' lived. He used to visit them when he lived in New York and later when he bought a nearby farm.

I suppose that for my Uncle Al I was the son that he never had. He was an uncle that I was glad to have had. Fortunately I identified almost completely with my father, certainly not an eccentric. However, I am grateful to have had my off-beat uncle as an influence in my life. I wish he were here to read this. I expect that he would deny almost all of it but would be pleased that he is with me still.

Life is a Supermarket

I know what readers are thinking: 'He's in his late seventies and has finally lost it. It must be a variant of Alzheimer's – the sudden type. He probably started to write this book a few years ago and now he is older. It happens to others so why should he be exempt?'

In my defense (or offense), let me say simply that my eccentricities have not matured or immatured into dementia – yet. Having said that, I remember what Victor Hugo remarked: 'If you are rich, you are eccentric; if you are poor, you are crazy.'

Several years ago and when I say 'several,' it was decades, Mitzie Maybe (alias Nicola Howard), a songstress from the UK, delighted audiences with her signature rendition of 'Life is a Cabaret, Old Chum.' The obvious implication was that life is filled with exciting joys. For some it is but my aim here is not to dispute or support that analogy or philosophy. I would offer a different comparison or to be precise, an additional comparison: Life is a supermarket. By that I mean that while knowing what to buy is important and is the ostensible reason to go to the supermarket, knowing what not to purchase is equally important. For those who have the wisdom and discipline to concentrate their efforts and energy on what should be foremost to them will most likely be successful and happy but only if their aspirations are realistic, commensurate with their abilities and circumstances. Studies have shown that men, in contrast to women, are more likely to buy items that are unnecessary and expensive and may never be used.

I realize more than I did when much younger that the art of living resembles a work by Matisse, who was able to accomplish his visual as well as his emotional effect by putting less into his pictures, which were brilliant in their apparent simplicity. Matisse is elemental and elegantly uncluttered. Could we do this with our lives? Henry David Thoreau thought he could do it and he did, **Walden** being his testament.

How many of us could write the following and mean it: 'I went to the woods because I wished to live deliberately, to front only the essential facts of life, and see if I could not learn what it had to teach, and not, when I came to die, discover that I had not lived.' That kind of decision takes more courage than most of us have. We comfort ourselves by thinking that in Thoreau's time it was easier to 'live deliberately,' if one decided to do so. I am not sure about that because relative to his era, he was unusual and most of his fellow citizens were likely rushing about as madly as do Americans today.

Trying to simplify our life within our culture requires massive willpower and Herculean daily screening of seductions (I am not talking about those that are sexual), needless emails, telephone calls, bombardments from the media, and all enveloping consumerism – a tsunami of stimuli. We are fighting to keep our heads and souls above water. If we are not being inundated, we are certainly being tweaked and we react consciously and unconsciously to losing our direction and our individuality, too willing to become marionettes, pulled this way and that way, often simultaneously, by a society which seems to have lost its way.

Robert M. Goldwyn

You Can Retire but you Can't Hang Out

Early in practice I used to see physicians who had just retired come to the hospital ostensibly to attend rounds but, in actuality, to hang out. They were very artful in the way they did it. The reason given was to earn CME credits in order to maintain their licensure. Why would they do that? I understand now that it was not to admit to oneself that one is no longer a doctor able to write a prescription even though the occasion would seldom arise – something I have observed during the five years I have no longer treated patients.

The older doctors (I dislike the adjective) would enjoy more what followed the lectures and the rounds: namely, meeting their peers.

When I first retired, I would 'drop in' to see my friends and the operating room staff but the emotional pressure is now less to do so. With time, the bonds to past activities and people with whom you have worked daily weaken. When you are active and doing something, there is no time or need for nostalgia.

A few recently retired doctors used to eat in the hospital dining room. I wondered then whether they felt out of place. As the months went by, I would see them less. They probably realized that those who were working were too busy to kibitz. Inexorably one's peers also retire; the new staff you do not know and share too little to form friendships although good manners usually guarantee sociability.

In any activity, whether medicine or business or sports, friendships arise from challenges, tasks, stresses, pleasures and experiences you have in common: the trauma patient you worked on together, the difficult patient that almost robbed each of you of your sanity, the threat of malpractice, the difficulty in scheduling patients in the operating room and the malpractice suit that threatened you both. Hopefully you still have the esprit but it is not de corps.

I fear committing the worst social crime which, according to Oscar Wilde, is being a bore. The corollary is not to overstay one's time.

Once you are gone, you are gone. My mother used to say that nothing is more tedious than yesterday's newspaper. In college or in medical school if you return to reunions, you are welcomed but these occur only at periodic, stipulated times. While you are at the college, you are not part of it. Soon you find yourself looking at students who resemble your grandchildren and faculty, your children.

I remember when I finished my plastic surgical residency at the University of Pittsburgh Medical Center and went back to say goodbye the day after our graduation dinner. I did so because it was hard for me to separate. I recall the feeling of even then having achieved an outsider status. Everyone greeted me enthusiastically and wished me well but they were immersed in their work. In short, my presence was extraneous, irrelevant. While I added a social moment to their schedule, I contributed nothing to the group's purpose. The truth in Ecclesiastes is harsh in its reality, there being a time and season for everything. It is hard to acknowledge that in our own lives but slowly the realization comes to everyone that he or she is here and not there and that others, if not we, will recognize when we are passé.

I also remember, painfully, when Dr. Hermann L. Blumgart, the legendary and long serving Chief of Medicine at the Beth Israel Hospital, returned to accompany one of his friends to the Emergency Room after he had been retired for about ten days, one of the residents said: 'Who is that old man? He seems to know his way around the place...'.

Béla Schick (1877-1967) of Mt. Sinai Hospital in New York expressed it best: 'Every Chief of Service should have a pet dog, like Ulysses had. When he retires from the hospital he should leave his dog on the floor of the department he served, because when he returns the only one who will recognize him will be his dog.' This is the medical version of what Thomas Wolfe summed up in the title of his powerful novel: **You Can't Go Home Again**.

Retirement not only involves a loss of recognition (from who's who to who's he) but generally means loss of power and that is seen most clearly not just with a chief of a service but with the most powerful of the powerful – a former President of the United States. Bill Clinton, for example, may have undiminished popularity but not so his power.

When a surgeon retires, he relinquishes the manual part of his identity. This is not so with a retired internist unless he had done cardiac catheterization. A surgeon cannot do in retirement what he did in his work unlike a croupier who can still play cards with his friends, even for money although he may no longer work as a professional in a casino. A master chef who might have run his three Michelin Star restaurant can still cook at home. I have yet to meet a retired surgeon who is operating at home unless he removes an occasional sliver from the hand of one of his grandchildren. While that may be the end of surgery it certainly is not the end of life. Milton Berle once remarked, 'You're young only once but it is enough if you work it right.'

Come to think of it, one is old only once.

The Importance of Pat Boone

Some of you older – note I am avoiding the word 'old' – readers will remember Pat Boone, a very popular vocalist in the late '50s. One of his signature songs, which I particularly liked, was 'Love Letters in the Sand.' Why would I be writing about him, particularly for this audience? The reason is simple, almost humorous but stark: I was whistling that song a few days ago and I suddenly panicked when I could not think of his name. In fact, my inability to recall his name lasted for 48 hours but then, thank God, it came to me, not in the middle of the night, as the cliché would have it but at supper time. To anyone else, not being able to remember the name Pat Boone would not be a shocking event but since I am 77 whenever I detect evidence of aging mentally, it is upsetting, annoying, and frankly angering. That I should expect to differ from anybody else is, of course, ridiculous, pretentious, stupid and worse, boring. Yet, knowing that intellectually does not help me emotionally. Any 'senior moment' is threatening. Whoever originated that term was a genius because it makes it sound as if it is only a second when, in fact, these seconds or moments can add up.

During the 48 hours that I could not bring to the fore Pat Boone's name, I asked a number of people, most of whom were about my age, but they were of no help. A few had vague recall but most, none. Some thought that I was asking them about the other Boone – Daniel. At least I knew the difference.

I then gave myself the ultimate test: I tried to name the line-up of the 1946 New York Yankees and the Boston Red Sox. I did moderately well but nothing like the performance I gave when I was sixteen. I even fancied myself then a minor Einstein – of baseball statistics. Perhaps one of the reasons Einstein achieved so much was that he did not bother with baseball and trivia.

During my approximately 40 years in practice, I was never facile in recalling patients' names. One reasons, I suppose, was that I had so many but another – more honest – was that I did not take the time to remember their names when I first met them. Like most plastic surgeons, much of my practice was short-term relationships. With children or others who required years of treatment, their names stayed in my mind and still do. It is interesting, however, that now being retired, occasionally a name of a patient surfaces and I am not sure why. In most instances, I have noted that the name is not just uncommon but bizarre: e.g. Amy Lizard.

I recollect a television program which featured a 'memory expert', who was able to recall the names of what appeared to be randomly selected people from an audience of 300 Polish women to whom he was introduced five hours before. I need not remind you that it is a rare Polish person who has a simple name – all this made that performer even more remarkable. When the host, whose name I have forgotten – as I have that of the 'memory expert' – expressed his wonder at his guest's ability, he said – and this I do remember: 'Most people do not forget names because most people do not take the time to remember them when they first meet a person.' That probably is true. We are concerned more about our impression on another people than with that person. Our narcissism limits us, as is true in other areas.

Pertinent to getting older is what Talleyrand said about the Bourbons: 'They have learned nothing and have forgotten nothing.'

I had intended to stop here but a few days later I realized that the reason I am adding the following is that my anxiety about losing my memory is doubtless due to the fact that my mother, in her late eighties, developed Alzheimer's and died from it at 94. I thought I had self-awareness but, like most others, it disappears when it becomes too threatening.

My mother was a remarkable person in many ways that will become apparent throughout this book. As she was showing relatively marked symptoms of her dementia (and it is interesting that I conveniently ignored them in their early stages) she managed to maintain her caginess – the confabulation common to many with Alzheimer's. In addition she kept her humor and her ready repartee.

I remember that we had come to that point when I, the only child, had to obtain power of attorney. We had a gathering at the house, where she still lived about ten years after my father had passed away at age 84 – and where I had spent my childhood. My mother, then 88, was flanked by her accountant, Johanna, a long time friend as well, Sam, her attorney and my boyhood pal, and my wife Tanya as myself. We had hoped to present persuasive reasons for her to sign the paper. My mother was still sufficiently aware and competent to execute such a document even though she was forgetful in certain areas. She told all present that she did not want to sign because my father had warned her 'never to sign anything'. Whether that was true I do not know but she adeptly played it as her trump card.

Johanna asked her whom she trusted more than anyone in the world and she replied that it was me.

'Why, then don't you want to sign this piece of paper? I really do not understand that.'

My mother's reply will stay with me as long as I have a functioning memory: 'There are many things in life that we do not understand: this is yours for the week.' We all were somewhat frustrated but I secretly was proud of her for her humor and spirit; it continued my delusion that she would live forever, as most children who love their parents hope. Six years later, she passed away in a nursing home but memories of her are still vibrant, for which I am thankful.

'There is Still Good Water in the Well'

This morning I heard a radio interview with a man, a laborer, from Indonesia, whose village the tsunami had destroyed. Fortunately his family survived but not his home except for the foundation. Remarkably he was not bitter but grateful because 'there is still good water in the well.' This was his version of 'not half empty but half full.' One either has or lacks this kind of philosophy and I wish I could cultivate more of it for myself.

It seems to me that in America the poor who have more legitimate reasons to complain do so less than the middle or upper classes, who have carried whining and entitlement to historic heights. Why am I surprised after living more than seven decades that those who have more want more and believe they deserve more?

Very few complain at McDonald's, not so at a two star restaurant. I have friends who pride themselves on being malcontents. They exemplify the kind of person my mother described as seeing only the thorns in a bouquet of roses. The Yiddish language has a wonderful word for a chronic complainer: kvetch. In Leo Rosten's book, **The Joys of Yiddish**, he has this sentence: 'There is a prized lapel button that reads:
FRANZ KAFKA
IS A
KVETCH

We have become a nation of kvetches and our legal system reflects it. People have not accepted the reality that bad events can occur and will always occur. An accident – free existence is impossible for any living organism. Even a tree is not exempt from lightning.

Instead of wrestling with one's self on the intangibles in life, we grapple over minor tangibles: the steak that we return because it wasn't cooked to perfection; the adequate kitchen that we redo; the salary that is never high enough; the car that isn't this year's model; last year's clothes that have supposedly outlived their usefulness because they have outlived their style; our bodies that we overhaul relentlessly. There is always so much to be done and most of it is unnecessary.

Robert M. Goldwyn

Part of the reason the human species has been successful (one might debate the adjective) is our core dissatisfaction. We are seldom satisfied. Likely in the genes is an impetus that pushes us to do more and, for example, fosters technological process but also personal dissatisfaction and restlessness.

Americans distrust anyone who is content although we repeat the Biblical injunction to be content with our lot. Not only might we distrust a person who appears happy but we dislike it: e.g. 'Mary (or Martin) thinks that she (he) is happy but she (he) really isn't. Just look at the face and you know.'

The words of Rabbi Levi Olan of Temple Emanuel in Worcester, where I grew up, often come back to me: 'The person who pursues happiness is condemned never to find it.' I believe that his emphasis was on the word 'pursue.' My father used to point out that when we went to Maine to go fishing, the fishermen in the town always told us that the best fishing was 'further North.'

In retirement if one is 65 or certainly if one is older, you have done what you will do and you have what you will have. You had your chance to be a millionaire, a Hemingway, a Louis Pasteur, an Abraham Lincoln. Why count yourself short if you are 'just' yourself? While you could have done better in many areas of your life, it is more likely that you could have done worse. If you have your health and your loved ones, 'why be a pig?' a quote from my good friend, a general surgeon, Clinton Koufman. I am assuming that almost all my readers have adequate food, shelter, and are not depending upon a monthly Social Security check for survival. Remember that a large percentage of the American public lack these basics.

Most of us have more possessions now than we did when we were young and are likely de-excessing 'stuff' through yard sales, charitable donations, and gifts to children or friends who are doing you a favor to accept. You have gone to too many funerals of those who have had to leave behind big homes, large pensions, and too many loved ones.

'There is still good water in the well' – as long as we know where to find it and don't poison it.

Little Acts of Random Surgery

No longer an operating surgeon, I still keep in practice surreptitiously and vicariously.

I perform surgical acts: I cut bread, slice turkey, tie my shoes, fasten my wife's necklace, sometimes with great difficulty. Despite temptation, I am precise more than most in dividing a dessert. And I have a talent in removing slivers from children and grandchildren, even friends and neighbors.

Admittedly the challenges are not the same and the satisfactions, fewer. The risk of malpractice, however, is negligible.

Today's medical students and residents, once able to learn surgery and practice skills on dogs or even patients, are being trained more in virtual surgery via the computer. Since that instrument and I have yet to become friends, I maintain my status as a surgeon in more subtle ways, some of which I have already mentioned, but not with the same exhilaration. After all, how many pieces of bread can I slice (and eat) for my wife and myself?

An obvious suggestion from many readers would be for me to take up carpentry. My grandfather was a carpenter but not of the cabinet sort. He built homes and worked in the Boston Navy Yard, even into his seventies. A couple of my surgical friends, retired as surgeons, now make furniture and even sell it. I prefer less challenging substitute surgery. The reason is that through many years in practice, I treated scores of people, some even skilled workmen, who had lost digits and even hands to saws. Surgery without a patient, even a complaining one, to a once practicing surgeon is like climbing a mountain via a television documentary. The older we grow, the more substitutes we use; surprisingly many, if not most, are enjoyable even though they are stand-ins.

Robert M. Goldwyn

Am I an Original or a Copy?

In retirement I have found or made the time to study myself in the sense of trying to determine whether I have more of myself in me than of others, whether I am an amalgam and, if so, of whose ingredients?

Most people are reluctant to study themselves or engage in too much introspection either because it is boring or hazardous. Who knows what lies within?

The easy answer to this question is that we are an original and a copy, a unique mixture – unless we are one of identical births. Each of us has had a childhood and life experiences that can never be the same as anyone else's. This would be true also with identical twins.

For some reason, perhaps it was due to my being an only child and my having the time to observe others, not just my parents, that I became fascinated with human behavior. I remember this being true even when I was five years old. I was not alone in imitating the mannerisms of my parents but I went beyond that. I enjoyed the attention that my mother and father gave me for my minor thespian talents. On occasion I carried it to an extent that distressed them as, for example, when an aunt or an uncle by chance overheard themselves being imitated (a euphemism for 'being made fun of') by their little runt nephew. Fortunately by the time first grade was over, I had learned the boundaries and realized that good acting could be in bad taste. My delight in speech and words, however, has never waned – hence, this book.

I was always better at languages, French particularly, than math or science. But it was not just the language that intrigued me, more so the images, especially those romantic which foreign speech evoked. Whether a French phrase spoken or thought, I assumed the role of a boulevardier like Maurice Chevalier or Charles Trenet. Not surprisingly I became more grandiose, fancying myself in the future as another Rousseau or Voltaire. When I was less megalomaniacal, I transformed myself into one of the many odd characters in the novels of Balzac.

Fortunately I was sufficiently rooted to reality that despite my leaps into fantasy, I had sufficient contact with the world about me. Sometimes when thinking of a world apart from my own, I would stare and my father, a psychiatrist, would worry that I might be an incipient catatonic, not a foolish anxiety considering the fact that my mother's side of the family, thank God not my mother, was rich in mental illness, unfortunately not in valuable, tangible assets.

When I was about twelve, I read **Prue and I** about an elderly couple, pre-TV, who travel the world from their modest living room, in their minds' eye and reveled in what they experienced – all this without physical exertion, risk or cost. Through books I did the same until I was older and could do the real thing.

One of my close childhood friends, Sam, still a friend and a family lawyer, was someone whom I admired. He was tall, competent, and modest. My father noted that when I was about thirteen, I was talking like him. I had realized it also but thought my father would not perceive it. What hubris on my part considering that my father was a psychiatrist!

Frequently I still see and hear in myself patterns of behavior, speech and thinking that I have adopted consciously or unconsciously. I have borrowed minimally or heavily from those whom I value in my life, those who have made an important positive difference. On the other hand, I never had much sympathy and certainly no affection for Adolph Hitler: when I joke and act like him to get a point across, he is living peculiarly through me – an enormous irony that he should survive in a Jew!

Does there exist a person who carries no traces of the influences of others in his or her development? I think not. Even somebody raised by a wolf – and there have been a few – have qualities of this early parenting or whatever you might call it. Propinquity is powerful but so is distance. I have known many friends who became doctors in the image of their fathers even when their fathers had died shortly before their birth or who had deserted their household.

Reading for me and certainly movies and TV for others of a younger generation mould us. Certain writers and their novels have changed my way of looking at the world and writing about it. Some writers – I am not one of them – refuse to read because they fear being inculcated to the point of losing their originality, the implication being that they have some to lose.

Robert M. Goldwyn

One of my mother's favorite sayings was: 'There is only one original but many copies. Do not be a copy.' I am sorry that I have betrayed my mother to the degree that I did not arise *de novo*, something that my mother certainly understood.

Thomas Macaulay, the 19th century writer and statesman, described Samuel Johnson as a 'man of many parts,' paying homage to his copious talents. I also am someone of many parts but not like those that brought Johnson to the pantheon of human accomplishments. I am unique in the many aspects of my non-uniqueness, all brought together through purpose or accident. It is interesting at this stage of my life to try to determine who has been part of me and to what degree. Even when I am dictating this, my secretary notices that I sound like people we have both known. Sometimes my wife asks in jest (more truthfully, in desperation) whether I am the Bob Goldwyn that she had married and not a person who carries the name but is not just a copy but is a multiple.

John Donne's remark, worn almost beyond use, was extremely perceptive: 'No man is an island, entire of itself; every man is a piece of the continent, a part of the main...'. As far as I can determine, each person is not just part of 'the main' but has elements in him or her of brief encounters with out-of-the way islands.

On his 70th birthday, S.J. Behrman remarked: 'I have had about as much of myself as I can stand.' I have lasted longer without that sentiment and the reason is that myself is not myself but a multiple of selves to the point of amusement but not psychosis – as of yet. Nobody has more than one body but the mind has many subsets. 'It takes a village.'

With me and I suspect with many others, the older I am, the more I think about the influences on my life, some of whom are disproportionate in their power compared to the time spent with that person. And certainly many have made their mark on me without my actually having met them, e.g., F.D.R., Hemingway, Marie Currie.

It would be unfortunate if we had to postpone until we are older the delightful trip backwards to revisit those who have helped make us who we are. That is why loved ones no longer with us are still fellow travelers.

Retired Not Dead

Retrograde

Among my favorite books are those by Marcel Proust (1871-1922), his series *Remembrance of Things Past* (A la recherche du temps perdu). The literal French title differs from that in English by its emphasis on search or quest (recherche) for the past and without stipulating possible categories: things, people, events, sounds, smells. As any Proustphile knows, it was all these and more. Now with leisure I can dip once again into this masterpiece without adhering to a rigid schedule as in a college course with the prospect of exams.

I am not an expert in French or its literature although I can speak French continually but not fluently and certainly not faultlessly. But I can remember and have had my fantasies about what I could, would or should dredge from my past if I were to devote the rest of my life to such a project. How much of the present would I fail to notice or enjoy or experience if I relentlessly pursued what went before, with the purpose of entrapping it by recording it? Embarking on such an inward voyage of self-absorption would be easier for someone younger who, paradoxically, would have less of a journey and distance but perhaps a greater one in depth.

'Thus it came about that, having unlimited time at his (Proust) disposal, he embarked upon a long and leisurely work, full of minute detail, in which was imprisoned, as in a net, his whole experience of life...' [*Encyclopaedia Brittanica*, H.S. Ashmore, Editor In Chief, Chicago: 1962, volume 18].

For an obsessive plastic surgeon, a thought of advancing retrograde into one's frontal lobes is a tempting prospect, overwhelming to the point of impossibility, at least for me. My family and readers need not worry that I shall attempt it.

Our memories permit us to bring the past to the fore, almost always incomplete and distorted yet those remnants are better than nothing. Remembrances for psychoanalyst's anamnesis is an occupational activity but for most of us, our reminiscences may be therapeutic but they certainly are wells for nostalgia. We can retrieve, without the computer, lost loved ones and close friends, who rejoin us either in our conscious mental meanderings or in our unconscious dreams. It is hard to make yourself dream anything but one can lower the blinds, lie on a bed or on a reclining chair, close one's eyes and let the past take over – a simple nudge of your mind in that direction starts the motor and you go in reverse. I tried it the other day and put myself back temporarily into a busy day as a resident:

An image of myself, young doctor rushing, in my whites, black hair (now the situation is reversed: hair is white and clothes are dark), hearing myself paged (no beepers then), faces of the boys of summer (no women then as house officers), a retired chauffeur complaining of back pain with a diagnosis of metastatic prostate cancer (would the fact that I have prostate cancer be related? The question is as laughable if it were not so serious), running to the dressing room to change, the smell of the anesthesia, the sights of attending surgeons and anesthesiologists now gone, the young nurses (one of whom I liked) now grandmothers or worse, the patient being wheeled in, scrubbing at the sink – the entire operating suite now demolished but not its memories...

I could go on longer and Proust did but I lack his talent or his persistence. That so much can come back so quickly is miraculous as it is mysterious. Where do the memories come from in our brain and where have the years gone in our life? Even a geologist who in his work might think of billion year intervals would not do so in thinking about the number of years he has lived. For the individual life and death are personal matters. It is little consolation that our life span is vastly longer than that of a Mayfly.

But returning to Proust, who lived 51 years, he got more out of his past than many who lived twice as long. The more important question, however, is how much did he get out of life as he was experiencing it while wallowing in the past?

W & W

Since my retirement, I have cultivated W & W, not wisteria and water lily but walking and whistling, both accessible, and even better, both free, and perhaps good for one's health: e.g. whistling requires pulmonary excursion beyond that required for walking.

Although anyone with a little effort can learn to whistle and many women do, whistling remains primarily a male rite passed from fathers to sons, from older brothers to younger. My father taught me when I was seven and I recall my exhilaration at finally being able to do something he did.

A quasi-vocal art, whistling is a private enterprise but it need not be a solitary act. Its simple power can affect others. By merely pursing the lips and emitting a breath, one can call a dog from afar, find a friend in a crowd, register appreciation for an art work of the opposite sex. How cruel and isolating it would be to deprive hard-hats of their right, even duty, to whistle at something extraordinary that the Lord built.

Whistling requires no equipment. No Walkman with its ear plugs, wires and batteries encumber me. I can whistle as I promenade. Whistling is much different from singing. Passersby smile at a whistler but fear a singer. Others would even regard someone with the powers of a Placido Domingo as a premature discharge from an asylum.

I am now a 77-year-old whistler. I have been whistling for more years than I have been a husband, father, doctor or taxpayer. With whistling I can evoke the various eras in my life. 'Begin the Beguine' and 'Don't Sit Under the Apple Tree With Anyone Else But Me,' for example, bring back the tumultuous days of the Hitler era and World War II. 'Buttons and Bows' has me whirling again with Ethel at the high school senior prom. Four years later in college, it was Ellen and at the prom the band played 'Getting to Know You' and 'Come On-a My House', both ironic titles for what happened to us after in that distant age when moderate petting seemed a federal crime.

I usually whistle to myself but sometimes to others, I confess, as they approach me. The requirement for them, however, is not to be tuned into

Robert M. Goldwyn

their headsets and tuned out from the world. Do I tend to whistle more to women passing by than to men? I have never done a study but perhaps depending upon the age of the person, I select a song that might be in his or her era. It is easier for me to whistle to people of my vintage.

I realize that with each year my audience is dwindling.

I am usually unaware of my whistling, sometimes with an odd effect. Yesterday, the garage attendant leaped from his cage and grinned foolishly saying, 'Oh, doc, it's only you whistling. I thought a bird flew in.'

While that incident was humorous, another was sobering. As I was whistling and walking, a young woman sitting on the bench gave me a grand smile and proclaimed: 'I have heard you whistle a few times. My grandfather used to whistle some of the same tunes.'

So, there it is. I am an older (not old, of course) man whistling, a grandfather figure to my daughter's children's generation, most of whom have never heard of the **Seven Dwarfs** or saw them marching off to work whistling. That's another virtue of whistling: you can do it before you work or while you work; it leavens the task and also celebrates its completion. Whistling is more fun than chewing gum and infinitely better for your teeth. If whistling could be shown to have aerobic benefits, it might replace jogging and the Nautilus. Instead of the gasping and the grunting, we would be serenading each other.

Although I am the quintessential amateur whistler, I do pride myself on a few breath pirouettes – with an occasional arpeggio or trill.

In this age not known for its powers of self-amusement, whistling is vestigial. Even with men, fewer are doing it. Why whistle, when you can listen? I will tell you why. For me using my built-in fife is more than fun and it is more than nostalgia.

It is a form of protest, meek to be sure, against the increasing media-induced passivity. Although I admit that my whistling can no more reverse this trend any more than did the whistling of 'Dixie' a century ago prevent Appomattox, but, at least, I too will go down fighting – and whistling. I confess that I enjoy being among the last of a breed. There is a peculiar grandeur in that sort of futility. However, my generous nature makes me willing to share this perverse satisfaction with others. Let other males who seem preoccupied more with whetting their whistle rather than exercising it join me. If we whistlers of the world can unite, we will prevent that other sex from taking over what we have so foolishly forfeited.

Long after the tennis players have laid down their rackets and the golfers have sold their clubs, I will still be whistling. I will be able to do it even from a wheelchair or hospital bed. Whistling then would have a utilitarian value: at least, I could summon a urinal.

In fairness I must acknowledge one disadvantage of whistling. If you do it on the streets of a town that has no leash laws, you will soon attract a devote but chaotic phalanx of canine followers. Their howling and your whistling would never, as they say, make it to Broadway or even off Broadway.

'Plastic Surgery is Moving More and More in the Direction of Aesthetic Surgery'

Recently I heard a senior plastic surgeon known for his work with cleft lip and palates and craniofacial anomalies say that publicly. He added: 'You can't make enough money in reconstructive surgery.'

I realize that although he cast this as a global sentiment, he was talking about himself: the common phenomenon of the aging reconstructive surgeon doing increasingly more of aesthetic surgery.

I remember when Dr. Francis D. Moore, then the Moseley Professor of Surgery at Harvard Medical School and my chief at the then Peter Bent Brigham Hospital, observing that 'gynecologists are aging obstetricians.'

The specialty of plastic surgery is rife with cosmetic surgeons whose early careers were in microsurgery. Is this shift bad? Not necessarily. Is it good? Not necessarily.

The plastic surgeon whom I quoted was American and from a large city in the South. From his perch, what he said was undoubtedly true.

Robert M. Goldwyn

Is American plastic surgery shifting to become more aesthetic and less reconstructive? I am not sure. More than 80 percent of board certified plastic surgeons in the United States do both reconstructive and aesthetic plastic surgery. Beyond argument is the fact that the cosmetic component is more remunerative than the reconstructive. As malpractice premiums rise, as the bureaucratic hassles multiply and, as payments for the surgery of necessity decrease, plastic surgeons in the United States will be going where the money is – proving that one does not need to be a bank robber like Willie Sutton whose professional career was built on this premise.

When I was Editor of **Plastic and Reconstructive Surgery** (1980-2005), I was always mindful that throughout the world, especially in less affluent and technologically advanced areas, reconstructive surgery is much more important, really crucial, than aesthetic surgery. As long as there are congenital anomalies, cancer ablations, trauma, including burns and injuries to the upper and lower extremities, there will be a need for reconstruction. Whether those who do it will be plastic surgeons I do not know but I am certain that the concepts and techniques that characterize our specialty of plastic surgery will still be useful in any arena. In short, the need for reconstructive surgery will not disappear. True also is that as long as there are human beings, there will be concern and dissatisfaction with physical appearance and the desire to improve or embellish it. Whether some might call this vanity or a necessity or self-actualization is inconsequential. What is important is that from the beginning of recorded history, human beings have never been completely satisfied with nature given physical appearance and have sought to modify it. Why not look younger or better or different if you wish? But those who have had cosmetic surgery are not immune from the necessity of having reconstructive surgery.

Contrary to teachings of Karl Marx, not every aspect of society and not every citizen is motivated by accumulating money. I grant, however, that Tennessee Williams was right when he had Ann Margaret in **Cat on the Hot Tin Roof** say: 'You can be young without money but you can't be old without it.' The point being is that those who lack something think more about it than those who have it.

I predict that plastic surgeons or whatever we may be called in the future will continue to do reconstructive surgery because it interests them and/or they feel they are contributing more to society and their own inner being by doing work that is a necessity not a luxury and that for them reconstructive surgery is more intellectually challenging than rejuvenative surgery, for example.

But could we be approaching the time when reconstructive surgery is done largely in academic centers and aesthetic surgery outside? The place is less important than the need and whenever there is a need, a place will always be found as will those required to do the task.

Overhearing

You will note that I have avoided the word 'eavesdropping.' Even better than 'overhearing' would have been the phrase 'happen to have heard.' Where am I going with all this, you may ask? The fact is that retirement offers a person so inclined an opportunity to intrude stealthily into the lives of others. Many of the skills and traits we acquired in childhood come to the fore when one is 'on the social,' as they say in England. I use that expression even though, thank heaven, I am not receiving welfare, unless one considers social security a form of it.

When I was about nine, I sent away for an Orphan Annie ring, which had a mirror that enabled one to look straight ahead but also to see what was happening behind. This became a constant companion when WWII began. I was convinced that I would find a spy. So obsessed were my playmates and I with that possibility that several of us crept to the window of a German speaking immigrant. When we saw that he had a shortwave radio, we called the FBI. I am not sure what happened subsequently but he and his family lived for many years afterwards in the same neighborhood. I now recall this incident with embarrassment and guilt. It made me realize how easy it is for people to stereotype others and cause them pain.

Robert M. Goldwyn

But getting back to what I am trying to say – in a roundabout fashion – is that my fascination with spy stories and my being a rabid reader of Sherlock Holmes combined to make me cultivate skills that once I thought were clever and now I think are foolish but nevertheless have added a bit of zest to my day – only a bit, nothing sufficient to put me in the realm of the grossly abnormal – only the obviously eccentric.

For example, when I was about twelve, having read many spy stories (and I continue to do so), I learned how to push my chair slightly backwards in a restaurant so that I could overhear the conversation behind me. I also mastered the peculiar skill of being able to speak, then pausing, so I could catch a phrase or two from an adjacent table. These machinations my parents thought were an annoying hobby. They considered my behavior a rude, stupid waste of time and definitely not what our Founding Fathers had in mind. Since they could readily see me relocate my chair and by the slightly distracted look on my face perceive that I had lessened my attention to what was happening at our table. I underwent a Darwinian adaptation: I learned to do two things at the same time: talk and listen both to those in front and behind me. The relevance of this overly long prologue is to reveal that now in my retirement, as I walk around the reservoir, I am able to 'overhear' parts of conversation from those who are near me, coming or going. Here are a few that I have collected in the past year:

'I told my daughter she would have an uphill fight. He may be nice but he is an alcoholic. Why pick him?' said by a 50-ish woman to an older woman.

'My Henry doesn't need a leash,' said by a small woman about 70 to a much younger man concerning her dog, the size of a mini-horse. At first I thought she was referring to her husband.

'You live and you die and no one can tell me different,' said by a long haired 20-or-so-year-old to a woman of approximately the same age with a purple streak in her hair and a shrill laugh.

'I'm not going to vote for Bush because I know what he stands for. I'm going to vote for Kerry because I don't,' said by a 60-or-so professorial looking man, about six feet tall, to his companion, an elderly woman, severely kyphotic.

'He's crazy but at least you know he is,' said by a woman in her fifties to a man about the same age concerning a jogger dressed in shorts on a February day, the temperature 30°F.

'I'm someone who isn't afraid to talk,' said by a 50-or-so woman to a man of similar age. This couple and I passed four times and on each occasion, her friend was silent – and he was not dressed like a Trappist.

'This town has a leash law. I would like to shoot every dog who isn't on a leash as well as its owner,' said by an angelic looking woman about 60 to her friend, a nun.

Admittedly what I have recorded would not interest any reader of John Le Carré but gathering this material sharpens my senses while not being an actual violation of the Privacy Act.

'Virtual Medical School'

In some areas of the country, and at Brown University in particular, there is a 'trend toward Internet-based education' (M. M. Bombardieri, E-School would teach Medicine from Afar, **Boston Globe**, Wednesday, July 30, 2003). Although to me at my age this idea is surprising even shocking, I suppose one might have predicted this concept in view of the power and influence of the Internet.

The article further states, '[S]oon medical students...can study medicine for two years without getting near a cadaver, a fellow student – or even Providence [where Brown University is located].' What is peculiar is the statement by Dean Smith, who designed the program and who desires it to 'replace the conventional lecture – and textbook approach of medical school,' which he calls 'dehumanizing.'

The first point in rebuttal is that not all lectures in medical school have to be 'conventional.' I certainly had many that were not. Furthermore, I would dispute the assumption that reading a textbook is more dehumanizing than using a computer. Maybe Dean Smith might have 'chat rooms' in mind. At this writing, I do not believe that those who one meets via the computer are able to talk to you in person or even shake your hand.

Society criticizes physicians for not being able to interact with people. In response some medical educators are trying to evolve a system that does little to nurture the skills of human interaction. I realize, of course, that one does not relate in the usual fashion to a cadaver as one would have when that person was alive. However, the feelings that seeing a once living human being and being permitted to dissect that individual in order to learn to help others is a kind of a epiphany for the would-be doctor. Although I have forgotten more anatomy than I care to admit, the initial introduction to the human anatomy lab will never leave me. So also the interaction of the three others who constituted 'our anatomy team.'

Even when a lecturer was dull and the required memorization, formidable, one could find inspiration not just from the information but from the caliber of the person who presented it. I have seldom met someone whom society has designated as a teacher who has not known more than I in his or her particular area.

Without question the years have taken away much that I have learned and relearned but fixed in my mind despite the shifting sands of memory is what I remember about my teachers as people: what they looked like, how they talked, their mannerisms, and their dedication.

In fact, even today, I find myself consciously or unconsciously imitating them. When I catch myself doing this, it brings about a smile but sometimes also a bittersweet feeling. My youth is gone and with it many who inspired me to do better, to become what I am today or was in the past. As far as I am concerned, it would be folly in the name of efficiency to have someone begin his or her life in medicine by spending the first two years of post graduate training interacting with a mechanical device instead of a living human being, no matter how boring or colorless that individual might be.

That type of person might be our first patient.

Length of Life

No surprise that when one becomes old, not just older, one thinks about death. Kafka's stark comment 'The thing about life is that it stops' is an indisputable fact. Most beyond infancy know it but prefer to shelve that knowledge to the brain's back burner. There are some who look forward with enthusiasm to that event, such as suicide bombers and also those who seek final relief in their last earthly act.

Despite an extensive search, I have found little information about whether living creatures, aside from human beings, have an awareness of death even when they become injured or ill. If they knew that their days were numbered, would their behavior change? Ours certainly does although with inconsistency. Indisputable is Samuel Johnson's remark that 'when a man knows he is to be hanged in a fortnight, it concentrates his mind wonderfully.' Do Mama and Papa Robin know that they are building a nest for the last time? They certainly sense the passage of the seasons but are they aware of how many they might have left? Even we cannot be sure about that. A house sparrow chirping outside my window led me to the computer to find information provided by Patuxent Wildlife Research Center. Under 'Longevity Records,' I found that a house sparrow might live to be more than thirteen years old. One gray catbird made it to eighteen years but most hummingbirds burn themselves out before they are twelve, longer than I had thought.

When I was growing up, I knew a neighbor's parrot who could talk and did so for 74 years. Since that is my age range, I think of that parrot more than I have done in a long while.

Let me give you more disorganized data about longevity: gorillas, 50 plus years; whales, 40 to 100 years; elephants, 60 to 80 years, the Asiatic or Indian variety living longer than the African.

What is interesting but not surprising is that within a species, life spans may vary considerably: e.g. from five to ten years for warblers, as an example. Some mammals do surprisingly well with regard to their life span. The average bat is with us for three decades; perhaps their sleeping all day is a vital factor.

Robert M. Goldwyn

When I was a college sophomore, a common question we asked each other was 'If you knew you were going to die tomorrow, would you do anything different today?' There were variations on that query. Most of my friends replied that they would change their behavior – namely having more fun and doing so with women. In that era of relative deprivation, fantasies of the depravity occupied a large segment of our fantasies.

Residents have asked whether I would 'do the same thing over again.' My answer is that I have no regrets professionally although in my personal life, I could have behaved differently with advantage.

A patient told me about an unmarried friend whose doctor give him a grave prognosis in a newly discovered lung cancer and told him that radiation treatment and chemotherapy would likely not cure him. He sold his business and his home and like Gauguin, whom he had admired, he went to Tahiti. The weeks became months and soon two years passed. His fatigue did not worsen; his chronic cough, which had occasioned his visit to a doctor – his first in a decade – went away. Family matters relating to his estate which he had planned to distribute among his siblings and their children caused him to return reluctantly to the United States. Not to prolong what must now be obvious, he thought he would see his doctor who with considerable apprehension and embarrassment told him that his laboratory findings as well as the X-ray results had been confused with someone else of an identical name and birth date. This might be only an urban myth but it does make us think about whether we are doing what we want with our life.

Much of our activity and most of our novels come from our pervasive awareness of death. What would be the quality of our life and what kind of world would we have if we did not have the need or awareness to number our days.

Is Truth Always a Virtue?

I have done many things in my 77 years which, as I calculate, comprise approximately 28,000 days, or about 40 and a half million minutes. I could give you the number of seconds and nanoseconds if I had help from a mathematician or a computer. The point I wish to make is remarkable at least to me: I do not believe that I have ever gone through a full day, including sleep and dreams, without having expressed every thought that I had – in an unadulterated form. I do not consider myself a liar but I am certainly not someone who tells it completely the way I think it or feel it. I played the game we all do, replete with manners, enough so that people still invite me and my wife (perhaps it is my wife primarily) to their homes. Yet, this script is common:

The host and hostess when you arrive: 'It's good to see you and we are glad you could come.'

Myself: 'Thank you. Thank you for having included us with your guests.' (I am tired and wish they never had.)

Similarly when I had patients. I managed to get myself sufficiently together to greet everyone warmly, welcome him or her and make the patient feel comfortable. There is nothing wrong with that and it is what the role of a good physician requires. However, that is exactly what I am saying: It is a role. Good physicians are not only competent and available but to be successful they must be aware of their idealized role in their interaction with others. To put it bluntly, they must be actors. As far as I can determine, the greatest actors are those who go through life without being professional actors. The overworked mother who warmly embraces her little son despite his throwing his food on the kitchen floor; the husband who, despite his feelings, remains unperturbed when his wife for the third time in their ten year marriage accelerated her car forward in the garage.

Examples of what might be called altered expressions of feelings are infinite and probably should be for society to function. Road rage, for example, is acting out what most of us would like to do but have the restraint not to. The line from **Oklahoma** of 'Doing what comes naturally' has a powerful appeal especially to the civilized repressed (Freud had a lot to say about that) but chaos would result if even a small segment of our population behaved extemporaneously. Why wait in line at the stadium to use the loo?

While lying is not a virtue, neither is telling the total truth. Truth can be a lethal weapon if used for that purpose. Imagine a 50-year-old wife asking her husband, 'Honey, how do I look?' The usual response has a degree of truthfulness hopefully: 'You look fine.' Is there any gain for either of you to say: 'You look tired and you have gained a lot of weight. Your sagging cheeks make you look dowdy.' Even if you follow that indictment with 'but I still love you,' the damage is done with regard to her and your relationship.

Should I now at the age of 77 decide to be a modern Diogenes, seeking the impossible or if I decided to be a Mr. or Dr. Truth, how many would I punish in my wake? Mark Twain was right when he said that 'Truth is a national resource; use it sparingly.'

Regarding the truth, Emerson believed: 'The world does not know what to do with an honest man.' Perhaps someone totally honest, if there is such a person, would not last long with regard to himself, never mind others.

Are physicians always honest with their patients? Generally yes. However, the exceptions are numerous and significant. To a patient with extremely advanced cancer who asks whether there is hope for recovery, how many of us would say 'No'? Most of us, I would hope, would shade the bad news, perhaps with something like 'There is always hope although I admit that we don't seem to be on the winning side right now.' May destiny spare me from a doctor who is 'brutally honest.' I would hope that one could be honest without being brutal and, if there is any art to medicine, that would be its realm.

A Counterproposal to Looking Younger

Looking younger: is it worth it? The ready, though not necessarily right, answer is 'yes'. It must be since so much effort goes into that objective. As an operating plastic surgeon for about 40 years, I was part of the anti-aging industry. It was not all my professional activity but a sizable segment.

Since, and even before, Ponce De Leon tried and failed to find the fountain of youth, the human species, with rare exceptions, has been a slave to the ideal of youth and its perpetuation. The reasons, I believe, are not difficult to understand: youth is synonymous with life although not a guarantee, namely, the heavy toll that trauma, suicide, and war takes of our youth. But someone who is young is supposed to be vigorous, optimistic, totipotential, primed to explore and discover the world and themselves as well as their opportunities.

Though enthusiastically undertaken, the attempt to stay young or to look young is a losing battle but so are many other activities. Who can keep up with one's laundry?

Never once in my professional career did I have anyone ask to look older. As far as I know, we have hundreds of techniques with endless variations, for example, of facelifting but not a single operation for face-lowering. Who would want it? The advantages of appearing old before one must are decidedly limited. Perhaps a teenager might want it in order to buy alcohol or cigarettes or to romance someone older. But probably from economic circumstances no patient desiring that transformation ever came to me. I would not have known what to do. One possibility, in retrospect, would be to stretch the skin of the face by weights, attaching them at night. However, if the would-be Casanova or Casanovess is attempting this for somebody else, the important other could not be in the same room.

Some practical ways to age prematurely would be to illicit the help of a stylist to thin or color hair gray or white, a dentist to yellow teeth or to remove a few, an audiologist for a mock hearing aid, a physical therapist to teach a faltering, bent gait, a medical suppler for a cane and a walker, and an actor to instruct how to feign a tremor of the head or hand or both or to speak in a reedy falsetto.

But unless one is collecting for disability, being infirm has little advantage.

All this I believed until the other day when, like Newton whom an apple supposedly fell on the head and generated his brilliant insights, I, without the falling apple, suddenly saw the world differently. After much thought and more fantasy, I realized that our present thoughts about how we look are totally wrong. What the world needs is to start a pro-aging movement, with myself as leader, of course. I have already a couple of suggestions for the slogan: 'Become Old Before Your Time' or 'Old is In.'

With our electronic capability, we could scour the world and then flood the media with images of successful, famous people who are old and look old and have never indulged in anti-aging stratagems, either operative or non-operative. Key to the success of this revolution in the United States is the well known agility of the American public to change its mind and its direction in response to savvy PR. Our government can never maintain a consistent policy through two administrations. This gives me not just hope but assurance that the pro-aging crusade will be successful. I admit that it will take time but not so much as one might think. At first, there will be the predictable laughter, scorn, anger and, inevitably, fierce vocal opposition. All that will wilt because of the fact that there are many more old and old-looking people not just in our country but throughout the world than there are young and young-looking.

Plastic surgeons will find that their practice may diminish because of the public's indecision about what to do, whether to look younger or older. But, as certain as is aging itself, patients will return, the first being former patients to reverse the rejuvenation that you effected. Rare will be the person who can keep pace with the redos. You will experience a new kind of patient dissatisfaction, however. Not the previous 'Doctor, I expected you would make me look younger than you did,' but the opposite.

'Doc, you let me down. I paid a lot of money to have your Methuselah operation but I am really angry because I don't look as old as you said I would. My friend saw Dr. Ageim and he came out fantastic. He is 52 and looks 85. I should have gone to him. He even charged less. What's wrong with you? I'll tell you something else. I hate to say it out loud because the very thought of it kills me and when I repeat it especially to somebody else, it's like I've been murdered twice. But two weeks after your operation, I went to my pharmacist and you know what the guy said to me? "You look rested. You look younger!" I could have shot him. I paid you seven grand and I come out looking *young*. My luck to have a doctor who did the wrong operation. I go through all the expense, the time, the pain and come out looking younger. It's an outrage. Not only do I want my money back but you'll have to pay for my next procedure. I want to be real old. I want to be taken for my father, or better, my grandfather and at least I should look older than my brother who is ten years my senior...'

Imagine the trend! No, it is more of a tsunami, sweeping in its path everything that should be anachronism: no more anchor women and TV personalities who have the same frozen plasticized faces, no more wives of politicians and even the pols themselves sneaking off before the campaign for two of three weeks to get rejuvenated, no more vapid Barbie Dolls lounging around the pool or in the game room at the country club, no more need for wasting one's energy to postpone the inevitable – aging. 'Bring it on.'

What the prophets have done for religion is what we, if united, can do for appearance. People will be happy to age and even accelerate the process. Soon in America age will be as respected as it is in China. If you are jogging and look like 88 when you really are 50 and tell someone your age (no longer a need to hide it), you will get surprise, even praise, and certain respect because you 'look so old.'

Surgeons are optimists but we are also realists. And we are relentless, not the sort to falter and capitulate. If we persist, we will profit from a sure thing – aging. Instead of battling what nature has ordained, we should embrace it and speed it on its way.

Polaroid and I

If readers think they are going to get a history of the Polaroid Corporation and its internal workings from me, they would be wrong in the extreme. On a few occasions, however, my life and that of Polaroid intersected. I remember; Polaroid never noticed.

The first instance was when I was a junior at Harvard College in 1951. Someone knocked at my door and told me that he was promoting the stock of a company that made 'instant film cameras' which had come to the market three years previously.

Robert M. Goldwyn

I had heard of Edwin H. Land (1909–1991), who had left Harvard at the age of seventeen (later returned to continue his research) to start a company whose original product was polarized sunglasses. I knew nothing about the instant camera, which, my visitor told me, would soon win universal acceptance. His message was obvious: buy shares now and enjoy the windfall later.

'You will never have this opportunity again,' he said.

I frankly cannot remember the price per share then but I recall thinking that a few hundred dollars would give me more than just a few. Like most of my peers, dutiful in those days, I told him I would call my father and discuss the proposition with him.

My father, always a conservative investor, was on this occasion most conservative.

'No,' he concluded but his reason was not simply the amount of money involved.

'It is a good lesson for you to learn early in life that you should not be so impulsive and respond to any suggestion you hear like the one you just told me about – someone whom you do not know comes to you trying to sell you stock in a company you know nothing about.'

I need not belabor the obvious: a few hundred dollars in Polaroid then would have grown astronomically.

I should add that when Dad died 33 years later, he did have Polaroid stock, most probably purchased on the advice of a financial planner long after I had graduated from college and medical school.

Like many plastic surgeons of my era, I used the Polaroid Land Camera in my practice, mostly for patients contemplating a rhinoplasty so that they could show me during this initial consultation what they had in mind and I could give them my thoughts. In this digital age some might not remember that we used film and its development could take weeks.

Another group of patients who benefited from my having a Polaroid camera were women wishing breast reduction. Soon after they had left the office, I dictated a letter to the insurance company and included photographs in the hope of lessening the time to get their verdict on coverage.

I used to fantasize what the early explorers with a Polaroid camera in their hands could have achieved when they first encountered the so-called primitive tribes.

As some may remember, Polaroid defeated Kodak in a patent battle in 1986, forcing Kodak to abandon the instant camera business. Polaroid developed an instant movie system, Polavision, but it was too late to market and compete with the new video based systems. So also did Polaroid miss exploiting digital photography.

As investors might have predicted, Polaroid became officially bankrupt in 2001 with the result that the new Polaroid company was reformed and placed under the management of Bank One. The thought of Polaroid bankrupt seems incredible to me and those my generation to whom the company was an icon. Even more incredible and infinitely more tragic is the fact that thousands of stock holders as well as current and retired employees were left with nothing, whereas executives jumped to safety in diamond laden parachutes.

In an article in the **Boston Globe** (April 27, 2005), J. Krasner reported that about 6,000 retirees would be receiving a total payout of $47. The chairman who was with the company only three years would receive $12.8 million for his shares and the Chief Executive, only two years in his position, would get $8.5 million. The egregious disparity and injustice are sad and that our laws allow and encourage this phenomenon is obscene.

Polaroid was once considered an ideal place to work because of its family-like environment, where each person was valued for his or her efforts and ingenuity and treated with respect and dignity. Fortunately, Land did not live to witness his dream turn nightmare.

Hospital Politics: A Nosocomial Disease

Among the most useful advice my father, a neuropsychiatrist, gave me was: 'Stay away from hospital politics. You'll be fighting endless battles that will divert you from what should be your major concern – optimal care of patients.'

Robert M. Goldwyn

I am thankful to be able to say that I followed his counsel as much as I could. I kept in mind his admonition particularly during the 24 years I was Chief of the Division of Plastic Surgery at the Beth Israel Hospital. While I did not avoid problems with strong political overtones, I never rushed into bureaucratic skirmishes that were certain to enervate all participants. With a Zen-like power I never knew I had, I detached myself from *sturm und drang*. My recurring thought was that it is a miracle hospitals can help even cure patients when so much effort is misspent, for example, on issuing and complying or avoiding to comply with countless, often absurd directives most requiring documentation by overworked nurses, doctors and staff.

One had a better chance of doing one's work in the age of paper than in this paperless era. Formally sending a simple letter required effort, usually a secretary but now anyone who can tap on the computer can send droves of messages. Who are those with the desire and time to spew forth distracting trivia? Frequently the culprits are physicians and nurses who have left the bedside or the operating room to find a niche or a haven in administration. Their self-importance is proportional to their distance from patients. They find conferences irresistible and cause them to multiply faster than rabbits. We have all had to attend some and the scene is usually the same: a long table with comfortable chairs, occupied often by those who have their eye and soon their hands on another table, almost always in the corner, laden with refreshments. The chairpersons have a genius for scheduling a meeting at times most inconvenient for those who are directly involved in patient care.

I lack data but my impression is that some doctors in their late forties or early fifties tire of taking care of sick people although that was their goal when they entered medical school. Some secretly would have preferred attending business school in order to make more money, to have fewer emergencies, no risk of malpractice, and to have a more convenient, self-centered life style. Some doctors transform themselves into commissars and identify more with the trustees of the hospital than they do with medical colleagues. This would be acceptable if their actions improved the lot of doctors, nurses and hospital employees.

My fantasy is that if patients were magically to disappear from the hospital, the administration would be oblivious for several weeks.

Many who seek power within a hospital do so under the guise of 'what is best for the patient,' selfishness wearing the mask of selflessness. Most depressing is that many believe what they say and what they are doing but are bereft of introspection.

Spare me from the doctors who have abandoned patient care and have not succeeded in administration. They may wear the garb and retain the mannerisms of a clinician but they have greater things on their mind, mostly concerning themselves rather than the patients or staff who should be the recipients of their best efforts.

When I was a medical student, a common sight was the venerable doctor, 65 or older, still taking care of patients with enthusiasm, wisdom and empathy. That species has almost disappeared and those who remain are less a role model than an object of amazement and sometimes even of scorn because they are regarded as people who have over stayed their time even though they may still be excellent doctors.

What Peggy Noonan observed about some politicians I found to be true of political doctors within a hospital: 'Beware of the politically obsessed. They are often bright and interesting, but they have something missing in their natures; there is a hole, an empty place, and they use politics to fill it up. It leaves them somehow misshapen.'

When I began my surgical residency at the then Peter Bent Brigham Hospital in Boston, Adolph Watzka, who used to be the great Harvey Cushing's orderly, told me in his less than fluent English: 'Be like a beaver. Do your work. Keep your mouth shut and do not waste time.'

My father would have enthusiastically agreed.

Ethics: The Non-Abstract Kind

The popularity of discussions about ethics in our society is testimony to its unfortunate absence. Every institution, not just religious, gives seminars on the subject. The Mafia probably have a 'crash course'

– literally. Mark Twain understood the reality: 'An ethical man is a Christian holding four aces' (substitute any denomination).

Even at this distance (wherever I am) I hear the collective groan of readers who are thinking 'this guy is really old when he starts talking about ethics.' In fact, they are right since those near or in their dotage whose ethical behavior was likely lacking now foists its consideration on those much younger.

A story comes to mind of a grandfather who owned a department store and dreamed of passing it to his grandson, then age eighteen. Mindful of ethics, the grandfather queried his grandson about a possible dilemma:

'What would you do,' he asked, 'if a lady's bill came to $100 and when she paid, she gave you unkowingly two $100 bills? Would you tell your partner?'

There is an enormous difference between the work ethic and ethics at work. The former refers to the Judeo-Protestant conception that if you work hard, God will reward you tangibly and intangibly, the implication being that when one labors for oneself, he or she is laboring for God – a win–win situation, unless, of course, your business fails.

Without doubt this thinking contributed to progress and also remorse in the form of runaway materialism. When the means vitiates the end, an individual or a society must confront another set of problems.

During a discussion at a recent meeting of plastic surgeons, I posed this situation: A woman with breast cancer has been scheduled for a mastectomy in a week. She has been referred by her general surgeon, who plans a skin-sparing mastectomy and wants you to do the reconstruction, which the patient also desires.

In the course of the consultation the patient asks you directly whether Dr. ____ does a 'good skin-sparing operation.' If that doctor did, your answer would be easy. In this instance however, the surgeon is known for struggling with a skin-sparing procedure and has had an inordinate number of skin flaps necrose.

The patient senses your hesitation in responding and asks: 'If I were your wife, would you want Dr. ____ to do the skin-sparing mastectomy?'

Not to put the sole burden of response on the reader, I had this situation and I told the patient that I would prefer to have another surgeon operating.

Admittedly this is not an easy circumstance to be in but it happens more often than one would like. Since I believe that my major responsibility is to the patient, I believe also that I have to tell the patient the truth even if it means I would be jeopardizing my relationship to that surgeon who would never send me another referral.

For completeness, I wish to add that I called that surgeon to inform him what had transpired. It was not the easiest phone call I ever made or the surgeon perhaps ever received. No surprise that referrals ended from that source, a consequence that felt like a liberation. It is easy to discuss ethics – proper behavior and morality – in the abstract than in the specific. I wish to make clear that the story I related should not be taken as permission or even encouragement to disparage a colleague. That is an entirely different matter. The surgeon in question was perfectly capable of doing a modified radical mastectomy but for some reason had not properly learned how to perform a skin-sparing mastectomy with fewer complications than other breast surgeons in the hospital.

I have never believed that one could or should elevate oneself by bringing down another person. When a patient with a complication seeks your help, you should give it without indicting or even lightly censuring the other surgeon. You should be like a relief pitcher in baseball called hopefully to solve a problem without railing against the previous pitcher for having produced it.

It is impossible to discuss ethics without considering truth. That five letter word causes enormous problems if not spoken and sometimes if spoken.

The 19th century poet, physician and Dean of Harvard Medical School, Oliver Wendell Holmes wrote: 'Truth is tough. It will not break, like a bubble, at a touch; nay, you may kick it about all day like a football, and it will be round and full at evening.'

Robert M. Goldwyn

Progress Is Not For Everyone

The title not the subject came indirectly from Oscar Levant (1906-1972), pianist and actor: 'My psychiatrist once said to me, "Maybe life isn't for everyone."' With a psychiatrist like that, it is no wonder Levant was a frequent patient in mental hospitals.

Progress demands change, which can be arduous and not to everyone's liking. This is true for myself in some areas. An example is that I am retreating from computers when it would be better for me to embrace them (not in preference to my wife). For short-term ease, some of us delay, reject or dismiss what would be to our long term advantage.

A spectacular example of this phenomenon relates to cochlear implants for children. These electronic devices have been available for two decades but only in the past five years have they received approval from the United States Food and Drug Administration (P. Davies, Aural Argument, the **Wall Street Journal**, Tuesday, March 28, 2005). One would think that parents would be delighted to have their children benefit from these implants, which can be inserted at age twelve months before imperfect language patterns develop. Not so when the parents are deaf and fear their children will not learn sign language. The fact that children can be trained in sign language and have also better hearing through cochlear implants would seem a logical compromise. Again not so. Enter the factor of 'deaf pride', which causes many who are deaf to fear that the emblem of their culture, sign language, will disappear.

I recall in the 1970s when I was among the first in my area to do breast reconstruction I spoke at a symposium, where a woman in the audience stood up and proclaimed: 'I have had a mastectomy and I am proud of the fact that my absent breast is like a badge of courage. Women should look upon loss of their breast as an opportunity to show their courage [approximate quotation].' I forget what else she said but I remember replying, 'Not all women choose to show their courage by living with a deformity that a few hours of surgery can correct.' I made the point that 'having cancer itself is enough of a challenge to a human being – why create a further obstacle to maximizing the quality of life?'

Compared to many my life has had less tragedy although it has not been without it. The journey from birth to death is sufficiently formidable and grueling without our devising ways to make it more onerous for ourselves and others.

Spare me from the doctor who is a masochist or sadist or alternates between the two.

Community Service – Medical Style

Either by design or chance I thankfully have never committed a crime to warrant community service as penance. If that were to happen, I can think of a few activities that would make jail almost preferable. Note that qualifier 'almost.'

I remember during my plastic surgical residency at the University of Pittsburgh Medical Center my rotation to the maximum security Western Penitentiary. While I found that experience instructive and fascinating, the inmates certainly did not; most would have preferred any community service on the outside looking in. I met, however, a desperate few more comfortable being the quintessential insiders. They would craftily engineer a violation of their parole to return them to prison, occasionally to their previous cell.

In lieu of imprisonment, what kind of community service would I consider acceptable? Anything to do with care of patients. Unacceptable would be serving on a committee to revise the medical school curriculum, a seemingly endless task for the Sisyphi among us. After a new curriculum has been in place for about three years, it is deemed out-of-date by those who have been waiting impatiently to overhaul it.

That change may not necessarily be improvement is a concept that the curriculophiles (don't bother trying to find this in the dictionary) refuse to acknowledge. They are the true revisionists who function in that role despite being officially retired.

Anyone who has persistent or possibly prurient interests in the curriculum will always have something to do. One advantage is that if you have championed a change that proves disastrous, the realization will take years. By then no one will know who is responsible and you might have exited the earth.

Other kinds of medically related community service that I would abhor would be to serve a long stint on the hospital Quality Assurance Committee or, heaven forbid, the Medical Records Committee.

Please understand that I do not think less of those colleagues who are devotees of medical education reform or hospital committees. To attack them would be like railing against the Sisters of Mercy. In a peculiar way, I admire their purpose but as another Goldwyn said – Sam Goldwyn, unfortunately no relation – 'Include me out.' As this book testifies, I preferred to put my energies, to direct my obsessiveness toward writing. One of its enjoyments for me is that it is a solitary activity, appropriate for an only child. Committees, through necessity, are inherently slow-paced and painfully deliberative and ponderous, earning its definition as 'A group that takes minutes and wastes hours.'

Even better: A committee should consist of no more than three members, two of whom are absent.

Take My Identity – Please!

Dr. I. Gott Tsuriss was now alone in his office. His last patient, Mrs. Sue N. Quvetch, had left. Thank God! Her one half hour appointment, the last of the day, stretched to two hours of interminable torture. Tsuriss admitted to himself that she did have something to complain about: in the course of her facelift, the mandibular branch of the facial nerve on the left side was injured. 'No,' he thought further, 'I injured it – it didn't happen without me and unfortunately I can't do much about it.'

Her words resound in his beaten brain: 'Now look, Dr. Tsuriss, I came to you because you had a good reputation. Lord knows how you got it because look what you did to me. And for this, I paid you $20,000.

You mugged me. I could have gotten that free just by walking in Central Park, not even at night. Now you tell me to be a patient patient. I am not a martyr and look what happened to them.

'I faithfully use this crazy device (an external nerve stimulator) that you gave me. It makes that side of my face twitch and my husband can't stand it. In fact, to tell you the truth, we haven't been intimate since the operation. To be honest, we were never that close in that way before the operation but this is even worse.

'The other day I was using that stimulator and my grandson, little Jonathan, ten years old, a true genius, came into the room, saw me twitching away and streaked to the phone to call 911. I never realized he knew the number but why not, he knows everything else. I also never knew I could run so fast and I tackled him. Can you imagine I tackled my own grandson. That kid has a sense of humor. He said to me "Nana, you should play for the New York Jets."

'As much as I love him and I like to tell the story, it is ridiculous that I should be punished in this way. You don't have golden hands; they are made of lead. I looked you up on the Internet and you are 55. Who knows if you're telling the truth. Maybe your eyesight is no good. In the meantime I walk around with my right hand covering the right side of my mouth.

'The other day, when I was about to get into the car and Lena Schrier, the world's biggest gossip, saw me and I couldn't take my hand away from my mouth to get into the car. She kept talking until I thought I would lose my mind. Finally she went away. As a matter of fact, I never give anybody a ride because they'll see what I look like. I gave up playing bridge, going to the beauty parlor – Marcel comes to the house and I'll tell you the truth: this is what he said to me about you: "How did you find a butcher in a penthouse and a fancy office building. All the butchers I know are on the ground floor." Marcel thought it was funny but a comment like that really hurts. Furthermore, I didn't find you. You found me. Quite simply, you ruined my life – that of my family and everyone else I know. Even the Rabbi asked my husband why I don't go to services anymore. In that regard, it's my bad luck that I am Jewish. I can't even become a nun to hide away. God knows how many of those nuns you're responsible for.

'I am grateful to you that at least you see me – four times a week. There are some people who would run away but maybe you had no place to go. You also were decent – you gave me back my money but don't think that this is the end of it. My son-in-law is a lawyer – he works at a big firm and he loves litigation like the Democrats love Clinton – the male one.

'I've had all kinds of thoughts about this. In desperation, the other night my husband, Sol – as if I have any other husband – thank God I am married because no one would want me – suggested that we move – to be specific – that I move to Casablanca and wear one of those burkas that Muslim women wear. Between the jokes and the reality, I could go crazy. And you just sit there – nodding your head like a shrink and shrinking into your chair. God knows how I can still make a pun after what you did to me.'

Tsuriss had noticed that indeed he seemed to be losing height. His wife also observed that he had aged and was 'withering away.'

'I am between suicide and homicide,' Tsuriss thought to himself. 'Not a good place to be. I can't survive this – not even the guy that climbed Mount Everest – Hillary – could have lasted under these conditions. If I could escape, I would. The nut that Kafka wrote about – the one who turned into a beetle. It would be a relief. If that happened, my wife could give my clothes away and even take the tax deduction. I'm thinking ridiculous things but I have to get out of this somehow. Perhaps I could pay someone to take my place – some extreme masochist. Mrs. Quvetch wouldn't know the difference. She is so angry that she would say the same things to anybody sitting in this chair. There must be a way out...'

The phone rang but Tsuriss was no more interested in answering it than in looking for an Italian deli in Chinatown. He could see that the call came from his home, his wife probably wondering why he was so late. It's sometimes useful to have caller ID – 'ID, ID, ID,' he screeched in his Eureka moment.

Tsuriss, not a man to move quickly, nevertheless, leaped from his chair and began to dance around the office. The last time he danced was at a summer resort and he was in bed for three weeks with sciatica – that was twenty years ago.

'I got it, I got it. Thank God for my brain, still brilliant. I am a minor Einstein – very minor,' he thought again.

'The Lord has delivered me. I will change my identity. I should have thought of it before. I'm glad that I was driving home from the hospital when I heard the report of that Romanian who was stealing people's IDs. With my luck, he is jailed but I am sure there are plenty of other illegal immigrants like him who will do it. I will go into an ATM, cough and pretend that I am older than I am – senile and repeat to myself but so everyone can hear me – my code number. Naturally, I will move everything out of that account before I do that and I will wear a long-sleeved jacket so that when the money is supposed to come out, I will give it to myself. I know that crazy tune that the machine plays and I will start singing it – just like Placido Domingo. Come to think of it, if he is ready to retire, maybe I could take him with me. Now I am really getting foolish…

'Perhaps I will be lucky enough to find out who stole my identity and ask him – it has to be a male – to continue. I could have him sit in the office whenever Mrs. Quvetch comes and she'll think that she is losing her mind because someone else has taken my place. If her husband is thinking seriously of sending her to Casablanca, he will not worry about having her hospitalized on a psychiatric unit. Maybe by then, with the help of the Lord, her nerve will come back. That's funny: her nerve will come back and my nerve will come back. Maybe we can have a party together; she and her husband, my wife and me, and the identity thief and his "significant other" as they say today.'

Tsuriss picked up the phone eagerly with an enormous smile on his face. He dialed home and his beloved Irma, his spouse for more years than he wants to count, answered: 'Dear,' he said, 'have I got news for you and for me! There are some big changes ahead. Your husband is never too old to think differently. I can't wait to get home to tell you,' he said putting down the phone, leaving his wife trembling not from passion but anxiety.

'Is the world ready for a new me?' he thought as he skipped from the office, closing the door with a defiant bang.

Robert M. Goldwyn

Can I Age Without Becoming Cynical or More So?

To be honest, I am not sure whether I am a cynic or a realist or a cynic-realist-optimist. I know that most people would prefer the label of realist or, better, optimist to that of cynic, which connotes an individual chronically sour and dyspeptic. Who would want to exemplify what Oscar Wilde wrote, 'A cynic knows the price of everything but the value of nothing'?

In retrospect I believe my mother was 70% optimist, 30% realist. My father, a neuropsychiatrist, was 70% realist and 30% cynic. Having to listen to patients undoubtedly accounted for that ratio. However, he must have been somewhat of an optimist because he dug dandelions, an act that according to the comedian Henny Youngman defined an optimist.

Proportions of cynicism to realism to optimism vary in most of us depending upon what is happening in our lives with reference to home, work, or the world.

On 9/11, the realism and cynicism in most of us, unless we allied ourselves with the perpetrators, hit an uncomfortable high.

Like most surgeons, part of me has to be an optimist. If I were not, how could I stick a knife into somebody and expect, not just hope, that the outcome would be excellent?

As far as patients are concerned, especially those for aesthetic surgery, they are optimists even when they have been properly informed about possible complications, including death. Think of it: a person pays money, risks his of her life, endures discomfort, mental and physical, frequently goes against the family in the quest for an improved appearance – and expects that all will be well.

I pity anyone who begins life as a cynic because, with time, he or she will become more so. Why does that happen? It is probably due to the fact that when we were young, we thought we could change the world and now we know that it has changed us more than we it.

Retired Not Dead

One antidote against cynicism is to marry or at least to associate with someone more optimistic than oneself, perhaps less realistic and certainly not pessimistic. Perhaps the proper definition of an optimist is someone who marries a pessimist. One might think that a good sense of humor would an effective prophylaxsis against pessimism. Many comedians, however, are funny because of their cynicism and pessimism. Listeners have a happier time with them than do their mates. Yet, from a practical standpoint, a good laugh, no matter how occasioned, leavens one's mood. Possibly because of their long history of suffering, the Jews have generated a disproportionate number of professional humorists.

Contributing to the phenomenon of becoming more cynical with age is our tendency to praise one's peers while denigrating those younger, just as previous generations had done with us.

In his autobiography, Buckminster Fuller has a drawing of what an archeologist had found in Egypt from 2000 BC – the sentiment (in hieroglyphics) that 'the youth of today offers no promise for tomorrow.'

I suppose that a principal for cynicism increasing with our age is that we understand that death is nearing. If we are older than 45, we know that we likely have fewer years, that we have past the point where we have more years ahead than behind.

Is this being cynical? Perhaps, but it is certainly realistic. Unless one believes in a splendid afterlife, where the unfair imbalances will be righted and we and our loved ones will be reunited in eternal joy. Unfortunately one cannot at the end of his of her life suddenly adopt that kind of thinking unless it has been previously present. Now with each birthday I am more willing to believe in the worth of Pascal's (1623-1662) wager that if God does not exist, the skeptic loses nothing by believing in him but if he does exist, the skeptic gains eternal life by believing in him. Note that we have added skeptic to our list of cynic, realist, optimist and pessimist. If one were to assign percentages to those ingredients in one's personality, the only certainty would be that our estimates would differ significantly from those closest to us. We are what we are and usually not what we think we are.

Robert M. Goldwyn

Compensation and the Computer

Written more than 100 years ago, Ralph Waldo Emerson's essay on 'Compensation' is one of the glories of American literature for its clarity, wisdom and relevance.

'Polarity, or action and reaction, we meet in every part of nature; in darkness and light; in heat and cold; in the ebb and flow of waters; in male and female; in inspiration and expiration of plants and animals; in the systole and diastole of the heart... The same dualism underlines the nature and condition of man. Every excess causes a defect; every defect an excess. Every sweet hath a sour; every evil its good. [...]For every thing you have missed, you have gained something else; for every thing you gain, you lose something...'

An article in today's ***Boston Globe*** bemoaning Internet pornography and its deleterious affects on children as well as those older recalled Emerson's words. What surprises me is our surprise. Why should momentous technological advances be problem-free when they never were? Progress always has its downside. Man has always had to adapt to the negative consequences of a much heralded achievement.

In that article [The Secret Life of Boys, B. English, the ***Boston Globe***, Thursday, May 12, 2005] a Boston area family therapist is quoted as remembering 'getting into his father's girly magazines, when he was a boy... My father's and uncle's magazines were basically stripped down pin-up girls. There was no simulation of sex, there was no bondage, no water sports or scatology. There were no sexual aberrations. Now, any kid can go online and find women and men having sex with animals, they can find torture, they can find simulated rape...'

Maybe it is my age but this news amuses more than outrages me. I am more accepting than angry, having decided that I have as much ability to defy or control the computer and its ramifications than I have in regulating the tides. I predict that soon without much Internet effort we shall be unearthing almost everything about anybody. Our curiosity and initial excitement will succumb to boredom, which not even massive doses of Viagra® can reverse.

Whereas once I was getting mail on how to learn the computer, I now receive advertising on courses or devices to 'manage' the computer so that, like a runaway horse, it will not kill the rider. Although there may be a solution for every problem, there is certainly a problem with every solution, insuring that we always have something to do.

'Burglarious'

The Tab newspaper, which comes weekly at no charge, is published in my town (people here are quick to emphasize that it is not a city) of Brookline, with a population of about 60,000. One feature is the 'Crime Watch,' a report of the police department. I read it because of a juvenile fascination with activities outside the law, things I have never done but perhaps unconsciously wish I had. But I am unwilling to spending hundreds of hours and thousands of dollars for a psychoanalyst to explain my behavior.

The point with perhaps too much prelude is that frequently I read in the police column about a person in 'possession of burglarious tools.' The word 'burglarious' means exactly what one would think but it's attraction for me is that it seems wonderfully old fashioned, like finding a still functioning ice cream parlor or soda fountain of my childhood. To be honest, I never used or heard the word 'burglarious' when I was growing up. It is a word that I doubt would appear in the **New York Times**.

For years after I left Worcester, Massachusetts, where I was born, I would speak about going to the 'filling station' to get gas. In fact I would use that phrase even when I knew that others might not know it to emphasize that I was not from 'the big city.' I was an in-betweener – not a city slicker and not a country hick.

Until my grandfather died at 88, he would refer to a car as a 'machine.' Having spent most of his life with horses and buggies in Austria and then in the United States after he immigrated, he had never come to terms emotionally with the products of Henry Ford's genius. Similarly he was never at ease with Alexander Graham Bell's legacy. He would hold the telephone at arm's length and yell into it, almost as if he were dealing with a grenade.

From that era I remember people from small towns around Worcester visiting their children or grandchildren in New York City apartments and asking them whether they had 'enough water pressure.'

An older cousin, Danny, when his Worcester friends were ill and facing surgery, would ask: 'Do you think they'll have to go in,' an unambiguously graphic term about entering of the peritoneum. Though an outdated expression, it definitely conveyed the fact that the surgeon does invade a place that welcomes no visitors.

I am reminded of age gaps when I hear residents presenting a patient in letters comprehensible only to those under 35. I exposed my Jurassic past when I ask the meaning of these acronyms. I am old enough, confident enough, to inquire openly and not to ask in a whisper the person next to me.

From time to time I unmistakably show my disconnection from this century and unfailingly elicit blank looks when I compare someone to a celebrity of my boyhood.

Keeping up with the Joneses in terms of time is more exhausting and more likely futile than keeping pace with acquisitions. It took effort but I have adapted to the present mores of no longer wearing a tie and jacket to every restaurant. Though my wife and I might be conspicuous because of our age, we blend with our clothes. Have I progressed or capitulated or both?

Returning to where I started – with 'burglarious' and its evocation of the past. Here is another: Icebox. At home we had a refrigerator but during the summer on Cape Cod, we had an icebox. I remember clearly when the 'Ice Man cometh,' which excited us kids because we could get chips from the truck, a delicious beneficence on a languid August day. On one occasion that same grandfather looked intently at a block just delivered and said to my mother and me, 'You are being robbed. This is not 25 pounds. Weigh it.' Of course and unfortunately he was right – only eighteen pounds.

In those days I can hear my grandparents and their friends talking about the 'crystal set' not the radio. What we now call a porch, they termed a verandah. It extended across the front of the house and along its sides and in the evening they would sit holding hands and watching their form of TV – cars and people. They were from Europe, the Old World, and created for me what is now my old world. My friends, secretaries and typists, Jane and Frank Sivacek, have offered more old-timers: The mudguard, now fender. The mudguard would block the mud from being flung up at the passengers during wet weather as the horse drawn carriages traveled the dirt roads. Some grandparents, not mine, used the term 'spell' for any illness no matter what its cause.

The world would be dull indeed if we eliminated everything and everyone old-fashioned like myself.

The Holding-on Generation

Last week I went to a get-together because a friend, a psychiatrist, had just published a book. It was not a celebration because unfortunately he had died of cancer before he could complete this project of 20 years. His wife, also a psychiatrist, and her son as well as a colleague, finished the task.

The author I had known for 40 years; he was my age, a member of what I call the holding-on generation but was not able to hold on. Except for a few children and grandchildren, most at the party were my generation, in their late sixties or seventies, and were psychiatrists, still able to continue their work – to hold on professionally. In another five or ten years I expect they will be trying to retain not so much their professional niche but their place on earth, a morbid but realistic thought.

Like myself, what I saw around me were people in the summing-up phase of life, having passed through the parental stage, into grandparent or great-grandparenthood. We like to think that we are dispensing wisdom, experience and generosity to those younger, a debatable point.

Robert M. Goldwyn

For that to happen requires not just our ability and willingness to do so but the designated recipient must also have the willingness and ability to accept and to learn.

Jean Anouilh, in the **The Waltz of the Toreadors**, wrote this relevant passage: 'And under this carnival disguise the heart of an old youngster who is still waiting to give his all. But how to be recognized under this mask? That is what they call a fine career.'

At this point in my life, I am more calm than I had thought I would be. I do not dread death but I am anxious about what form it might take. I have never liked pain for others and certainly not for myself. As a surgeon I realize that for me to help patients, I had to inflict pain but I always tried to minimize the agony as best as I could.

At the book party, as we paid tribute to the debut of this volume and the demise of its author, I realized that those who were purchasing this first edition were later editions of themselves, people I remembered from three or four decades ago. Some made a point to avoid saying that they had retired and if they had, they emphasized 'but I am still active' usually without clarification. I could sympathize with them because I did not enjoy saying to those I had not seen for a few years that I was retired; throughout my professionally active life I prided myself on being just that – professionally active. The reason that was true for me was why I assumed it was true for them: an affirmation of being useful to others, of making a difference. While one might argue that an elderly person in a nursing home still 'makes a difference,' that thought is harder to accept than if one were referring to that individual still functioning in his or her work or within the family.

That we were there to purchase the book of a dead friend and colleague was less an occasion of sadness than of awareness, the acute realization that our days are numbered and we should 'number our days.' And for me this book is an expression of that perception. I hope I can complete the task without leaving it to others, as did my friend.

Horror of Horrors: A Sick Doctor Among Us

I saw a friend, a senior plastic surgeon, at a national meeting. Three years previously, he'd had a cerebral vascular accident, which left him unable to walk but able to talk. Assisting him in his wheelchair were his wife and a daughter. His recovery and his coming to this meeting were the enterprise of a devoted family. While I considered that his effort to be there was admirable, several others did not. One person said: 'He really should not be here. It makes it too difficult for the rest of us.'

Rightly or wrongly I have interpreted this reaction to be the discomfort of witnessing a colleague, like ourselves, who could suddenly become devastatingly ill, an unwelcomed testimony to our vulnerability, something we did not wish to confront but prefer to believe emotionally that sickness should happen only to non-M.D.s, who constitute most of our patients.

Stripped of our degrees and our clothes we physicians are like everyone else, with more knowledge, more defenses but still trembling inside.

I do not doubt that if that afflicted colleague had not been a physician and a patient and if we had encountered him in a social setting, the reaction would have been different. We would have found shelter in distancing ourselves while maintaining our professional, sympathetic attitude.

Some doctors are uncomfortable when dealing with illness within their family, as for example, a spouse. In a sense discomfort is appropriate because one should not be the physician to a loved one. However, our malaise may be that we cannot accept the reality of illness in those whom we love, reacting as if it were an imposition or, worse, an outrage – the 'How could it happen to us or me?' syndrome. Perhaps we believe that as doctors doing good for others we shall escape harm. Rationally we know this is irrational, an example of magical thinking. As physicians we see daily that nobody is exempt from the human condition but denial is powerful and convenient.

Robert M. Goldwyn

Among the billions who witnessed the long illness and suffering of Pope John Paul II, there were likely many who were discomfited but many more, especially the ill, were inspired and strengthened by his example.

In the United States the elderly and disabled are commonly sent to nursing homes or similar facilities but in those countries too poor to provide this care, they live out their days among their family. Our society seems to say: 'We know that people sicken and die but we do not want to witness it.' This culture which prides itself on its rational thinking and technological progress is, in this instance, unfortunately selective about what it chooses to avoid. Eventually, however, the ball we used to dodge as kids will find us.

▲▮▲

Cosmetic Surgery with Spirituality

Mark R. Tur, President of Celestial Practice Enhancement, Inc., was addressing those who had registered for his course at a national meeting of plastic surgeons:

'I am glad that you and I could meet. You will note that there are only twenty of you in a room that seats a hundred. I compliment you for your courage and foresight in spending your time here. The fact that there are relatively so few is testimony to the fact that you will have an unusual opportunity to enhance your practice – an opportunity that most of your colleagues have not yet realized. Let me make my first point – look at how I am dressed. Nothing trendy, nothing to suggest that I am a habitué of Armani or Saville Row. Far from it.

'You,' Tur points to a bespectacled person in the front row, 'tell me what you immediately thought when you saw what I was wearing.'

'Well,' he slowly replies, 'I thought you looked like an undertaker – everything you're wearing is in black.'

'Very good,' Tur answers. 'In fact, that is exactly the impression I want to give.'

'You can't think of death without thinking of spirituality and spirituality is in today. I want to make clear at the outset that I take no political positions. I am not on the far right or middle right or far left or middle left. I am simply an observer who has, I say humbly, the ability to see a direction the world is taking and, more specifically, as far as your practices are concerned, a direction that will either leave you on the crest of the wave or drowning behind if you fail to take advantage of the opportunity you have.

'What do I mean by this? People, as evidenced in the recent Presidential election, want something more than being perceived as hedonists. Even those who are on the far left, and perhaps especially those, want to feel that their life has meaning – that they are doing something everyday that is not superficial. And, if you forgive me, those who do only cosmetic surgery have been accused of doing luxury surgery – the surgery of non-necessity. It takes no Einstein to realize that obliterating wrinkles and creases on a face is not so important in terms of survival as is obliterating a cancer in the breast. True, I am making a value judgment but I would say to you that if your spouse or partner or important other had to deal with a condition which threatens his or her life, you will admit that it would take precedence over having some bags removed from below your eyes. As I glance around the room, I sense your discomfort but I am not here to make you comfortable. I am here to tell you the way it is and give you an opportunity that hopefully you and I – my company and I – can take advantage of together.

'Even when somebody is seeking something frivolous or doing something frivolous, that person does not want to believe that he or she is frivolous. By now, you must be wondering what I am talking about. Sometimes I wonder myself (laughter).

'I realize that some of you are residents or have just finished your residency and others have been in practice more than ten years. What I am going to teach you this morning – or try to teach you – is that it is never too late to start, the earlier the better, to change your image with regard to patients.

'Let me be specific. "At last" you are probably saying to yourselves (heads nod affirmatively). Consistent with the concept of infusing spirituality into your practice, hopefully into your lives too, but I am not talking about that, that's your personal choice, I shall now tell you how you should appear to your patients and how you should interact with them.

'To begin, do not, do not, have an ostentatious office. Try to have plain furnishings. Do away with anything that bespeaks money or, worse, wealth. Get rid of everything that is ultra-modern and overly up-to-date except, of course, the equipment in your examining room or treating area or in your own operating rooms. Obviously this will be easier for those of you who have not started your practice. And, for heaven's sake – I mean that literally – do not, do not rent or buy an office in the most expensive building in town. That would shatter the image that we are trying to create.

'Your furniture should not be dilapidated, of course. Any good office supply company will give you what I like to call standard – competent furnishings. No patient wants to go to a doctor whose office is sloppy or run-down or where, as Erma Bombeck said, "The plants are dying." However, people today, and I emphasize today, do not want to think they are in the lap of luxury and the expensive lap is the surgeon's. I am sure you get my meaning: a reasonable office in an accessible location – safe and convenient – near public transportation – an office that is current but not, not trendy.

'Now a few remarks about personnel. Here again downplay everything. Do not hire people who look like Britney Spears and who dress that way. I am not suggesting you have only have unattractive people in your employ but avoid those who look like Kelly Ripa or Tom Cruise. There is no way that even you with your brilliant skills can transform your patients into that kind of actor or actress and you do not want to give the impression that you deal only with that crowd.

'As a matter of fact, my company has a small subsidiary called Suitable Vestments, it is a good name because it suggests investments but concerns only apparel. We can dress all your employees, including yourself in what I call era appropriate suits, skirts, jackets, etc. These clothes will have a clerical look but I assure you that you will not be impersonating a priest, mullah or a rabbi – certainly not an orthodox rabbi (smiles in the audience).

'We also do environment consulting – not interior decorating nor

Feng Shui. I abhor the word "decorating" because it suggests the opposite of what we do. If there could be a word, it would "de-decorating." The emphasis is always on playing down any sign or suggestion of high pressure business or personal vanity or material indulgence. We can arrange meaningful small touches that reinforce the effect that we are trying to make – perhaps having the garb of a Franciscan monk quietly displayed in a partially open closet. For those who are more Eastern minded, we do have saffron robes suggesting Nepal and Tibet. And that brings me to another suggestion – only a suggestion and I emphasize that it is only a suggestion. It would do you no harm to have symbols of the Eastern religions in your office – a tiny Buddha, a prayer wheel. And do not buy expensive originals. They would cost a fortune but it would suggest opulence and that would be not only unnecessary but counterproductive. You can go to museum shops and get replicas and make sure the replicas look like replicas. In that regard, some background music – atonal, of course – can enhance (I avoid the word enrich) the ambiance.

'You have to have computers – everything technologically up to date – but they should not be too obvious. If you must have a bookkeeper, look for a retired nun and have her dress as such. That will emphasize integrity and a slavish devotion to ethical standards. You can see the direction I am going – a direction that is absolutely opposite from the way of most of your colleagues. They are misguided and will find themselves with empty offices – large expensive baroque warehouses while you will be pushing ahead slowly, then more rapidly in your more modest surroundings.

'And before I forget, do not have any advertising that you think is subtle but is not subtle or informational on your call waiting. It is crass, definitely not in the Hippocratic – Oslerian – tradition and is an anathema to anyone who has any degree of spirituality. If you need to have something, a Gregorian chant without the words. An alternative some of our clients have found helpful are dirges. And while I am on this subject, it does no harm to have the hours in your office marked by a church bell, muffled, of course. We can provide these touches for you at a small cost.

'When I said the word "cost" I am reminded of another way you should do business. It is a business, of course, even though it is in the spiritual as well as the surgical realm. Your bills should sent hand-written. Hand – I emphasize hand-written. People want stability and stability comes from thinking of the good old days that may never have been good but they were definitely old. That's why people are mad for things from the past – an old Victrola – a rebuilt radio from the '30s – you know the kind where your grandfather or great grandfather used to sit around while Franklin Roosevelt gave his fireside chats. Never underestimate the power of the past while you are embracing the future – and I should add, that embrace must be very cautious.

'Now, do you have any questions?
'Yes, the lady at the back.'
'Mr. Tur, what you are suggesting is so different from what everyone else is talking about that it makes me skeptical. I have to be truthful with you. Can you give me the names of some of the people you have advised?'

'I appreciate your honesty. Indeed, I can and I will do so after the meeting. I have their permission and, in fact, a couple of them are so enthusiastic that it might make you suspicious that they were either being paid for what they will tell you or they are members of my family (considerable laughter)'.

Someone in the back raises his hand. 'Mr. Tur, and I hope I can call you Mark (nod from Mr. Tur) could you send a representative to survey my office and my style of practice including the way I dress (laughter)?'

'Of course, that is what we usually do. We do have videos but the person – to person approach is the most effective and it is also the most old fashioned – time proven.

'I see that we have a coffee break and we have another hour after that. Please prepare your questions. For those of you who have not signed up for the additional hour, let me say at this juncture that you must never underestimate the power of spiritual thinking. What you may consider an act, certainly a change in your behavior, will soon become, if practiced rigorously, a part of you to the degree that it will not just transform your professional life but your personal one as well. Patients will come to you not just for your skill but for your spirituality, your core values which, if not ostentatiously displayed, will give them security and inspiration. They will tell others who will tell others and so on. One of my clients, now a close friend, told me that just the other day a patient said to him: "I came to you for a facelift but you did more than that – you gave me a soul-lift."

The audience leaves quietly, overwhelmed and transformed by their new insight and knowledge and eager for more.

The Charity Conundrum

A story concerns the wealthiest man in town who had never given to charity. When pressed by a small group of fund raisers seeking his help, he replied: 'I have a mother who is in a nursing home; I have a disabled sister who is divorced with seven children; three of my own children are sick, out of work on hard times. Why should I give to you? I don't give to them.'

That man did not believe even that 'charity begins at home.'

For those who have money but for whom philanthropy is never an option, the decision about giving is easy even though you and I might consider it wrong. At the other extreme are those who accept the principle and principal of philanthropy and also give a generous percentage of their annual income.

Most of us are in between: we want to give to good causes but are uncertain about which.

Our country makes it easier to give or harder to refuse because the Internal Revenue Service allows tax deductions for donations to 'qualified organizations.'

Since I have retired, I have more time to sort my mail. Everyone is after your money, at least mine. Seemingly infinite are the requests for unburdening one's wallet to investments, legitimate or not, publications, and charities. Because I am home more than I used to be, I am fair game for fund raisers who find me by telephone and doorbell.

Robert M. Goldwyn

For me it is a rare charitable cause that is not worthy although it might not be one of my interests. Can I honestly say that it is not a good idea to give to a medical school, a hospital, a museum, a peace or environmental group, an alliance that seeks to improve the health and well-being of firemen, policemen, and citizens here and everywhere?

Yesterday I received a form letter, with a personal salutation, from a recently graduated Ph.D. extolling the institute in which she had done her work on what I considered an abstruse subject: English colonialism in mid-19th century Africa. She and the university obviously deemed her project of sufficient merit to earn an advanced degree. While I accept the proposition that all knowledge is useful, I do not believe that all knowledge is equally useful. The playwright, George Kaufman, parodied this point: 'One man's Mede is another's Persian.' But even Bill and Melinda Gates have to make choices: why not I who have far less in the bank?

If one donates money, one should accept the fact, albeit reluctantly, that some causes and institutions use it less wisely than one would like. A professional society, for example, that counts every dollar may spend thousands on a project that I would consider frivolous and foolish. Universities may shift contributions so that they end where the donor least intended, calling to mind Gertrude Stein's remark that 'The money stays the same; only the pockets change.'

Despite my occasional cynicism, I continue to give with the realization that I can no more control the destiny of my contribution than I can my own destiny and often that of my personal investments. Some of my friends who give only to their family would be surprised if they lived to see what their heirs will do with it. The uncertainty of when and where to give and how the money will be used should not be an excuse not to give, a philosophy that I confess I have to reiterate to myself. The process of giving, independent of the recipient, enlarges ourselves, increases our awareness of those with whom we should feel a greater kinship, those less privileged and fortunate than we.

I have talked about monetary giving but equal in generosity, or more so, is donating one's time and energy to a cause, like raising money for breast cancer, helping the elderly and disadvantaged, or serving without pay as an advisor to charitable agencies and institutions.

A retired doctor might think that he or she has done enough for the human species but that is a mistake not only with regard to benefitting others but with respect to helping ourselves. I feel younger and more useful if I do something for others; even the smallest act counts. Taking without giving is the surest way to spiritual desiccation. For a physician to spend the final years of his or her life in a way not consistent with a career dedicated to helping others would be unfortunate. One's obligations do not end with the last patient.

A World of One's Own

Although few remember the name and many accomplishments of James Russell Lowell, the 19th century New England poet, critic and diplomat, most recognize one of his verses:

And what is so rare as a day in June?
Then, if ever, come perfect days.

As I left the house at the beginning of summer, I recalled Lowell's couplet. My world, even the universe, seemed at splendid peace. Forgotten were the screeching headlines and unpleasant stories of the newspaper I had just read. I surrendered to nature's balm and for a moment I did not notice a truck of the company that sprays our trees. Tending a long yellow hose that emanated from it was a thin man, about 30, wearing glasses. I ask him 'how things were going' more as a greeting than a query but he certainly had an answer.

'It's a good thing we came today because so much bad stuff is going on.'

He noted my apprehension and explained in more detail than I needed about the various plagues jeopardizing our greenery. I can't recall the scientific names he gave to these creatures but I had no doubt that he saved my property from ruin and me from extinction.

As he was talking, I realized that he viewed the world and this magnificent June day primarily as a haven of malevolent beasties. I am not sure how much he knew about Darwin but he was reciting an epic tale of survival of the fittest. In a way, he was doing for trees, vines and shrubs what in my career I had done or tried to do for patients. The living and dying were different for each of us but important to each of us. His profession had advantages: no emergencies at night, no CME re-certification, no hassle with third party payers, and little chance of having to defend himself in court against a malpractice claim.

Each of us has his or personal world which holds us prisoner and confines our vision. I remember that about a year after my first wife, Roberta, died in an auto accident, I encountered a funeral director from my hometown of Worcester. He asked how my life was going and when I told him about my loss, he immediately responded 'who did the funeral?' The comedy of the moment fleetingly lightened the sadness of the event.

George Bernard Shaw wrote: 'A man's interest in the world is only the overflow from his interest in himself.'

'Live Richly' !or?

Many will recognize the source of the title: it is the television logo for CITI, which not surprisingly urges all of us to 'live richly' even or especially if it is beyond our means, beyond our ability to pay off our credit card debt to CITI. We can then enter in the club in which few would want membership: the 18%-ers, the average annual interest rate on unpaid amounts.

The modern American way is to consume above one's ideal weight and income. We are continually exhorted to be 'all you can be' and more – in fact, all one can't be. And we plastic surgeons, with respect to the aesthetic component of our work, if we are not careful might subtly preach and practice this gospel.

What is good for the CITI group is not necessarily good for the rest of us; it could prove disastrous. But even if our fiscal assets were vast, should we 'live richly' or even try?

I can understand CITI's motivation in their choice of adverb. For me and my family, I would prefer others: wisely, carefully, compassionately, moderately. Note I did not stipulate ascetically or 'poorly.'

It was said of the nineteenth century novelist, Balzac, that he had to go to extremes to live moderately, a possibly fatal way to reach the golden mean.

If one spends too much money, one may end not richly but poorly, i.e. poor. It is easy, too easy, to do so, especially if one is a young plastic surgeon just setting forth: expensive office or offices, expensively decorated, excess personnel, expensively clothed (or mini-clothed), an expensive marketing-publicity firm whom you are employing but who really is employing you – all prompt the hope that looking rich will attract the rich and enable the plastic surgeon to charge more, a plan that can literally pay off but only if the surgeon is available, competent and has enough of a clientele of sufficient means so that expenses do not outpace income.

'Live richly' is another of the many mantras that bombard us through books, mail and the media. All offer hope of some sort but one has to be careful of which to heed. 'Be all you can be' is worthy advice but only if we fulfill our potential in what a sane society (is there any?) would consider healthy and helpful behavior. It would be absurd to believe that 'be all you can be' would sanction a novice car thief to become a professional. A super performer in a career most would consider destructive is a deplorable waste of a life. I state this knowing that our culture prides itself in avoiding value judgments to the degree that a few readers might find something redeeming in the act of purloining a vehicle. I recognize that the perpetrator might find redemption in a church rather than in a car not his own.

Paradoxically 'to live richly' is easy for someone to do for a short time until the money runs out. To live well in the best sense of the word is much harder and takes longer to learn and some, maybe most, never do.

Robert M. Goldwyn

Saving Money During Retirement

A humorist clearly understood the problem: 'I have enough money for retirement if I don't spend a nickel.' Unless they have been fiscally reckless, few physicians will have to suffer the ordeal of a majority of their fellow citizens: an inadequate nest egg to last them until death. Some have not even had a career in the middle-class meaning of the word. An obvious solution to older age money problems is to have amassed enough for the necessities as well as a few luxuries. A maxim, clichéd to the point of being ignored, is to spend less – harder to do than to lose weight.

Some retirees are more clever than our CIA in discovering secret ways of saving money. Early bird diners are in queue at 3.30 p.m. having gone to their bank for coffee and cookies, then to a specialized food store for samples. One of my patients had an aunt and uncle, whom she classified as 'multi-multi-millionaires' whose daily schedule was a series of nutritional freebies.

Calvin Coolidge, a Vermonter and 30th president of the United States, was so laconic that when Dorothy Parker was told that he had died, her response was 'How could they tell?' Nevertheless, when he spoke, however, he usually gave good advice: e.g. 'You don't need to take back what you don't say' – a sound caution that unfortunately from time to time I have ignored. He might have remarked but as far as I know he didn't: 'You don't have to pay for what you don't buy.' And that is exactly what I thought about today.

For example, in my fantasies, I could have bought a Maserati, whose retail value, I am told, is about $80,000 to $100,000, depending on the model. I turned down in my imagination a power lawnmower; refused to hire a chauffeur, valet and cook; decided to make do with the suits and jackets I have; bought a Doctor Scholl foot pad instead of having my shoes custom made; did not seek membership at a country club or health spa because I realized that walking two to three miles a day would be as good or at least what I would do; put aside a Sotheby's catalog – do I really need a Cezanne or a Matisse?; settled for watching the Red Sox games on TV rather than season ticket seats; abandoned in my mind plans for

Retired Not Dead

building a wine cellar and a swimming pool in my house; decided not to employ an executive assistant to answer my phone at home and sort the mail; concluded that I would go to my barber (not a hair stylist) instead of his or her coming to me; determined that I could drive myself and my wife to New York and not hire a driver and a stretch limousine; made up my mind to have a moderately priced room in a Manhattan hotel instead of two adjoining suites; accepted the fact that my body could survive well or better in restaurants lacking any Michelin stars; realizing what many of my friends cannot believe: people do eat in places un-rated by Zagat's and even enjoy their meal!

Think of the money I saved recently: I rebelled against the environmental zealots and purchased non-organic produce; turned down a super-luxury around-the-world private jet adventure limited to 'eight discerning people' (I was discerning enough to reject it); realized that my house did not need annual painting unlike the place where President Bush lives; declined hiring a personal trainer, masseuse, bodyguard; reconciled myself to the fact that the computer I have was sufficient for me (I am not sufficient for it); decided against tearing down my house to build another one with eight bedrooms for my wife and me and occasional visitors; told the realtor that I would not purchase a pied à terre in Paris, a villa in Corsica, or a fishing camp in Wisconsin; informed Tiffany that I do not need a watch that tells me not only the time but my blood sugar, cholesterol, height, weight, mood, cardiac status, and meteorological readings for all the United States and Central Africa; told Cartier not to go ahead with a jeweled ring in a Roman era setting with a cameo of myself in a caesar-like profile.

To every surgical retiree, I recommend this kind of daily cutting of expenses. Then when you and your spouse go out for dinner, at the usual hour for non-retirees, the cost will seem trivial and the pleasure, greater.

Robert M. Goldwyn

When Residents Graduate...Finally

Some days are unique in the life of physicians: when they get their medical degree; when they begin their training; when they finish it. The last happened this week when our chief residents in plastic surgery said 'Goodbye to All That,' the title of Robert Graves' memoirs about trench fighting in World War I, a comparison most residents would consider appropriate.

There were the final presentations in which the residents summarized their operative experience, gave their impressions of their training and of Boston, and thanked their mentors, some giving and receiving more gratitude than others. The parties, informal and formal, followed as did the awarding of certificates, with some residents receiving theirs six years after their medical degree and a couple, about twelve years later. I recall that when I was a surgical intern, my chief resident was in his fifteenth year after graduation, partly because he had served in the Navy. What I remember most about him was that the white trousers he wore (in those days we were dressed totally in white uniforms) were so short through so many washings that they looked like peddle-pushers!

All of this years residents, and their parents, some of whom attended the farewell banquet, as did spouses and important others were pleased with what they had accomplished thus far in life and considered themselves now qualified to begin the practice of plastic surgery. Being qualified did not necessarily mean being ready emotionally since many confessed their anxiety about leaving the cloister, where someone senior was always there for support, advice and assistance in the operating room as well as in their personal life. During their talks and social events, I found interesting and revealing not just what the residents said in their valedictory remarks but what the attendings responded. There were gentle and not so gentle jabs, verbal repayments for being slighted or misunderstood, tidbits of mockery all under a cloak of humor which did not always cover bare spots of aggression. I doubt that Freud would have been surprised.

The older surgeons who were there likely recalled their final days of residency, the culmination of enervating striving and stress. Thoughts were not just of career but of family, life's vicissitudes in which chance played a much bigger role than we ever considered when we were young.

For us older than 60, residents are a composite of students, younger colleagues, our children, even grandchildren. As surgical teachers, we note their brightness, ambition, and hard work – also their usually prompt obedience which we take too often for granted. We should know better since we do not always see it in our children. To a significant degree how we react to them reflects our relationship with our children and how they relate to us, their relationship to their parents.

As surgical educators we are required to have supervised their career, in the operating room, in the hospital and even outside the hospital with respect to their skills and character. Periodically we must complete evaluation forms which are more circumspect than in the past when residents were not permitted to see them. Only rarely, however, are residents requested to evaluate us, their teachers; we might benefit from their criticism if we were willing to listen.

Long after the techniques that we laboriously learned have become obsolete, we remember those who taught them and continue to gain from our teachers whom we admired when we were residents. When I trained they were father figures but now with more women in every stage of medicine, mother figures are also important and not just to female trainees. Although one cannot chose or easily discard one's parents, one does have options in whom to emulate not just with regard to skills but to character. The resident, if perceptive, may eventually learn the difference between knowledge and wisdom, between ambition with regard to patients and genuine commitment to them, and the importance of integrity especially when it is not convenient or rewarded.

The training of residents is not one way: we to them; it is also they to us. Compared to older surgeons, most residents know more about basic science and more about all areas of medicine and surgery. In these respects, they have much to teach us. If we are receptive we can emulate them, particularly their enthusiasm for what is new and unexplored. For those younger, the most disheartening aspect of their training is to have mentors who are uncaring, punitive and cynical. While we who are older cannot regain the years that we have lived, we can do better with the years that we have yet to live.

Every July 1st, when a group of residents departs and another arrives, I realize how fortunate I am to be part of the shifting scene. Although I am no longer in practice, I can teach outside the office and the operating room, hopefully imparting a perspective on medicine and life that they might not receive from those who like them are overly busy. However, I try to remember but sometimes forget that being older does not give me the right to invade, even with good intentions, an individual's inner sanctum. Much better for him or her to approach me. Rare is the person who can resist giving advice.

I hope that one of my heroes, Henry David Thoreau, was wrong when he wrote: 'I have lived some thirty-odd years on this planet, and I have yet to hear the first syllable of valuable or even earnest advice from my seniors.'

He may have been right but he has not dissuaded me from continuing to try – if asked and sometimes, I confess, even when not.

Brevities

From time to time I have the urge to purge – in the literary sense (I am glad Freud is not alive to interpret this) – all the accumulated snippets of interest that form a disquieting heap on my desk. My aversion to computers means I cannot store these digitally, so inevitably newspaper clippings, scribbled notes and references pile up on my work space. From the dust jacket of a book I recently read:

> **Crime, Mystery and Detection** *is an absorbing experience on a number of counts. Treason, grand larceny, petty thievery and even the stealing of affections appear in this book. What these acts all have in common is that fascinating pursuit of*

> justice – detection. We are all caught up in the brainwork of snaring the criminal, whether he is the cleverest Communist agent in America, the most detestable murderer or the most debonair jewel thief. Here the reader can probe and speculate to his heart's content. Richard M. Nixon.

At the time of publication, in 1965, Nixon was former Vice President of the United States. His remarks, in retrospect, portend his role in Watergate.

> In one's youth every person and every event appear to be unique. With age, one becomes much more aware that similar events recur. Later on, one is less often delighted or surprised but also less disappointed.

Albert Einstein to Queen Elizabeth of Belgium, January 3, 1954. Einstein Archive 32-408, in A. Calaprice, The New Quotable Einstein, Princeton: Princeton University Press, 2005. Another universal principle enunciated (not discovered) by Einstein, who died the following year.

Elsewhere in that book are these two absurdities: one comic, the other, evil:

> **Nobody in Football should be called a genius. A genius is a guy like Norman Einstein**, said by former player Joe Theisman.

> **Not Yet Hanged** the Nazi regime's caption under the photo of Einstein in its official book of **Enemies of the State**, 1933.

From a prayer book at a Reformed Synagogue:

> *The eye is never satisfied with seeing. Endless are the desires of the heart. A life, at its best, is an endless effort for a goal we never attain. Death finally terminates the struggle, in joy and grief, success and failure, all are ended. Like children falling asleep over their toys, we relinquish our grasp on earthly possessions only when death overtakes us.*

Robert M. Goldwyn

Rabbi Michael once said to his son: 'My life was blessed, because I never needed anything until I had it.' – Chasidic 18th century.

'He looked at his face (in the glass) looking back at it. He looked like someone other than the person he thought himself to be' – P.Steiner, **A French Country Murder.**

We plastic surgeons have heard this sentiment frequently from our patients. The fact is that we are who we are and who we are not.

I received this email from a classmate: **An Ode to The Old** (author unknown):

>… Sure, over the years my heart has been broken. How can your heart
>not break when you lose a loved one, or when a child suffers, or even
>when a beloved pet gets hit by a car? But broken hearts are what give
>us strength and understanding and compassion. A heart never broken
>is pristine and sterile and will never know the joy of being imperfect.

>I am so blessed to have lived long enough to have my hair turn gray, and
>to have my youthful laughs be forever etched into deep grooves on my
>face. So many have never laughed, and so many have died before their
>hair could turn silver. I can say 'no', and mean it. I can say 'yes', and
>mean it.

>As you get older, it is easier to be positive. You care less about what
>other people think. I don't question myself anymore.

>I've **even** earned the right to be wrong.

>So, **to** answer your question, (how do you feel about getting old?), I
>like **being** older. It has set me free. I like the person I have become. I'm
>not **going** to live forever, but while I am still here, I will not waste time
>lamenting what could have been, or worrying about what will be! And
>I shall eat dessert every single day.

Would such an attitude were purchasable on eBay!

'You make a living by what you get, but you make a life by what you give.'
– Winston Churchill

In D. J. Garrow's review of L. Greenhouse's book, ***Becoming Justice Blackmun: Harry Blackmun's Supreme Court Journey***, one finds this interesting paragraph: 'She (Greenhouse) depicts Blackmun as unusually self-preoccupied from early life onward. At the age of fourteen, he underwent an appendectomy, and "for the rest of his life, Blackmun would mark the anniversary of his own surgery; March 8 attained a lasting significance." Indeed, when Justice Sandra Day O'Connor had the same operation in 1988, Blackmun wrote her to say that "sixty-five years ago today I had my first surgery."' – The ***New Republic***, June 27, 2005

'New Releases', Relational Perspectives Book Series: Volume 27:
> What can contemporary psychoanalysis bring to the understanding of Generation X, a cohort for whom the trivialization of a dizzying array, of possible experiences teamed with the pressure to lead spectacular lives often leads to diffuse feelings of confusion, depression, and disorientation? In ***The Designed Self: Psychoanalysis and Contemporary Identities***, Carlo Strenger explores the psychology of young adults for whom the weight of cultural, familial, and religious traditions has seemingly vanished. These young people have grown up in a cultural universe defined largely by their contemporaries, and their maturational path is charted less by conflicts with authority than by the imperative to 'design thy self'.

Is the designed self the same as or different from the contrived self?

Olaitan, P.B. and Ogbonnaya I.S. Masquerades: Highly Flammable. Two Case Reports of Flame Burn Injuries Due to Masquerades. ***Annals of Burns and Fire Disasters*** 17:121, 2004:

> Masquerades are a common cultural practice in Nigeria, and especially in Eastern Nigeria. Often these masquerades are

performed during social functions, burials, house-warming parties, at Christmas and Easter, and indeed during most festivities. However, in relation to such events, some people accidentally suffer flame burns and present to our burns centre.

Case 1: The first patient we present is A.O., a 29-yr-old trader who presented to our centre 24h after suffering burns. He was being initiated into the 'masquerade world' – while dancing around a lighted candle, his costume accidentally caught fire. He was not culturally allowed to remove the burning costume, as this would have been regarded as cowardice.

Were Oscar Wilde alive today, he would have been delighted with this perfect illustration of his observation: 'Because a man is willing to die for a principle does not make it right.'

I. Kaplan (Now retired from plastic surgery) *The Wondering Jew*, Teper Publishers Ltd., Israel, 2004, p140

'Long Life'

Now the longer you live the older you get
And the older you get the more you forget,
And the more you forget the less you recall
Until you remember nothing at all.
Now when that happens, for the rest of your life
You reluctantly become an assistant housewife.
So you take down the washing and throw out the trash,
And go to the bank to withdraw some cash.
And you go to the post to collect the mail,
And here and there you knock in a nail.
And you help clear the table after you eat,
And think what to say when your friends you meet.
And when they come you offer them drinks,
And refrain from smoking 'cause your wife says it stinks. And so life passes by with little to do,
And you wonder why all this has happened to you.

'Cause the original sin your wife tries to repeat,
So she constantly gives you apples to eat.

From **Dictionary of Last Words**, E.S. La Conte, New York: Philosophical Library, 1955: 'Is there anybody in the room?' John Abernethy, English surgeon (1764-1831), the first to ligate the external iliac artery for aneurysm. – Not an unusual question for a surgeon.

Marie Antoinette, having stepped accidentally on the foot of her executioner: 'Monsieur, I beg your pardon.'
No one has ever accused the French of not being polite.

Jacques Casanova (1725-1798): 'I have lived as a philosopher; I die as a Christian.'
The world only remembers him as a libertine.

Edward the VII, King of Great Britain and Ireland (1841-1910): 'No, I shall not give in; I shall go on; I shall work to the end.'
These could be the last words of a few surgeons I know.

James Joyce (1882-1941): 'Does nobody understand?'
He might have been referring to the books he wrote, **Ulysses** or, more likely, **Finnegans Wake** or to Gertrude Stein, the writer and Joyce's contemporary, both of whom lived in Paris but never met because of their mutual dislike. Her last words were: 'What is the question? What is the question?'
If there is no question, there is no answer.'

It's the Mission not the Money

'What do you think this'll be about?' Myrna asked Joan, both secretaries, looking at the office bulletin board with a large lettered notice: 'Office staff meeting: 4 p.m. today.'

Robert M. Goldwyn

'Who knows what the Reverend Doctor will say but I bet it'll be one of his pep talk sermons,' Joan replies.

The 'Reverend Doctor,' their boss, was not a reverend but a doctor, a 55-year-old plastic surgeon, who was secretly ordained 'Reverend' by residents, some colleagues, and his employees, partly because of his name, Godfrey Gottlieb, but more, because of his ecclesiastical speech and demeanor. To his intimates (he had only a few) and his wife, he was known as 'G.G.', a name he intensely disliked but endured as just another of life's many trials.

4 p.m.: The chairs in the conference room are occupied by two secretaries, three nurses, the receptionist and the bookkeeper. Gottlieb, who stands facing them, is somberly dressed in a black suit, a dark gray tie on a high necked, super starched white shirt, remindful of Herbert Hoover, whom nobody in the room but Gottlieb ever heard of.

'I realize it is Friday afternoon,' Gottlieb begins. 'I thank you for your willingness to come (as if they had an option).

'We are approaching the end not just of the week but of our fiscal year. It is bonus time and, of course, each of you will receive your particular bonus (everyone notes the word *particular*) and a raise, whose amount will depend upon the advice and calculations of our accountant (everyone shudders) Mr. Monte Monetary (known to the staff as BAS – Born Again Scrooge).

'Monte, as he always does, will take into account not just the income of our office (all note the hypocritical *our*) and our expenses and everyone's performance and seniority and, I emphasize this, the gross national product of the United States and the world trade deficit as well as the factor of global warming (everyone is bewildered, as Gottlieb intends).

'Monte has suggested and I concur, as I am sure all of you will, that a sizable raise would be an insult to each of you so dedicated in the extreme to your work and to those who place themselves in our care (everyone thinks that the Reverend is at his best or his typical worst).

'Although money is the means of most transactions within our society, it should never be the objective. **Love of money is the root of all** *evil*, the Bible teaches us. No amount of money can ever replace the joy all of us experience in our daily, hour by hour, minute by minute, care of the less fortunate (the staff remembers several patients that day, all for facial rejuvenation or liposuction).

'If you could receive your salary without working in this office, you would refuse ("He must be insane," everyone thinks). Once again we can gain needed instruction from the Scriptures which warn us to be **not greedy of filthy lucre**. Money can never replace the spiritual high we receive from our literally hands-on relationship that each of us has with every patient. In that regard, how crass of me to use the word patient instead of what a patient is: a suffering human being (the staff's thoughts revert to those whom they saw earlier – none of whom looked like a sufferer).

'We have to remember that whatever we do for each of these unfortunate individuals who comes to us, we are helping not just that person but that person's family, children, grandchildren, great-grandchildren, friends, neighbors and relatives who may live not just in this country but throughout the world. You look astonished (and he is correct) but let me give you this example. I am sure that most of you remember Emily Knuckles. She was the seventeen-year-old with an enormous nose on her small pitiful face. It not only overpowered her looks but her psyche.

'When I first saw her, I said to myself: "Poor little Emily carrying the weight of the world on her nose." (Nobody in the room thought of Emily that way.) Well, as I was doing her rhinoplasty, the realization came to me that I was not only giving her a better looking nose – and I modestly say that it was a superb result – but I realized that this transformation would influence whom she would marry and of course with whom she would pass on her genes along with those of her husband, perhaps a better choice for marriage than she would have been able to make without our rhinoplasty (that *our* again) – those genes will pass from generation to generation. In effect, I was operating on her nose but affecting incalculable generations descending from Emily Knuckles. Long after we are gone, that operation that I did – that all of you helped her achieve – will have its effect. I call it a subtle Tsunami, so powerful in its consequences and ramifications. Can anything duplicate the work that we are doing? Can a payment in money ever equal our payment in satisfaction? For you to think of your salary and for me to think of my income is almost a sacrilege.

'Let me conclude by telling you a story that concerns three medieval workmen who were asked what they were doing. The first replied, "I toil from sunup to sundown and all I receive for my pains is a few francs a day." The second answered, "I am glad enough to wheel this wheelbarrow for I have been out of work for many months and I have a family to support." The third proclaimed proudly, "I am building Chartres Cathedral."

'As far as I am concerned, we are doing even more than building a cathedral. We are building a congregation, many congregations who will in turn build cathedrals, fashion empires out of dust, and will affect mankind in ways that only God can discern. Imagine all this happening in this small office as a result of our humble talents, our unwavering dedication, all possible because of guidance from above.

'Enjoy your weekend and its repose. Return refreshed on Monday ready for new challenges, new opportunities to change the course of human history.'

With a beatific look on his upturned face and his hands clasped together on his chest, the Reverend Doctor walks slowly from the room, leaving behind an audience whom his words have anesthetized, at least for the moment.

No Hope, No Medicine

I am assuming that most people hope for the best and not the worst: i.e. when a patient goes to a doctor, he or she hopes for improvement and/or cure and the physician hopes also for that outcome. From my reading, I conclude that hope has receive too little attention from basic scientists although not from social psychologists and psychotherapists. Without hope or the expectation that something good will happen because of what we do, I doubt that we would undertake much. The world would be dreary and medical practice would be sparse if human beings were incapable of hope. Hope and the will to survive – to thwart death – explains why there will always be a place, an opportunity for alternative therapies when patients believe that the best effects of generally accepted medical practice will not be successful for them. Understandably they will turn to other measures alone or in conjunction with conventional treatments unless the patient and/or his or her family has accepted or even may desire the inevitable. With life waning, agnostics, even atheists, might find comfort in the visit of any representative of any religion. A dying patient might chose also among the many supposed cures offered via the media, the Internet, through books or word of mouth. And why should he or she not?

In ***Measure for Measure*** there is this line:
> The miserable have no other medicine
> But only Hope

That is true but not only the miserable have hope; we all do and not just when we are unhappy. In fact, we may have the hope that our happiness will not end soon or, with more hope, not ever end!

In short, hope is essential to life and to medicine. Ambroise Paré (1517?-1590), the Father of Surgery, wrote: 'Always give the patient hope, even when death seems at hand.'

Some doctors, the most properly credentialed and scientifically based among us, become annoyed and patronizing when a patient whom they cannot cure and expect to die goes to another person or place or finds an alternative treatment. When we have nothing else to offer, we should respect the right of that individual to seek help, even to facilitate it or, at least, not to obstruct it unless we believe that it is harmful to the patient with regard to health which, ironically, the patient no longer has. No physician owns a patient. What we might consider bizarre treatment might work to our amazement and to the patient's benefit. We doctors might even learn something. But even if other ministrations fail, the patient and his or her family might have the satisfaction of believing that they tried everything, they exerted all their options and did not accept death passively. The patient might feel that he or she was captain of the ship on its last voyage.

And let us not discount the value of a charlatan (from the Italian, a variant of cerretano, an inhabitant of Cerreto, a village near Spoleto, famous for its quacks). Why should our pejorative opinion of a charlatan preclude someone dying for whom all else has failed from benefiting from even a charlatan's attention if it offers hope without adding to the pain or accelerating the death of someone presumably at life's end? Quacks – the successful ones – are notoriously amiable, always available, and are extraordinarily capable of displaying any emotion the payer wants, especially a hopeful attitude. A good physician should show some of the same qualities of empathy, compassion, and friendliness but sometime the overworked doctor may not be easily available, especially to the point of making one or two house visits a day.

I realize that what I am writing would lead some to conclude or misinterpret that I am a champion of charlatans; I am not. I do recognize, however, the limitations of conventional medicine and that of the more accepted forms of alternative medicine. My point of view is that to someone dying, whom medicine has deemed unsalvageable, is it a great harm to offer some hope and pleasure? We certainly do it for children with visits by clowns, sports figures, other celebrities and even the Final Wish program that may give these children a trip to Disneyland – all of which I applaud and suggest that older patients be entitled to something out of the ordinary if feasible.

Some or many may quickly rebut my argument by saying that charlatans offer 'false hope.' That is true but is that necessarily wrong if it does not harm an individual medically or financially or in any other noxious way. For centuries religion has had to face the charge of false promises and false hopes. Not everyone who goes to Lourdes, for example, is improved or cured. Nevertheless, they may find some happiness and tranquility in the process. We are too quick to decide what is best for others even if we do not have a true conception of what is best for ourselves. Forbidding a dying patient to have available to him or her even an aberrant alternative therapy because we feel it is foolish or we believe that the patient's wishing it is a sign of weakness is, to me at least, an indication of our lack of generosity. It is in the same category of foolishness as denying pain medication to a terminal patient because, and I have heard it said by residents, 'He may get addicted.' Although we physicians have been trained in science, we should not let science limit our vision, particularly when science at a certain point cannot provide the answers or the help that a dying patient and his or her physician need.

Who Will Remember Us?

The will to survive and the desire to propagate are basic drives, instincts that we once called ingrained but now term genetically encoded.

In spite of or because of my marginal knowledge of the science of evolution, even less of the theory of creationism, I propose another deeply imbedded human drive: the need to be remembered and also to remember. Cogent evidence throughout history are memorials to the dead, ranging from elaborate pyramids to simple stones, from mausolea holding remains to urns containing ashes. The human species find it difficult accepting death as the absolute finality. For alternatives many or most believe in an afterlife, in resurrection, or reincarnation. In those societies without physical structures erected to the dead, they are remembered through prayers and other rituals and may even be worshiped.

In many traditions, certainly the Jewish, in its liturgy and literature, the theme of 'who will pray for me after I am gone' is a constant. Jews, like many other sects, are instructed to remember their martyrs, their parents, their grandparents, even their earliest progenitors, the patriarchs and matriarchs, e.g. Moses, Abraham, Sarah, Leah.

These thoughts occurred to me when I recently visited my parents' graves in Worcester, where I was born and grew up. I go there once a year but not on a fixed date. The last times my children were there was when my parents were buried. I am an only child and when I am gone, nobody else will likely visit the graves of my parents. Unpleasant as it is to contemplate, my children and their children and their children will have their own final places, probably at great distances from each other and from my wife and me.

I now envy (perhaps too strong a word) those families whose members were born, lived, died and are buried in the same graveyard. What once was common in this country, particularly in rural areas, is unusual now because families are scattered. I confess that I do not visit the graves of my grandparents. The reason is not just that they are in different cemeteries not nearby but I no longer feel the immediacy to them that I had when I was a child. I never knew my father's mother, who died when he was young, but I had considerable contact with his father and much more with my mother's parents. My selfishness or self-absorption has unfortunately overcome what should be a sense of gratitude or, at least, responsibility. I console myself, however, with the observation that grandparents for most of us become less important in our lives as the years pass. The reverse is not true and if a grandchild died, the grandparents would remember the tragedy until their own deaths and if the geography permitted, they would be more likely to visit their burial sites.

Life is for those who have life. Not remaining linked to the past, not mourning even the closest lost loved one to the point of emotional and physical paralysis are perhaps also under genetic control. Someone who grieves too long, admittedly an arbitrary assessment, is considered abnormal, requiring psychotherapy, to enable him or her to reconnect with life.

Emotional relevance determines who is remembered and who is not during life and after death. It would be unrealistic to expect that great-grandchildren or great-great-grandchildren who never knew us should feel an attachment and desire to resurrect us in their thoughts and even more unrealistic to expect that they would visit our graves.

And if they did, what would they remember about us? More people remember Hitler and Stalin than most saints. I was thinking about this the other day when I read about the death of a 75-year-old 'socialite and devotee to fashion' whose 'greatest quote was that "if there was no shopping in heaven she wasn't going..." She was just a very light-hearted charmer. She was painfully thin and wore clothes beautifully. She didn't take herself seriously like her peers in her social set... [she] turned her children's rooms into walk-in closets after they left home... She was just a lot of fun.' I suppose it is better to be remembered as 'a lot of fun' rather than 'a lot of misery,' but I hope that most of us would achieve something more than 'an unabashed clothes horse particularly devoted to designer Yves Saint Laurent' [obituary, Nan Kempner, July 6, 2005].

I am showing my middle-class, bourgeois background when I state that life is too short, too precious not to take it and oneself seriously. It is interesting that two people whose writings I have enjoyed and from which I have taken instruction, in their public stance trivialize life but never did, if we can believe their biographers, their own lives:

'Life is too short for men to take it seriously,' George Bernard Shaw, **Back to Methuselah** and 'Life is much too important a thing ever to talk seriously about it,' Oscar Wilde, **Vera, of The Nihilists**.

It is much easier to talk about life in the abstract than to confront it in the reality.

Memory: 'Don't Leave Home Without It'

On the 125th anniversary of its debut, *Science* devoted a commemorative issue (July 2005) to 'exploring 125 questions that point to gaps in our basic scientific knowledge.' As one might have predicted, most of the queries concerned physics, chemistry, mathematics, and biology. For me many questions themselves were sufficiently daunting to comprehend without attempting to give an explanation. One query however, I did understand and have long thought intriguing: 'How did cooperative behavior evolve?' In the single page allotted to her, Pennisi mentioned many factors and possibilities most of which I already knew but one I had never considered:

Robert M. Goldwyn

With regard to Cooperative Behavior Among Humans, 'Modern researchers have discovered that a good memory is a prerequisite: It seems reciprocity is practiced only by organisms that can keep track of those who are helpful and those who are not. Humans have a great memory for faces and thus can maintain lifelong good – or hard – feelings toward people they don't see for years. Most other species exhibit reciprocity only over very short time scales, if at all.'

When young, we assume that our memories are adequate for most tasks, except possibly taking exams when we become exasperated if we cannot summon a strategic fact. When we become older, however, a lapse of memory is not just annoying but foreboding – a possible harbinger of dementia in one of its many forms. Memory, like any asset, tangible or intangible, we fail to appreciate until we lose it. Buñuel, the Spanish film maker, in his autobiography, **My Last Sigh** (1983) expressed it correctly: 'You have to begin to lose your memory, if only in bits and pieces, to realize that memory is what makes our lives. Life without memory is no life at all, just as an intelligence without the possibility of expression is not really an intelligence. Our memory is our coherence, not reason, our feeling even our action. Without it, we are nothing.'

Unfortunately I saw the transformation in my mother as her Alzheimer's advanced. To me she was and will always be something, not nothing but she certainly was different in her ninties from what she had been even in her eighties. As I observed her deteriorate, my fear was first for her comfort and well-being with the hope that she would have some happiness and, indeed, from time to time she looked as if she did. My other fear, selfish admittedly, was would my memories of her final stage of life blot out the memories of what she was to me most of her life and all of my life.

Since her death, my recollections of her when I was young and middle-aged and when she was middle-aged and even older become stronger as the painful scenes of her last two years in the nursing home recede, a kindness on the part of my memory. Just as the ability to recall is essential to cooperation, so it was important to my mother's cooperativeness as a patient. Until almost the end of her life, my mother recognized hospital personnel in general as people who were trying to help her. She recognized me, my wife, and her grandchildren until the final weeks or so I would like to believe.

To conclude writing about memory without acknowledging a master of the past, not just a past master, Marcel Proust, would be not simply an omission but a sacrilege. *In The Sweet Cheat Gone*, he wrote: 'The bonds that unite another person to ourself exist only in our mind. Memory as it grows fainter relaxes them, and notwithstanding the illusions by which we would fain be cheated and with which, out of love, friendship, politeness, deference, duty, we cheat other people, we exist alone.'

⁂

'Getting to Know You...'

Other oldsters will recognize this from *The King and I* by Rogers and Hammerstein. The next line 'Getting to know all about you' is a prelude to some thoughts about an aspect of medicine that physicians take for granted until they retire: becoming acquainted in the strictest professional sense with another human being at the time of the initial consultation and subsequently. What emerges from just obtaining a history is not solely an accumulation of facts, medical and personal, but, ideally, the personality and character of the patient, his or her relevant, usually important experiences, and that person's way of living. Within ten minutes in a doctor's office the interested and alert physician will have an infinitely greater knowledge of that human being than most others in that patient's life. The usual social encounters at cocktail parties or dinners or even the workplace understandably yield little by comparison.

The physician has the authority to elicit pertinent information from the patient who understands that it is in his or her best interest to furnish it. The therapeutic setting permits questions the patient under most other circumstances would rightfully consider intrusive, rude or even obscene. Every new patient is an opportunity to meet and understand a human being who was previously unknown to us an occasion to widen our experience through that of another, to add to our knowledge, sometimes a fact or an insight that the patient has expended considerable energy and time to acquire and frequently under difficult circumstances. The physician who does not like to engage more than superficially with the patient and prefers to doctor at a distance, limiting his or her interactions to prescribing, treating or operating, would consider what I have described as chances for self-enlargement, a prodigious waste of time. For me it was one of the more rewarding uses of my professional time and not simply to be a better doctor for that patient but to be a better and wiser person hopefully to benefit myself, my family, friends and other patients.

Is it simplistic to think that a physician, supposedly someone inquisitive about the world and what is in it would not take advantage of the therapeutic setting to learn as well as to heal? The physician has a ringside seat, at least, and a participant's status at the greatest show on earth, the human one. The first step, however, is to realize it.

The plastic surgeon may do the same operation with variations several times a day but never on the same person. Differences of the psyche, far outnumber those of anatomy.

One of the reasons I believe I never burned-out professionally was my spectrum of interests, something that my father, also a physician, taught me to cultivate. Perhaps of even more importance was my interest in patients, as individuals, not as vehicles taking me to the operating room.

Willing Regression

I sometimes use the time between when I awake and get up to displace myself backwards to my childhood, the home where I grew up, the neighborhood, grammar school, prep school and particularly my earliest friends. I wonder what they are doing or, somberly, whether they are doing. I speculate about their careers but more about their personal journeys: relationships, marriage, children, their losses and gains, what gave them the most happiness or the most pain and whether they resurrect the old days and think about what they might have done better or worse. The long look back makes us realize that situations which once we thought important seem irrelevant but the reverse is also true.

In my morning recall, key players then remain so: parents, closest friends, teachers but others who, I once thought, were minor players mount the stage of the past in major roles. I did some of them an injustice since still vivid to me are their images, mannerisms and the circumstances that brought us together. Do they ever think of me and how would they react if they knew that I still think of them more than casually?

Why I spend much of the present thinking about the past and have done so from an early age I have never totally understood. Perhaps I am partly forever stuck in my childhood, which was happy and secure and which I know how it turned out, more so than I do with regard to the present and obviously the future.

Throughout my life I have had a recurring fantasy that on my deathbed if I were mentally competent, I would enjoy a prolonged flashback, a parade of people who were important in my life who made me happier even briefly. I have been fortunate that far more good people have affected my life than the few bad. I was fortunate that I did not have to run an obstacle course but I did have to stay the course and I had an excellent start and much help along the way. In these early morning reveries I remember and thank many who eased my life and consequently those of my family. My journey back includes encounters with patients memorable because of their surgical problems but also because of their courage, perseverance and humor. I helped them but they also helped me and continue to do so in my combat with prostate cancer and other ordeals that are the uninvited intruders into our life. It is remarkable how in a few minutes, even in seconds, the brain can summon so much, so quickly outpacing even the most up-to-date computer.

One might think that my retrograde interval would tire me. Quite the opposite. It gives me energy, calmness, and a perspective of the life I have led and of the day before me.

Robert M. Goldwyn

Jean-Paul, Simone, Albert and I

The first time I saw Paris was the summer of '47 on a student tour with six boys from Worcester Academy. Our leader was Eben T. Fogg, who had taught French and coached our fencing team. World War II had ended two years before. The first evidence we saw of it was when our boat, the Ernie Pyle, a 8,500 tonner, one of Kaiser's a ship-a-day, entered the port of Le Havre. War's residue was all around us: prows of sunken ships, fragments of buildings, rubble in the street, a few old cars among scores of battered bikes, and the worn faces of people who had experienced too much.

By train, which still had German signs in the compartments, we arrived in Paris at night. The city was electrifying for me then and is still so.

That summer, despite its run-down appearance and its post-war living: e.g. ration cards for bread, Paris was Paris and no conquering army could take away its past.

We stayed at the small Hotel L'Alma, at 17 rue de L'Exposition in the 7th arrondissement, metro stop Ecole-Militaire, named after the school that Napoleon attended and where a teacher evaluated him as 'poor in military tactics.'

Though it was almost 60 years ago, that part of my youth – the Paris days have never left me. I could well understand the feeling that inspired Robert Hillyer to write:

> Early in the morning
> Of a lovely summer day
> As they lowered the awning on the rue Francois – 1er,
> I was 20 and a lover
> And in paradise to stay.

I was sixteen and a lover, but only of Paris, the other kind had not yet come my way. We were teenagers and for the first time not just in a foreign city but in Paris. Hemingway understood: 'If you're lucky enough to have lived in Paris as a young man, then wherever you go for the rest of your life it stays with you, for Paris is a moveable feast.'

Unfortunately my stay in Paris was only two weeks but I believe that I experienced everything with a keenness and excitement that happens too infrequently in the lives of most of us. No sound, sight, person or event was too inconsequential for me not to seize upon, comment about, record in my diary, and so remains part of me for these many, many years.

Before I went to Paris and when I was there, I studied French as hard as I could and read as much as I could. Not surprisingly I found my way into existentialism through the writings of Jean-Paul Sartre, Simone de Beauvoir, and Albert Camus. I confess that what they wrote were less important to me than how they lived. I found more romance in their lives than they probably did. On later trips to Paris and in my first year at Harvard College, I went further into existentialism, trying to experience it as if I were dressed in a beret and a dark turtleneck sweater, walking through the small streets of the Left Bank near the Sorbonne.

I was trying to decide how I would live my life even though I had already chosen to become a doctor, a psychiatrist like my father.

L'homme est ce qu'il se fait – man is what he makes of himself... this is purely a consequence of the maxim that existence precedes essence – **L'existence précède l'essence** (L. Pollmann, Sartre & Camus New York: Ungar, 1967).

I was caught increasingly between two opposing prongs: One, each individual can and must determine his or her own actions. 'Nothing can save me from this inescapable momentous choice – no commands, no values criteria, not even other people's actions, no model I may follow.' (Idem, Pollmann). And the other – the Freudian view that although we ideally can act in any way, our earliest life experiences determine to a great degree our choices.

I understood how World War II, the occupation of France and the actions of its collaborators influenced the development of Sartre's philosophy when he was part of the Resistance and saw too many around him offering excuses for their behavior. I had not been in the army and was just a bystander, thousands of miles away from what was happening in Europe and in the South Pacific. Sartre did not even serve as an example because he himself had stated that no one could use anyone else as a model but had to set his or her own course of action. Whether or not

God existed also did not matter since the choice was ultimately that of the individual. However, in the midst of these philosophical discussions with others and myself, I could pursue some of the trappings of a Paris existentialist: e.g. wearing my beret, talking French and hearing French music whenever possible, returning to Paris to browse through the bookstores and to eat at the Deux-Margots, the Parisian café that Sartre, de Beauvoir and other existentialists, authentic or would-be, frequented. I never saw any of them but during my prowls I imagined I did.

The leading existentialists are all gone. Sartre and Castor (Beaver), Sartre's name for de Beauvoir, lie together in Pere-Lachaise. Camus, who denied being an existentialist and the validity of existentialism, died in 1960 in an auto accident when he was 47. Is it possible that my life is already 30 years longer than his?

In my late teens and early twenties, I searched on this side of the Atlantic for someone who might be my Castor until I realized that what they had done as a literary duo would not happen to me and, in fact, was not what I really wanted. True to Sartre but more true to myself, I made my own path with gratitude to the existentialists and their city and all that I continue to romanticize without regret.

The Art of Getting it Right

In reviewing a biography of William Osler, Teigen cited the Latin aphorism: Ars est celare artem – 'art consists in concealing art.' His point was that 'when a historian/biographer is successful, readers do not notice the skill that went into the research and writing.'[1]

The validity of that observation extends beyond literature and even art. It is certainly true for aesthetic surgery. Those having it should look better without the stigmata: e.g. a taut face or a cropped nose. Improvement not a peculiar transformation should be the objective.[2]

Knowing where to stop is almost as important as knowing when to begin. And sometimes getting to the end point is trickier. In that regard,

Lord Mancroft expressed it well: 'A speech is like a love affair. Any fool can start it but to end it requires considerable skill.'

How to navigate between doing or saying too little or doing or saying too much requires a subtle brilliance. This is true in almost any human activity. Too much water can kill a plant but so can too little. Not enough tightening of the SMAS leaves unwelcomed sag; too much pull creates a tell-tale bridle. Unfortunately experience alone does not confer wisdom unless one is willing to learn from experience and not just to repeat it. Would that we were as critical of our own results as we are of a colleague's. With the arrogance of the non-combatant, a listener at a meeting or a reader of a journal will condemn the work of a presenter without showing or even reviewing his or her own experience.

A basic problem is not only that the golden mean is elusive but it varies from person to person. What I consider loud when my grandchildren play their music is certainly not true for them. Although we may listen to our patients carefully and think we have an accurate idea of what they want and even if we achieve it, the patient may feel that we did not get it right.

As I have gotten older, I have come to realize that any success that I have had was the result of not only what I did but what I refrained from doing, from not nurturing the seed of self-destruction that Freud believed resides within all of us and needs very little to make it grow.

While I was in practice, I was too often called upon to reverse the unfortunate effects of what colleagues had done in their patients. The hardest problems I found not only with respect to the work of other plastic surgeons but to that of myself was to backtrack surgically. Far better and easier for all concerned if what was needed was to do something more. Getting it right does not mean that one has to achieve the goal in one operation. A surgeon who attempts to get a swift, spectacular outcome is likely to endanger the patient's well-being and his own reputation. How to know when less is too little and more is too much a surgeon should be pondering before entering the operating room.

References:
1. Teigen, P.M.: William Osler, Again. **Bull. Hist. Med.** 75:745, 2001.

2. Goldwyn, R.M.: When aesthetic surgery is not aesthetic. **Plast. Reconstr. Surg.** 86:548, 1990.

Why Be A Doctor When You Can Be An Endorser?

The other night on television I saw (I could not avoid) an ad featuring Tigar Woods endorsing a new Buick. I do not play golf nor do I own a Buick but if I did drive a Buick, would I now take up golf? Conversely if I did play golf, would I shed my Toyota to buy a Buick in the hope that it would improve my score from what would likely be 180 to 175 over par?

In a world where malnourished millions struggle to get a decent meal once a week, we, in the United States, are overfed, and are obsessed with shedding weight, acquiring luxuries and seeking diversions. To aid us in the pursuit of the trivial are the pop icons of our age: athletes, rock stars, film and entertainment celebrities. Why they and not I? Yes, I am jealous. I want to be a cult figure – any cult will do. I resent the fact the advertising firms ignore a 77-year-old professor of surgery; a retired plastic surgeon who was an editor. If given the chance, the world, I am sure, would want to know which bottled water I consume, which toothpaste and floss I use, not to mention more intimate items. Because I am so generous and put the well-being of others before my own, I would consent to endorse products and places for a financial consideration far less than what Tigar Woods or Celine Dion receives.

During the initial stage of my contact with the public, I would have to be know as Doctor Goldwyn. As my fame grows, I shall drop the title and become like other last named greats: Plato, Aristotle, Einstein.

'Dr. Goldwyn flies American' (or any airline that is still in business and gives me a cheap ticket).

'For Dr. Goldwyn, nothing can surpass a January vacation in Lapland

'For writing, Dr. Goldwyn finds essential Nike shoes with cleats.'

I would willingly appear in public information bulletins: 'Goldwyn advises seeing a doctor before your mortician sees you.'

'According to Goldwyn, nothing enrages the IRS more than the use of invisible ink.'

'Goldwyn has switched from 41 cent stamps to 42 cent stamps. Why are you behind?'

'Goldwyn has discarded his abacus in favor of a BlackBerry' (which he keeps unwrapped on his desk because he doesn't know how to use it).

'Goldwyn says, "Be patriotic and beautify yourself and you will beautify your country; see a plastic surgeon today."'

I have many other ideas but why bore you? It should be obvious that being an endorser is easier than being a doctor: better pay, no emergencies, no malpractice, even if a viewer buys an $80,000 car and fails to get the woman or man who the ad implies comes with it.

My motto (credo?): 'Endorse without remorse.'

Wanting More

At a recent symposium on risk management, the leading speaker presented the well-known paradox of today's public benefitting as never before from remarkable advances in medicine yet being more dissatisfied with their care than were their parents and grandparents. At first thought this may seem surprising but it is not; it is predictable. Most human beings expect more when they have more. Just think of our friends, family and ourselves. As parents, did we ever hear our children ask for less allowance? For most of our lives we think that more is better but as we get older, we should realize the opposite is true and embrace the ideal of less, but few patients and few physicians attain that perspective.

Robert M. Goldwyn

One of the reasons for the dynamism of our society is the fostering of malcontent. To be satisfied with what one has is not viewed as a virtue but more as a weakness, an admission of passivity and indolence.

I am not talking about those unfortunate people with too little to eat and nowhere to go who need shelter and food, which they should have. For them, getting more is synonymous with survival. Not so for the majority of our population, however, who are beyond subsistence living, who throng the malls, who prefer replacing to saving or restoring, who confuse luxuries with necessities. Imagine what would happen to our economy if, for example, women refused to relinquish last year's fashions or if we bought new cars only when the old ones collapsed. The absurd message to the consumer is that something is out of date the day it is purchased.

Although some objects become more valuable with advanced age, not so most of what we buy and certainly not life and the human body. In our technologically based society, whose citizens want and demand the best and the latest, which may not be the best, people expect medical treatment to be infallible: improvement and cure with predictability – and at low cost. Life and the human body sadly are not subject to the wishes of the mind or the mechanics of the computer. The fact that people sicken and die, sometimes without warning, many take as an affront, a perverse injustice.

'But he took such good care of himself. He jogged four times a week, avoided fat, ate oatmeal and gobbled vitamins.' Modern man's preventive medicine resembles the funereal rituals of the ancient Egyptians to guarantee life after life. We grasp not at straws but at gossamer.

I remember a patient complained that her dermatologist 'missed the diagnosis.' She was referring to a basal cell carcinoma on her husband's nose. I replied that it is sometimes difficult to make the diagnosis at a very early stage but did remind her that her dermatologist had referred the patient for treatment. I excised the basal cell, with all margins clear, but another focus, not grossly visible, was detected.

When I told the patient and his wife, she said: 'You would think that medicine had come a long enough way so that things like this would not happen.' She was upset that her husband had to undergo another procedure and did not want to hear that medicine, like most human activity, is imperfect.

Staying Power

In the hospital I saw a nurse, in her late seventies, bent and dwindling, coming to work. That it was before seven on a magnificent Saturday morning in September when others, including myself, would have preferred being elsewhere, did not diminish her cheerfulness as she conversed in the elevator. Her 'Have a good day' was heartfelt. Although I had never encountered her before, I was certain that she possessed a turbo which propelled her to find joy in her work. It has been said that nothing great was ever accomplished without enthusiasm; to achieve even the ordinary requires a minimum of zest. The world has many quiet heroes and heroines who labor with little respite and often without being recognized or even noticed.

In marked contrast are the celebrities, especially the athletes, like Cal Ripken, who set a new record for playing in consecutive baseball games, and Lance Armstrong, whose seven consecutive wins at the Tour de France will probably never be equaled. Although their feats and character deserve the high kudos they received, Ripken at age 37 and Armstrong at 33 were still kids compared to the elderly nurse and many who have been in practice more than 30 years. A plastic surgeon, who recently retired, told me that in three decades he had never missed an operation. For him the game was perennial not seasonal.

This may be the first time in the history of medicine in the United States when physicians in good health are retiring at a comparatively early age. Factors leading them to choose weekday tennis over daily rounds are decreasing remuneration, increasing legal tangles, and unbridled bureaucracy. Voluntary retirement is possible only if one has the desire and the money. It is surprising how much frustration we can tolerate if we must.

I once asked a patient, a town employee, when he planned to retire. His reply was 'Sixty-six months and twenty-seven days.' Obviously he delighted in his work!

When people retire depends upon their personal preferences, societies attitudes and the guild's rules – factors that determine when they began their career. Ralph Waldo Emerson, in writing about the youth of his day, commented on a nineteen-year-old who after the death of his father edited a newspaper and supported his family. Now we hear about those of college age 'needing more time to get their head together.' Together with what? I never determined the structure other than the neck which they would be using. Their attitude, of course, is a way of avoiding commitment.

The humorist, Sam Levinson, wrote about modern grandmothers not looking like those of yesteryear. When I grew up, if a woman of 80 walked into a supermarket in shorts carrying a tennis racquet, the local constable would probably be summoned along with a psychiatrist. Today she is admired for staying fit and being 'with it.' About 35 years ago when I began practice, an 84-year-old doctor examined me for life insurance. He had been a well-known hand surgeon and anatomist; his love of medicine kept him in the arena although he was no longer operating. He, nevertheless, considered himself a physician and examined me thoroughly. His respect for detail and his pleasure in meeting patients, even an unspectacular one like myself, were evident in how he conducted himself long after most of his medical school classmates had either retired or died. Today he would be considered a dangerous anachronism who likely could not obtain malpractice coverage.

I Laugh Now But Didn't Then

I wrote the following a year before I retired from practice:

It should have been an ordinary morning: Up at 5:30 a.m., out by

6:30 a.m., at the hospital by 6:45 a.m., breakfast, then the computer to locate the patient on whom I had done a reduction mammaplasty the day before. I had to discharge her, then change for the day's operations beginning at 8:00 a.m.

Time is a foe in the morning. I felt like I had an extra systole when I could not find my patient in the computer. I called the Admitting Office, which had no record of her. I rushed down to the Information Desk to speak to the woman who has been in charge almost since I joined the staff. She also failed to locate the patient.

'Dr. Goldwyn, shame on you for forgetting her name.'

'Well,' I responded defensively, 'that is her name. I remember it because it is unusual. How many Zelda Zagrebs (name changed) could there be in this hospital? Or, for that matter, in the world?'

'Well, Doctor, you can come behind the desk and look for yourself.'

'I believe you,' I said, my voice cracking with frustration. I was doomed to be late for the operating room.

'Dr. Goldwyn,' she said in an understanding, therapeutic voice, 'you and I have been here many years. You know and I know how tired we can get and sometimes forgetful.'

In spite of myself, I appreciated her gentleness, even though it was misplaced. Maybe I had forgotten her name or worse, perhaps I never had operated on her because she did not exist. My mother, I recollected with alarm, now 94, is in a nursing home because of Alzheimer's. Could this be its first sign for me?

But this old fox had another trick. I called the resident and almost genuflected with gratitude when he said: 'Oh, sure, Zelda Zagreb is still in the Recovery Room because no beds were available.'

'Ah ha!', I exclaimed to the woman who had just revealed herself as a false friend.

'Zelda Zagreb is here! She's in the hospital. She is here, yes, in the hospital.'

Passing patients were looking at me as if I were another patient desperately in need of psychiatric attention.

'Her name never made it to the computer because she never was officially admitted to the hospital,' I persisted mercilessly.

She was not to be outdone. 'As far as I am concerned, she is not here if she is not in the computer,' displaying a logic that would have defied Kant or Heidegger.

One speaks today with concern about a new morality but more serious is the new reality, equating it with the computer, where if it is not there, it is not anywhere.

Ponder the term 'virtual reality.' Something or someone is either real or it is not. To resolve the problem we need today another Einstein or Houdini; I am just a doctor.

The Age of Nefarious

A rear bumper sticker yesterday still has me puzzled: 'My Karma Ran Over My Dogma.'

I thought I knew the definition of karma until I looked it up in The American Heritage Dictionary of the English Language to be sure and now I am not sure: 'The sum and the consequences of a person's actions during the successive phases of his existence regarded as determining his destiny.'

What kind of karma or dogma did the driver have and what significance should his existence or essence have for the rest of us who view the back end of his car? More likely it was a sadistic joke: 'My Kar (MA) Ran Over My Dog (MA).' If that is what it meant, what kind of human being would advertise such an event?

I admit that I was paying too much attention to that statement when I should have been more concerned about saving my life in Boston traffic, where capriciousness and mayhem are the norm.

A few other things that week made no sense. For example, at the hospital a man in his late twenties was to have an inguinal herniorrhaphy. When the anesthesiologist was about to insert an intravenous line, he said: 'How will the needle hole heal? Will it leave a scar?' The anesthesiologist, to her credit, seemed not astonished and reassured him that it would be unusual to have a bad scar from this intervention.

I suppose the now plastic surgeon should rejoice in this obsession with appearance. It pays our mortgage and our children's tuition. But is this the direction our society should be going? The search for outer perfection has obscured the pursuit of inner improvement. How far can a narcissistic culture pursue its gratification's? Tune in next century and see – and cry.

Here in the United States, where hospitals compete ferociously for patients, we are contorting ourselves to please. While concern for the patient should always be paramount, we have taken it to an extreme. There is a cloying, unctuous quality to all this. When was the last time you saw a gruff doctor? The occasional gruff doctor, almost always a he, has been succeeded by an occasional brusque female doctor. This type has been replaced, however, by a new model – the model physician, solicitous, overly so, someone who has just attended a seminar or a retreat devoted marketing. That performances of doctors are now being rated by patients and their Health Maintenance Organizations will likely produce a 'best (or should it be better) foot forward' approach to the patient.

I do wish we had the opportunity to rate patients, especially those who turn minor problems into major events. I remember a 42-year-old school teacher who had an upper and lower blepharoplasty along with removal of two nevi from the chin. One of the incisions in her chin opened slightly, prompting two calls a day for a week. I suppose I should have been thankful that she focussed on her chin and not her eyes but dreaded that would be forthcoming (it wasn't).

I acknowledge that we obsessive plastic surgeons find it difficult to deal with the same trait in our patients – an observation that recalls what I heard on the radio recently: a patient advocate, a comparatively recent phenomenon of the health care scene. He was earnestly haranguing the audience to select a doctor who had the same illness or condition as they have. 'That doctor will be more sympathetic and knowledgeable.' I was wondering whether he made sure that his financial advisor's assets were the same as his.

Robert M. Goldwyn

If I were a forty year old woman with breast cancer, would I see only a physician of my gender with a known history of the same affliction? Think of the profiles that my state's Board of Registration in Medicine would put forth in addition to what they do now:

Richard P. Drownne, M.D.
Age: 57   Male
Regional ileitis (medication, no operation)
High Cholesterol (medication)
Smoker (Persistent despite hypnotherapy)
Moderate Hypertension (medication)
Anal Tags (excision)

Or pertinent to our specialty:

Marshah Lionz, M.D.
Age: 48   Female
Mammary hypoplasia (augmentation)
External nasal deformity (rhinoplasty)
Excess fat of the buttocks (liposuction)
Marital difficulties (counseling)

Cecil Soma, M.D.
Age: 54   Male
Dog bite of face (repair)
Gynecomastia (correction)
Basal cell carcinoma of nose (Mohs excision)
Periorbital wrinkling (laser resurfacing)

I am not sure whether in America it is our karma or our dogma that is the problem. I do not know which is running over the other. However, I am certain that given the reality of disease, decline and death, at least of the earthly variety, the most important things in life lie beyond anyone's control, even that of the Health Maintenance Organizations.

'Something Old, Something New, Something Borrowed, Something Blue...'

Some will recognize the title as the first part of a wedding rhyme but of unknown authorship and date, which became the formula for success of a well known band leader of the 1940s. I was reminded of its relevance to surgeons and their choice of operations at a recent Mortality and Morbidity rounds when a patient who had a failed deep inferior epigastric flap was presented – 'something blue.'

Breast reconstruction offers many surgical options, depending upon the anatomic needs of the patient, her preferences, and those of the surgeon.

Young surgeons, I have observed, are more likely to choose a more complicated and lengthy procedure, commonly involving microsurgery, than would older surgeons.

If the flap fails, younger surgeons are more readily forgiven or less criticized because of the presumption that they are learning; where as older surgeons, especially those who seldom do the procedure, would be judged, perhaps rightly, to be 'past their prime.'

Younger surgeons are more likely to devise and promote new procedures.

Young patients are more likely than those older to desire immediate breast reconstruction.

Young patients are more likely to want their reconstruction by autologous tissue, such as a free flap, without an implant; older patients are more willing to have reconstruction by rotation flap with or without an implant.

A patient at the time of the initial consultation who considers herself most informed on the basis of information from the Internet about a specific kind of breast reconstruction and insists on it is most likely to be a difficult and dissatisfied.

No surgeon performs equally well every type of breast reconstruction.

Surgeons doing the mastectomy vary in their judgment and competence, a phenomenon seen particularly with skin sparing mastectomy. A younger plastic surgeon may find himself or herself in a difficult situation (the patient is in a worse situation) if he or she is allied with an inadequate surgeon – a dilemma made more difficult if that person is older and a steady source of referrals.

And penultimate, as I have said for years, what begins as reconstructive ends as aesthetic.

Finally, as important as it is to improve and invent new ways of reconstructing the removed breast, it is of greater importance to discover ways of preventing breast cancer and saving the breast or, at least, recognizing the presence of cancer earlier so that extensive, complicated and risky procedures will be unnecessary.

Advice To The Lifeworn: Do Less, Live More

A reviewer of a biography of Johann Sebastian Bach referred to the fact that the great composer's life was '...the story of genius shining through the stupefaction's of quotidian existence...' (Butt, J.: The Saint Johann Sebastian Passion. Review of C. Wolff. **Johann Sebastian Bach. The Learned Musician.** *The New Republic*, July 10 & 17, 2000, pp.33-8).

While none among us likely qualifies as a genius, most of us confront the stupefaction's of everyday living and, if we are to preserve our souls, we must rise above them. Too often we allow details and trivia to overwhelm us; indeed, we often seek them to avoid introspection. We then lose our perspective without realizing it. Priorities are not just disordered but forgotten. If one has to fight to keep one's head above water, one cannot notice the beauty of the pond. In response to the common question of 'how are things going?', we hear 'I'm hanging in' or 'going on' or 'muddling through.' Sometimes the reply is 'I'm fine' but said without conviction.

This period in western civilization (civilization is not synonymous with civilized behavior) is notable for human beings doing more and contemplating less. People rate each other and themselves on how many things they undertake, with more points for simultaneity of tasks or pleasures. Julius Caesar and Peter Paul Rubens could do several things at once. Today we have many who are attempting the same but unfortunately they lack their caliber.

Our children and grandchildren now have become not the beneficiaries but the victims of being over-scheduled, especially if they are the progeny of a middle class home where both parents work in high paying jobs. As the parents become richer, the children become 'enriched,' a word to describe after-school programs that hopefully turn an ordinary child into an extraordinary intellectual who, if all works out, will become an Ivy League professor as if that is the highest of human attainments. I thank my parents in retrospect for their allowing me a childhood that did include work but did not exclude play or leisure, time to think, time to fantasize.

I remember a 45-year-old patient who came for removal of a basal cell carcinoma of her lower lid was concerned less with its excision than the challenge of scheduling it. Her appointment book made mine look skeletal. Although she worked as a real estate agent, it was in the realm of other engagements that she had somehow lost her way in trying to find her identity. Looking for an opening in her list of must-events, she read some of them to my secretary: 'No, that's not good. There's an exhibit opening that I have to attend. It's in my friend's gallery. No, there's the new play at the Schubert and my husband's law partner is having a party that night' – on and on it went. Despite her feigning being upset with so many commitments, she relished her role as a social dervish. She was a prisoner in her own jail, recalling Jean-Paul Sartre's observation that the guard has less freedom than the person he is watching. Sartre did not consider the existential situation of the guard and the prisoner as being the same.

The freedom to do as much as one wants can be a kind of slavery if we do not know when to set limits. The idea and ideal that more is better is inherent in a technologically driven society. I use the word 'driven' purposely. Some people rush into the car, drive furiously but fail to consider their destination. Do I really want to go there or be there? Is it worth my limited energy and time? In the supermarket of life do we have to buy every item?

Each religion demands from its adherents a break from the usual routine. This interval is not for devotion alone but for contemplation, renewal and the rearrangement of priorities. In our society labor has taken over; it has become the end in itself. Since work, if done well, begets money, the incentive to undertake more and more is enormous. The practice of medicine is demanding but rewarding as well. We earn not just a living but praise and respect if we do our work well. In the process our money grows; our leisure dwindles; and, if we are careless, our spirit withers. The irony is that some will earn more than they will ever spend. That the average annual vacation for Americans is two weeks may be good for the Gross National Product but is it good for the inner self?

Once I asked a friend, a psychiatrist, what he was going to do that Saturday afternoon. 'I am going to think,' he replied. That answer I have never forgotten. The usual retort would have been 'I will play tennis' or 'I will be taking the children shopping' or 'I will be visiting friends.' Not he, who had the courage to plan a period for contemplation, the greater courage to do it, and even more courage to announce it.

As much as we surgeons enjoy operating, occasionally when a procedure has to be canceled, the unexpected few hours are like a divine gift, recalling that delicious day when the teacher forgot to assign homework or even better, when the substitute teacher never appeared.

Allowing ourselves a work-free interval is not the same as being lazy. Paying attention to our emotional and spiritual life is not really doing nothing. It is doing something – very important. From our parents and society we learn early our values and pattern for life. A middle-class child who was over-scheduled at age nine will be so at forty.

Henry David Thoreau instructed: 'Live the life you've imagined.' One has to look away from the grindstone to imagine. It is sad that too many will have earned the epitaph: 'Here lies _____, who never took the time to live but found the time to die.'

The Sameness of it All

Spiro Agnew, a former Vice President under Richard Nixon, both of whom, as we know, were forced to resign, made the quintessential politically incorrect remark about slums when he chose not to visit one in Los Angeles: 'When you've seen one, you've seen them all.' His remarkable lack of sense and sensitivity in that comment made it and him unforgettable, at least to me.

I thought today about what he said when I was in the deserted offices of the Department of Surgery early in the morning. I was in my hospital but I could have been in any hospital in America. While architecture might vary, the general layout would probably be the same: an entrance, a lobby, an information desk, elevators, an operating suite, rooms for patients and locations for the many specialties that constitute modern medicine. Sameness, similarities, and differences must be defined not only in relation to place but to time.

If, for example, I had been in a hospital in the early nineteenth century, before Roentgen and his discovery of radiation (1895), there would have been no radiotherapy, a marked contrast to what we find today. There would also have been no radio therapy, which came after the Curies isolated radium (1898). Hospitals were structurally simpler, suffering worse and, by comparison to today's statistics, morbidity and mortality were horrific. The great surgeon, Guillaume Dupuytren (1777-1835), reported a 25 percent mortality at the Hôtel Dieu following open reduction of zygomatic fractures. What is even more remarkable is that it was not higher, considering the fact that he was operating long before Lister's concept of asepsis and Fleming's discovery of penicillin.

Robert M. Goldwyn

When I talk about the 'sameness of it all,' it is patent hyperbole restricted in time, our era, and in place, America.

Wherever I have gone in this country as a visiting doctor or as someone seeing family or friends who are ill or on a few occasions, as a patient, I have found the relative sameness of the therapeutic ambiance comforting. For patients and physicians, surprises in the environment are disconcerting and possibly fatal. While we want our doctors and their treatment of us to be up-to-date, we do not want them or their hospital or even their office, to be unbearably dissonant with our expectations, presuming they are reasonable. No patient, except a dying one, would like to hear a doctor say that 'I have an idea about a treatment that is completely new. Let's give it a try.'

There is comfort in predictability.

Through my decades the hospitals with which I have been most closely associated have grown in size, facilities, and staff. New names are on the doors and people I never met are now the healers of patients for whom I no longer have responsibility or even relevance. But if I were to become unconscious and placed almost anywhere in any hospital in the United States, I believe that if I were to wake, I would know that I am in a hospital even if I did not see a doctor or a nurse. The dull color of the paint – the usual hospital hue would be sufficient for me deduce my surroundings.

Primum Nocere, Secundum?

Attributed to Hippocrates, Primum Nocere, First Do No Harm, is or should be a guiding principle for the practice of medicine. It is relevant also to the conduct of our lives. But what comes second? Hopefully, do good – for our patients and others. Although societies may differ in what constitutes good and bad, they recognize the difference(s). No family or any group, small or large, could function without having standards of behavior for its members even though not all will heed them. Despite my high titer of cynicism, I believe that most people do more good than harm in a lifetime.

Concerning the famous and infamous, biographies detail actions commendable or not. The life of almost every human being is a mixture if that person has lived long enough to have been able to make a difference. No matter how lengthy, no book and certainly no obituary can encompass all that a person did for 'better or worse' (and I am not referring only to marriage). Like most, I am a potpourri of inconsistencies, more of which, I hope, are deemed good rather than bad (I am talking in terms of 'good' and 'bad' because I find no synonyms to be as clear and powerful).

But whatever we have done with our lives or whatever our attitude toward death, the end must come to all, plastic surgeons or not, as it does to our patients. Whatever others will say or think about us after we are gone, we will never know. Their thoughts about us now are not always evident. Pertinent is John Wilson's obituary code, which though humorous, is sobering and instructive (cited by C. M. Ward, **Br. J. Plast. Surg.** 38:84, 1985):

> He did not suffer fools gladly
> He was the rudest bastard in miles
> His surgery was charged with idealism
> He took outrageous risks with human life
> He generously encouraged his juniors who benefitted immensely from his sage guidance
> His juniors did all his work and he took all the credit
> He was a man of Christian principles
> He was a transparent hypocrite
> He was a connoisseur of fine wines
> He drank
> He had personal problems
> He drank secretly
> His wife remained an inspiration all his life
> (God knows how the poor woman stayed with him.)

For some individuals their obituary should say something without saying anything:
- He (she) paid his bills promptly.
- He never shot a neighbor or a neighbor's pet.
- He drove on the right side of the road in the United States.
- He never pushed a cripple down the stairs.
- He never ran naked or screeched expletives in his place of worship.
- After his divorces, he was respectful to each of his seven wives.
- He never knowingly passed a counterfeit bill.
- He voted in each Presidential election.
- He made an occasional charitable donation upon the advice of his accountant and did so with neither rancor nor joy.
- He was proud of his modesty and careful not to boast about it.
- He never littered a highway.
- He believed in the golden rule – in reverse: he never did anything for anybody or wanted anybody to do anything for him.
- His shirts were clean and his shoes polished.

With a modicum of imagination one can construct an obituary or a eulogy consistent with the advice of Chilon of Sparta, known as 'one of the wise men' of sixth-century BC Greece: 'of the dead, [say] nothing but good.' But if not good, at least nothing bad.

The British Prime Minister, Harold Macmillan (1894-1986), observed: 'Memorial services are the cocktail parties of the geriatric set.' Since the deceased cannot enjoy the occasion, why shouldn't others?

Retirement: Time for Savoring Tidbits

I just finished reading Louis Buñuel's autobiography, *My Last Sigh*, which he finished a few months before his death at 83. Among his accomplishments as a director were the **Adventures of Robinson Crusoe**

Retired Not Dead

(1952), **Wuthering Heights** (1953) and my favorite, **Belle de Jour** (1967) featuring Catherine Deneuve. While my life has not been that of a Spanish film director, the process of aging which he described and I am experiencing has similarities. We both have had a past and, as we are fortunate, a memory of it. Buñuel wrote:

'[M]ost of the time I prefer a slower death, one that's expected, that will let me revisit my life for a last goodbye. Whenever I leave a place now, a place where I've lived and worked, which has become a part of me – like Paris, Madrid, Toledo, El Paular, San José Purua – I stop for a moment to say adieu. "Adieu, San José," I say aloud. "I've had so many happy memories here, and without you my life would have been so different. Now I'm going away and I'll never see you again, but you'll go on without me." I say goodbye to everything – to the mountains, the streams, the trees, even the frogs. And, of course, irony would have it that I often return to a place I've already bid goodbye, but it doesn't matter. When I leave, I just say goodbye once again.'

I am fortunate to be in good health despite a few medical problems which my doctors have helped to control, and am not at the stage when I am saying goodbye 'to everything.' But, I confess, that when I go abroad, especially to a place remote and exotic, I wonder whether I shall have the chance to return. When I was younger, I was presumptuous to believe that I would always make the pilgrimage again if I chose. With age comes the realization that one is in control less of one's actions but hopefully more of one's reactions. We become more mindful that we are no longer the captain of our own ship – in fact, we never were. We sought comfort in denial but eventually the truth of Victor Hugo's observation become irresistible: 'We are all condemned but we do not know when our sentence will be carried out.'

The last paragraph of Buñuel's autobiography expresses well my recurring thoughts: 'Only one regret. I have to leave while there's so much going on. It's like quitting in the middle of a serial. I doubt there was so much curiosity about the world after death in the past, since in those days the world didn't change quite so rapidly or so much. Frankly, despite my horror of the press, I'd love to rise from the grave every ten years or so and go buy a few newspapers. Ghostly pale, sliding silently along walls, my papers under my arm, I'd return to the cemetery and read about all the disasters in the world before falling back to sleep, safe and secure in my tomb.'

In another passage, Buñuel wrote: 'No one's really interested in other people's dreams...' Certainly psychoanalysts are as is anyone whose life is entwined with that of the dreamer. The 'Greatest Show on Earth', in fact, is not the circus but life around us. If one is interested in people and enjoys paying them attention, study, and possibly help, one will never be bored. Admission is free and the 'show goes on' all day, everyday, in every season and without the need to other than watch, listen and think. Other human beings provide endless opportunities for instruction and even detection, the last in reference to their motivations that might explain their behavior. Sometime it gives one so inclined even more opportunity to savor life's tidbits. As an example, before I began reading **My Last Sigh**, I spent time and got pleasure from thinking about the inscription on the inside cover of the book: 'Vic – LETS [sic] SEE THE REST TOGETHER ~ ,' signed 'Whitney' with a heart drawn beside her name.

    If I were running to the office or to the operating room, I doubt that I would have speculated about Vic and Whitney. What happened to their relationship? For some reason I believe they were not married when Whitney wrote what she did. How did their lives turn out? Did they see together more of Buñuel's 32 films? If, by a miracle, either Vic or Whitney or I hope both read this, would it cause a smile, tears, anger or indifference? Always a romantic, I believe that when Whitney expressed 'Lets [sic] see the rest together,' she was wishing for more than sitting in a movie theater.

    My copy of the book that Whitney presumably gave to Vic was published in 1984. Now, twenty years later, Vic and Whitney are likely in their forties. Do they believe, as do I, that although life has a multitude of choices and circumstances, we are never totally free to make a choice although we are permitted and encouraged to do so.

Buñuel's title, **My Last Sigh,** brought to mind the well known verse by Robert Frost:

> I shall be telling with a sigh
> Somewhere ages and ages hence:
> Two roads diverged in a wood, and I -
> I took the one less traveled by,
> And that has made the difference.

Did Vic and Whitney take a road less traveled and, if so, were they together?

※

Let Them Take Steroids

The title is a parody of Marie Antoinette's remark 'Let them eat cake,' (Qu'ils mangent de la brioche.) Louis XIV's Queen might not have been sympathetic to the peasants but historians doubt that she ever made that comment. There is no ambiguity, however, that she lost her head via the supposedly humane machine designed by the French physician, Joseph-Ignace Guillotin.

Whatever Marie Antoinette may or may not have said, I am stating 'Let them take steroids.' I am not talking about patients with adrenal insufficiency; I am talking about athletes.

'Finally,' some of you are undoubtedly saying, 'Goldwyn has gone bonkers. Tendencies in that direction were apparent to some of us but now his stupid statement leaves no doubt to anyone about the dismal state of his mind.'

What prompted my venturing into areas I probably should avoid was the disclosure this week that Ralph Palmeiro, the superstar first baseman of the Baltimore Orioles, someone who has chalked-up more than 3 thousand hits and more than 500 home runs, tested positive for steroids, specifically stanozolol, not available except by prescription.

What would happen if we allowed anyone eighteen or older to take any substance not prohibited by state or federal law to enhance his or her athletic ability? Note that I am not stipulating the rules of an athletic association but statutes of the federal and state government.

Robert M. Goldwyn

The immediate response to what I propose is likely 'There should be a level playing field.' I agree that the playing field should be level and usually is, at least for baseball and football players, but certainly not all athletes are born with the same physical, emotional, and intellectual capacities and skills. Furthermore, what is later acquired may be as important or more so than what is genetic. Not every athlete is privileged to have the same training and facilities because of where they live or how much money they have. Those who compete in the Olympics from the United States, receive much more to make them excel than most athletes in most countries. Should we attempt to equalize the trainers and training of all competing athletes?

To equalize mountain climbing, specifically the ascent of Mount Everest, should we do away with special clothing? Training, equipment, such as oxygen, and not try to obtain the most knowledgeable Sherpas? Do we think less of Sir Edmund Hillary and Tenzing Norgay for having reached the top of Mt. Everest in 1953 because they had equipment and know-how that their predecessors lacked?

I just read that professional tennis is allowing the use of rackets containing piezoelectric crystals inside the shaft: When the racket hits the ball, that instantly fires up the magnets and forces the racket back to its original shape, helping 'players add power and precision to their strokes' (E. Sheng, Nanotechnology Hits the Tennis Court, **Wall Street Journal**, August 25, 2005).

I mentioned about the now routine use of oxygen in climbing great heights but what should we do about the common routine of providing oxygen to football players when they leave the field? While oxygen in not a steroid, it does modify their metabolism to eliminate lactic acid and prepare them more quickly to return to the playing field, level to be sure.

Think about the common stimulant, coffee and other beverages containing caffeine. Should they be prohibited and athletes tested for their breakdown products prior to competing?

Perhaps smoking cigarettes before the game or chewing tobacco during it should also be banned and players tested for traces of nicotine.

And what about alcohol? Should athletes be given Breathalyzer tests? What would have happened to Mickey Mantle, the legendary centerfielder of the New York Yankees, whose ingestion of alcohol was as prodigious as his ability to hit home runs from either side of the plate?

If we offer the argument that athletes must be protected against hurting themselves, a likely long-term affect of steroids, then let us do away with boxing. It certainly would have spared Mohammed Ali his subsequent neurological problems.

As far as I am concerned, eliminating speed car races would not only save the lives of many drivers but would not encourage teenagers to imitate them and kill not only themselves but others.

If I were in charge of the Olympics or any organized sport, I would say to all participants over the age of eighteen: 'Show up on time. We do not care what you have done to your bodies, whether by substances not proscribed by state or federal laws, what you have modified yourselves by training or special foods, by psychiatric help or meditation, and the like. Do your best and we shall consider the winner the person who is the best no matter how it has been achieved without cheating, of course, and by respecting the usually accepted rules of the contest, such as beginning the race at the starting line when the gun sounds.'

While the running field may be level, those on top of it are not and it is only when we die that the field becomes level with us under it.

Driven Crazy

For some reason, known perhaps not even to God, I have had periodic difficulties with the Massachusetts Registry of Motor Vehicles. My first ordeal I described more than a decade ago (**Plast. Reconstr. Surg.** 94:361, 1994). The essence of that bureaucratic auto-da-fé was that I had been driving for five months with an expired license plate sticker that a policeman had observed. The Registry had sent my renewal form to an address in Littleton, Massachusetts, where I had never lived or even visited. When my daughter, Laura, who had been driving the car told the policeman who had stopped her that I never was a citizen of Littleton, he replied, 'Maybe your father has another life.'

Why the Registry did not mail my application to my home in Brookline I never discovered. Despite an agonizing sequence of telephone calls, letters, and even personal appeals, it took several weeks to convince the apparatchiks that this situation was due to their computer error and not my willful disobedience.

To recapture the moment, which has obviously never left me, I ask readers to forgive me for quoting myself: 'I asked to see the head of the Registry. She listens to my story and matter-of-factly says: 'Well, Doctor, when you didn't receive your registration renewal, that should have triggered something in your mind.' I felt as if I was again in the office of my junior high principal. I tell her that my life is filled with forms, that in my workday, my secretaries and I choke on them. How could I possibly realize that one less form arrived?' This is a tactical error of gargantuan proportions. To someone in her position, nothing could be more important than a form from the Registry.

'I will do anything,' I plead. 'I will even pay the excise taxes that I do not owe to a town where I have never lived.' My voice quavers like that of an aging castrati (or should it be castrato?). If only Kafka were alive, I think, to witness and record my agony.

The manager is now looking at me skeptically. She must be certain that I am not who I say I am. How could a surgeon fall apart so quickly when he must deal with life and death hourly? I am disintegrating like a meteor.

'How did this ridiculous situation happen?' I wail.

'We are all only human,' she says. This response brings me halfway back to reality. I also have used it on unpleasant occasions with patients. The difference is that she will not get sued and no one's health, except for my sanity, will be harmed. All this is a prelude to what happened a few days ago. I recount this episode as definite proof, at least to me, that the Post Traumatic Stress Syndrome does exist.

I recently received in the mail a notice to renew my license. I decided to do so on the Internet. Although I am writing this calmly, when the Registry sent me that letter, my peripheral resistance increased markedly because I remembered what had happened to me, The Littleton Affair in my mind's file. Even when I go to the supermarket to buy apple juice, which frequently comes from orchards in Littleton, I seek another brand from another source.

To be honest (and why not, since I can't think of a better alternative?) my wife, Tanya, is my access to the computer. For reasons that only a psychoanalyst could fathom, I have chosen to remain off the 'information highway.'

With The Littleton Affair in my memory, my wife and I completed the form obsessively, checking and rechecking to be sure that my name, date of birth, place of residence, and social security number were accurate. We sent it out and it was acknowledged but a few minutes later, we received another reply stating that 'No record exists of this person of that name at that address with that social security number.'

'How could this be?' I squeaked to my wife, 'They're after me again.' I can always depend upon my paranoia, to which my wife is almost accustomed.

'I exist,' I screeched. 'I have been on this planet for 77 years with that social security number. I just went to the bathroom. I am functioning and therefore I exist.' This outburst caused my wife to react with an indulgent look, as one would give to a lunatic. The startled concern in her eyes belied her outward saintly calmness.

'Let's repeat the process,' Tanya said logically.

'It will be Littleton once again,' I replied forlornly. 'I am not sure I can go through it again.'

Wisely ignoring me, my wife redid the form with the same data and off it went into the computerized interstices of the Massachusetts Registry of Motor Vehicles.

Almost immediately and mercifully the Registry accepted our offering. Perhaps the Lord intervened not wanting to put me through a trial for sainthood since obviously I am patently unworthy.

Exhilarated by having had my identity confirmed and my citizenship verified, I said to myself: 'I have renewed my license, therefore I am.'

Robert M. Goldwyn

For Some Another Obstacle on the Road to Cosmetic Surgery

In *Cosmetic Surgery Times*, the Medical Editor, Dr. Ronald G. Wheeland, Professor and Chief, Section of Dermatology, University of Arizona College of Medicine, (*Cosmetic Surgery Times* 8: Editorial, September 2005) called my attention to the following fact: 'Several states have now issued rules that prohibit patients on government assistance from having cosmetic surgery, even if they pay for the procedure themselves... instead of just recognizing that the patient seeking cosmetic surgical procedure should pay for it, government says that indigent patients who receive their health insurance coverage from state or federal sources cannot have cosmetic surgery even if they pay for the procedure themselves.'

The reason for this edict is the belief that cosmetic surgery is a luxury and unnecessary as are all luxuries, and that it is performed for vanity not survival. Dr. Wheeland concludes that the prohibition against indigent patients having aesthetic surgery even if they pay for it is 'unfair: ...when other groups receiving government-subsidized health insurance coverage, such as those on medicare and active-duty military members can have cosmetic surgery (some even at government expense).' I agree completely with Dr. Wheeland and his analysis as well as his conclusion, namely that indigent patients are 'easy targets' for this kind of ruling and that there should be 'flexibility' in deciding who is eligible or not for aesthetic surgery.

One can easily think of a situation, as does Dr. Wheeland, of someone who is receiving welfare but is given money by his or her family or friend for a procedure that might benefit that person psychologically and lead to an important change in his or her life.

Consider a family on Medicaid who may have a teenage daughter, an excellent student, perhaps interested in becoming a actress but has a large nose and wishes a rhinoplasty. The family, including that girl, work hard to earn money to pay for a rhinoplasty which they cannot have without jeopardizing the family's health insurance subsidy from the government. Does someone who is poor also have be or feel ugly?

The larger issue is what society and those with money think a poor person should have. Is someone on welfare allowed or entitled to have a family outing at an athletic contest? Are we so draconian that we deny the economically disadvantaged fun? Should someone poor, receiving financial aid, buy only a used car and, if so, how old and of what make? Those economically blessed either by inheritance and, or, their own hard work are often punitive toward those below them on the socio-economic scale, whether by circumstances beyond their control or by their own misguided or even foolish actions. Should those below the poverty level be allowed a hot fudge sundae when protein from a chicken would do them more good? Would we apply that same criteria to ourselves?

We have heard the refrain that if one gives money to the poor, certainly to a beggar, he or she will spend it on alcohol. Perhaps that is true but too often it is given as a reason not to help anybody whom we encounter, whose presence makes us uncomfortable. 'Why should I subsidize that person?' I have heard on many occasions. My response, either expressed or voiced to myself, is why should I subsidize a CEO's lavish lunch in a three star restaurant at which he has possibly arrived in a chauffeur driven new Maserati or an old yacht. Misguided society too often forgives even admires the excesses of the rich while condemning the same behavior in the poor.

An unpleasant feature of human nature, when exercising power over public funds, is our tendency to be mean to the have-nots but generous to the haves and have-lots.

'But Their Appearance Was Overrepresented...'

The title quotation is from John Ward, the trainer of Monarchos, the 2001 Kentucky Derby winner. As a happy coincidence I met this magnificent horse at a farm when I was in Lexington, Kentucky about a year ago. Mr. Ward was not referring to Monarchos but to some yearlings he had bought a few years before. They had undergone enhancement prior to having been sold – electrostimulation of muscles, straightening knees and legs, reshaping feet, receiving anabolic steroids and routine supplements, even having acupuncture as well as over-exercising in order to show 'their muscles rippling' (J. Drape, At Horse Sales, Steroids and a Little Nip and Tuck, **New York Times**, August 14, 2005).

Mr. Ward said also that 'time and exercise and genetics' would eventually prevail and return the horses to 'their normal state... There is a fine line between the showmanship of showing a horse to its fullest and fraud.'

Not all adjustments, a euphemism, however, are allowed. If, for example, a yearling has had electrostimulation of the throat to make it look fuller and to increase the breathing capacity, the 'horse can be returned for a refund, but only if what was done can be proven within fourteen days of purchase.'

Cosmetic surgeons are more fortunate with regard to our patients than are veterinarians and the owners and trainers of young thoroughbreds. We are allowed, expected, encouraged, and even paid to overrepresent our clientele. And if we do not, our patients would be not only unhappy but perhaps litigious. The fact that a spouse, for example, finds out that his or her mate has had aesthetic surgery does not usually lead to a divorce and the expectation of a refund. Numerous studies have shown, furthermore, that when observers who on the basis of photographs have ranked subjects highly in terms of their appearance, they do not change their ratings after being told that their favorites had undergone cosmetic surgery. Not just plastic surgery but much of our society and ourselves depend upon 'overrepresentation.' In our environment and in our personal lives we do not leave nature alone. That is the essence of a technologically advanced, albeit sometimes misled, society. Tunnels are pushed through mountains, rivers are diverted, lawns are mowed, houses are painted, heated and cooled and our bodies altered and not just cosmetically.

Do I overrepresent myself, and if so, to whom, because I take medications to lower my cholesterol or survive my prostate cancer? Am I a better or lesser me for having had medical and surgical manipulations?

Did the authentic Goldwyn exist only in his youth? – But even then, I had my tonsils, adenoids and appendix removed.

To pursue the absurd, does liposuction or correction of syndactyly diminish the true self? For most of us, these are inanities to be dismissed but for philosophers these questions undoubtedly would stimulate endless discussion and weighty (obese) books.

Imagine what Internet dating services would require for information to be shared with a prospective date: list all operations you have had; list all medications you are taking; check this box if you are presently dyeing your hair. If you have had cosmetic surgery, please provide details as well as preoperative photographs. If you have lost more than ten pounds within the past year (with or without surgery), please furnish pre-weight loss photographs.

One might speculate whether society could survive such openness. We have heard about the dangers of government without representation but could a society exist without overrepresentation?

My Shoes Were Too Big For My Feet

In choosing this title, I realize that the folk-saying would imply that I attempted a task beyond my ability. In this instance, however, I am being literal: I bought shoes too big for me.

This might have Freudian significance because I remember when I was about eight, I wanted to buy gloves that my mother and the salesman said were much too big for my hands. Perhaps I was fixated on another part of my body and wanting it more imposing. That event from 65 years ago I remembered when, about six months ago, I purchased shoes that I thought would be comfortable. At that time, the salesperson questioned whether they were too large but I persisted. Later when my wife saw them, she said they were 'much too big.'

Nevertheless, being an obstinate surgeon, I wore them for six months. One of my friends, also a surgeon, asked whether I had a problem with my gait since I plopped my feet in front of me as if they were snowshoes. 'Of course not,' I replied indignantly. What finally ended this macabre instance of ill-advised outfitting occurred at a meeting of The American Society of Plastic Surgeons in Philadelphia when, to my embarrassment, I could not extricate myself from the back seat of the taxi without the doorman helping to deliver me, almost like an obstetrician but without forceps. My wife was with me and, like the good wife she is, said nothing – which is worse than saying the obvious.

I did not enter the hotel but immediately went with her to a department store and bought shoes that did fit, a size smaller than what I was wearing. The saleslady asked 'How could you ever have gotten shoes so large for you?' I murmured something in futile self-defense. She advised me strongly: 'You are the type of person who should never buy anything without your wife being there.'

Why repeat such a comic story that reflects little good on me? I suppose that it illustrates how I, and I am sure many others, do something wrong, put up with it, try to adapt physically or emotionally and not take the obvious steps to correct it. It is embarrassing to be wrong. It is stupid also: I spent more than $100 for a pair of shoes that would do better on the feet of a Boston Celtic. The money, however, was a lesser issue. Admitting that I was wrong, bestirring myself to change were the real issues.

Currently I have shoes that fit. My friend, who had noted my almost syphilitic gait, no longer comments about my walking. I am still no Nureyev but I am making progress.

Names

When Juliet says to Romeo 'What's in a name?' she answers her own question: 'That which we call a rose/ By any other name would smell as sweet.' An answer both clever and immortal, as is so much of Shakespeare.

In almost every culture throughout recorded history, parents give names to their children, whose peers give them nicknames. Some countries, France and Germany, have certified names; parents cannot chose any name they want for their offspring. While the American Civil Liberty's Union would protest, some children have undoubtedly been spared terrible labels. On the other hand, some names have become clichés through overuse. Attributed to Sam Goldwyn (no relation) was this statement: 'Now why did you name your baby "John"? Every Tom, Dick and Harry is named John.' This famous movie director obviously anticipated Yogi Berra.

Where have some names gone: Prudence, Hope, Faith, Epiphany, Charity, Felicitas, and Immaculata? These were given to baby girls but now parents would be afraid that their daughters might grow up not possessing those qualities. Perhaps the safest name was one I heard the other day for a girl or it could be for a boy: Destiny, which has the added advantage of being politically correct.

We are in another era in which we should give names for qualities we want for our children but are afraid express: Entrepreneur, Top-of-the-heap, or Leader. Not so the many African-American parents who have had the courage to be clear in what they wished for their children: Lawyer, Doctor, Judge, Duke, King...

If we were to rename people after they have retired, we might replace William, with Spendthrift; Harry, with Philanderer; Sue, with Shopper; George, with Gossip. Fortunately for us, perhaps not for society, we usually live with the names we have received at birth and not according to the lives we have since led. To cite an extreme example, Adolph Hitler carried that name from birth to suicide. He remained officially Adolph even though the surname Horrible would have been more fitting.

If each of us knew that we would be assessed periodically, perhaps every ten years with a possibility of being renamed according to our behavior, would we act better toward our families, friends, and colleagues? Perhaps our society should adopt the practice of giving stars or noting absence beside our names, as does the **Guide Michelin** with restaurants. Think about the toasts and eulogies that might ensue:

'We are here to celebrate Bob Goldwyn's 77th birthday. He deserves the recognition, certainly from his family and friends. Although he has accomplished much in his life, we must take note of the fact that he had two stars growing up, three stars at 50 and at 60, but is down to one star now and is in danger of losing that. The reasons for this should not cloud this celebration. For the bean or star counters among us, the causes for his having lost some of his stars can be accessed on the Internet (comedycast.networth.org).

I once met a Chinese man, age 40, whom his village called 'Six Finger Lee,' because he was born with six fingers on one hand. Subsequently he had the supernumerary digit removed. He told me that the elders had discussed whether his nickname should be changed. For some reason he liked it since it gave him something to talk about when he met a new girlfriend. Think of the consequences if this same gentleman had several marriages and at age 55 was known as 'Four Wives Lee.' Anyone meeting him for the first time would not know whether the woman with him was his fourth wife or the fifth-to-be. But everyone would be forewarned.

Some people have directed their lives to live up to their name. A famous professor of psychiatry at Harvard Medical School was Harry Caesar Solomon. He achieved eminence without acting like the Mighty One from Imperial Rome. His parents placed a heavy burden on him which he managed to carry well. Furthermore, he did not hide his middle name but there are some who should. I had a patient who dropped his first name of Leo to assume his middle name of Napoleon. The only quality of Napoleon that he had was his height. He had to sit on a cushion in his job as a bank teller. It was as if history had gone awry – someone named Napoleon propped up to take care of customers who lined up in front of his small window. With the name Napoleon, he should at least have been president of that bank.

There are friends and colleagues that I have noted names but frankly have lacked the courage and intrusiveness to inquire, e.g., did Court Cutting became a surgeon partly because of his name? Did John Doktor become a physician so he could be Dr. Doktor? These thoughts remind me of a conversation that allegedly took place between James Joyce and his father when he told him that he had met a girl whom he might marry. When the elder Joyce found out that her name was Nora Barnacle, he said 'That's the kind of girl who'll stick to you,' and indeed she did.

When I was in practice doing a large amount of breast surgery, a new patient greeted me, 'Good to meet you, Dr. Breast.' I was amused not just by her remark but the fact that sometimes I would think of myself as Bobby Breast, a confession that I can make now that I am much older and no longer in practice. I wonder whether that patient ever had a similar Freudian lapse with her gynecologist.

The other day I found out the name of someone whom I had known for decades and whose name reflected the Waspiness that he radiated but was Jewish and never publicly admitted it until he died when he was buried in a Jewish cemetery. Did I think differently about him and less of him when I discovered his past history? Yes, because I thought that he had lived much of his life as a lie.

Thinking of him recalls a story about Charles P. Steinmetz (1865-1924), who was a mathematical and electrical engineering wizard at General Electric. He was also a hunchback and a Jew. One day while walking in New York City with Otto Kahn, the banker and art patron, Kahn pointed out some of the many buildings and charities to which he had donated, most particularly the Metropolitan Opera. Suddenly Kahn turned his head and bent down to whisper into Steinmetz's ear, 'I used to be a Jew.' Steinmetz replied, 'I used to be a hunchback.'

Vestigial Activity

Vestigial is a common word in biology and medicine, most frequently used in relation to the appendix, a rudimentary organ which in today's human being seems to serve no purpose. I think of that word frequently since I have retired because I see myself engaging in vestigial activity.

Let me go back to the time when a friend and I went to Tangiers; we were both twenty-five. We found a book by Major Melor, who had come to Tangiers immediately after World War II. We never met him but we fantasized considerably about his life, much of it might not have been true. We imagined that he had served in Burma or India, retired to Tangiers, where the cost of living was less and the excitement more

Robert M. Goldwyn

than he would find in London. We envisioned him as someone who rose early, marched not walked, primed for a dangerous event or perhaps another war, ready to defend an empire that no longer existed and would not call upon his services. Perhaps his wife has since died and on their anniversary, he dutifully visits her grave, where he now rests.

The fact is that a retired surgeon is like a retired major or perhaps a general, who has no army, the surgeon has no patients. Yet, he or she might engage in vestigial activity, perhaps encouraging friends and neighbors to consult him and, like myself, gives an opinion about whether to seek help and when as, for example, when a four-year-old in the house across the way fell on her face. I was sorry not to have been able to to suture her laceration in the emergency room.

I knew a retired internist, who had an enormous family and many, many friends to whom he was still 'the Doctor' and remained so to patients long after he had stopped practicing. His wife told me that he would spend about a half hour every day giving medical advice and guiding referrals. In that situation, the difficulty is not just to maintain one's knowledge of a field but knowing which physicians are doing what and how well. This becomes a harder task for a physician who has retired, like myself, who no longer is in the operating room where I can see and hear reports of other surgeons at work. One loses contact with personnel, nurses and anesthesiologists, who are in the best position to recommend whom to see and whom to avoid. The older doctor, whatever his or her field, finds himself or herself with a winnowing group of colleagues. When younger, we talked about schools and summer camps for the children, resorts and travel agents for us parents, then retirement living and possible nursing homes for our parents, all according to our age group. The most cogent reminder that each of us is like our peers is reading alumni notes: everyone is confronting similar problems and looking for solutions that sound familiar.

At some social events, people, usually women, come to me asking my opinion about plastic surgery or general medicine. I am careful not to pose as an expert in an area where I had only modest knowledge and even in plastic surgery where I was a specialist. I am leery of trying to maintain a position that is vestigial. Recent questions I have been asked are:

- 'Do you think Amy over there has had a facelift?' a question usually from a woman.
- 'Do you think that I should have a facelift – maybe a mini-lift?' a question always from a woman.
- 'My wife went to see a plastic surgeon for her face and he quoted a price of 15,000 dollars. I thought it was exorbitant. What do you think?'

If I think it is exorbitant for what is contemplated, I would avoid saying so. Even though I am old enough supposedly to speak my mind on matters about which I have some knowledge, I am careful not to criticize other physicians, those who are still in the trenches.

The longer that I am retired, the less I wish I was still in practice. I enjoy the pleasant change in being able to give advice but not be responsible for a patient or anyone else accepting or refusing it. Calmness comes when one no longer is a combatant but an observer, a status akin to that of a retired athlete who is now a sports commentator or a fan only.

The Joy of Being Unscheduled

When I was in practice just a few months, I had few patients and, like most doctors and certainly surgeons at that stage, I wanted more – many more. In fact I used to complain to my father, whom I mentioned was a neuropsychiatrist. He told me that I would look back on these days as being among the happiest. 'You are free to think new things and to plan projects and to have time for yourself and family (our only child, Linda, was then two).'

I did have some ideas for research, clinical and laboratory and although I applied myself as hard as I could, I still had unused time which my ambitious soul thought should be put to use. I was able, however, to exercise three or four times a week and I used to joke that I was the 'healthiest surgeon in the world waiting for patients.'

Robert M. Goldwyn

I remember that the Chief of Plastic Surgery at the then Beth Israel Hospital was Dr. Malvin White. When he was on the telephone and I happened to be sitting in the room, I saw him open his appointment book and tell his secretary that he could not possibly operate on another patient because he had 'six rhinoplasties to do' that day. I was still waiting for my first patient to request that operation and I confess that I forgot the tenth commandment – not to covet my neighbor. I said to Dr. White that 'someday I wish I had your schedule.' His reply was: 'How I wish I had yours!' Dr. White was then in his late fifties.

Of course, Dr. White proved to be correct but I did enjoy the fact that later I had patients booked for surgery six months or longer. Nevertheless, as much as I saw this as proof of my professional coming of age, I dreaded, nevertheless, looking at the book and realizing that the spontaneity of my life, at least professionally, had disappeared. In fact, I would tell my secretary, to surprise me and keep me unscheduled a day or so in the next three months. When she did, it was like a gift from God.

I recall visiting somebody at a very well known clinic and after having watched him operate, he told me that he knew exactly what he would be doing in the next four years because his schedule was fixed and 'relentless.' I was sorry for him and he later left that clinic and I understood why. Someone once said that while it is necessary to become part of one's time, one should not become 'a creature of one's time.' That was said in reference to the age in which we live but it applies also to the time that we have.

As residents, we thought that being overworked when one would be on his own would be a pleasure. For a while, even for many years, it continued to be a gratifying experience but on more than one occasion, this popularity was a burden.

One of my colleagues described the feeling of returning from vacation as if 'an iron hand was reaching out to grasp me.'

It would be hypocritical if I did not say that although I did not like to see myself scheduled every minute, I did crave structure. There is a difference and it is not simply semantic. I find pleasure and comfort in having at least a general idea of what the next day or week will bring but

I do not like literally the sensation of being locked into an unforgiving series of commitments. Even having advanced tickets to the Boston Symphony re-awakens the uncomfortable awareness of my having to make a mandatory appearance though it is for a pleasurable occasion.

By the time I retired, I was glad to be no longer 'scheduled out,' a lesser form of burnout. I did not dread the work, quite the opposite, but knowing that since kindergarten, I had never avoided a task or a commitment transformed the prospect of retirement into a relief.

Many physicians when younger and certainly when they are residents, myself included, would occasionally look at a patient in bed and for a brief second would have the thought that we would like to be that patient, just to be in bed but not with his or her problem. Sickness is synonymous with forced passivity. Even though one can help himself or herself get better, one is still on the receiving line with little latitude of action. One does what the doctor says because that is what the condition demands. It is also what society expects. The patient has a duty to get better.

Working, certainly for a physician, and being over-scheduled is the opposite of passivity. One is active even though in a peculiar way one might have been too passive in allowing himself or herself to become active.

For most physicians work is like riding a horse, who may be docile at first but soon can become a runaway choosing a direction the rider never intended or wanted. No patient and no physician likes to see laziness in a doctor. I have known a couple whom I would call lazy. Many may be inefficient but lazy is not an adjective I could apply to most of the people with whom I have worked, even those who pride themselves on having a 'good lifestyle.'

Although the 7/24 physician is not the norm today as he or she once was, medicine has not yet become a haven for the indolent. One is expected to be able to 'fit a patient in,' a common expression; that attitude of the physician coupled with that expectation of the patient makes it happen. No human being, even a physician, is infinitely distensible; something has to give, usually other aspects of a physician's life suffer: his personal relationships at home or at work; shortcuts are taken to the detriment of the patient; the physician's health deteriorates, physically and mentally, occasionally with the doctor becoming not just addicted to work but to alcohol, drugs, or other forms of self-destruction, perhaps an extra-marital relationship, gambling, reckless investing.

Unfortunately the list is too long.

Because so may people in medicine work so hard, it is difficult for many to realize it. When a colleague has a heart attack, for example, we all temper our pace, only to accelerate a few weeks later.

Although we could learn from the bad examples of some patients whose histories contain numerous illustrations of unwise, self-punishing behavior, we chose to deny or forget, consciously or unconsciously severing a link between their lives and ours. While it is necessary for a physician to detach himself or herself from the patient in order to be objective, that mechanism frequently masks our introspection, rendering us oblivious to our vulnerability and our not perceiving or admitting to ourselves that we share the same problems and could develop the illnesses that afflict those who have come to us for help. Retirement offers the physician the time and the opportunity finally to follow the injunction of Luke to heal himself (or herself). Paradoxically and sadly it comes when the doctor is no longer a practicing physician.

The good news is that he or she still has one more patient – himself or herself.

A Self-Made Self-Inventor

When my retirement as Editor of *The Plastic and Reconstructive Surgery* was immanent, I expressed my concern to our Coordinator, Susie O'Connor, about what I would with all the time I'd have at my disposal. Her suggestion was: 'This gives you an opportunity to reinvent yourself.'

Honestly I had not known that I had ever invented myself. I certainly never created myself – that was my parents doing or misdoing, depending upon how people think of me or I think of myself.

I gave Susie's reply considerable thought, as I have always done with her remarks since she is extremely insightful, as well as hard working, practical and with an excellent sense of humor.

Some possibilities came to mind. I list them without regard to possibility or importance:

- A writer of spy novels;
- A writer of haute cuisine pornography;
- A founder of a Medicare baseball team with myself as coach;
- A successful try-out for the Romanian gymnastics team being their only male and their oldest and heaviest member;
- A courier, with all expenses paid in addition to a salary and my freedom to choose when, where, and how to go and return...

But seriously how can a 77-year-old retired plastic surgeon reinvent himself? My solution, albeit fanciful, was to select and nurture one of my many selves, which each of us possesses.

Oscar Wilde [in *De Profundis*] observed: 'Most people are other people. Their thoughts are someone else's opinions, their lives a mimicry, their passions a quotation.' A. Sen wrote: 'We are influenced to an amazing extent by the company that we keep and people with whom we identify, and our lack of clarity about many of our beliefs and their underlying reasoning may arise, at least partly, from the fact that they reflect the views and judgments of others who have – perceptibly or imperceptibly – influenced us...' [*Beyond Identity: Other People*, The New Republic, December 18, 2000].

Sen concluded that 'in fact, we have plural identities even within competing categories.' Certainly with me and I presume with others these identities, these selves in someone healthy, whoever that person might be, worked more in harmony than in conflict and synchronously.

The contemporary novelist, Norman Manea, describing his vision of what happens in the world is that 'everything [is] compatible with everything else.' When incompatibility occurs, breakdown follows and can have serious consequences for the individual and others.

The sociologist, Goffman, talks about the presentation of self in everyday life [E. Goffman, *Presentation of Self in Everyday Life*, Garden City, N.Y.: Doubleday, 1959]: 'When we allow that the individual projects a definition of the situation when he appears before others (a group or another person), we must also see that the others, however passive their role may seem to be, will themselves effectively project a definition of the situation by virtue of their response to the individual...'

We are all aware of the role we are playing as we relate to others either in person or not, by phone or letter, now email. Every human being is like a CEO having to keep track of many aspects of his or her company, namely their many selves.

Each of us is like a giant piece of seaweed that arrives on shore bringing with it all sorts of things but since we are human, for us it is all sorts of experiences, memories, habits, likes, dislikes, beliefs and objectives, many of which we can never reach not just because of lack of will but of time. This book is evidence that I could not or would not reinvent myself; I could only recapitulate myself. As long as one is living, the recapitulation continues.

From my childhood in Worcester at Temple Emanuel I have the memory of Rabbi Levi Olan who, when officiating at a funeral, said: 'There is never a right time to die; there is always one more bar mitzvah to attend, another wedding, another new life to greet in the world, another task to do or trip to take...'

Every person, even someone whom we consider shallow, has sufficient depth to plumb, sufficient material to dredge up from his or her 'plural identities' to enjoy, regret, or to share.

Shredding

After my father died in 1985, when he was 84, I had the responsibility of the records of his patients from 55 years in practice. These charts filled seven large file cabinets. I did not want to intrude into the lives of those whom he had treated but I did look at three or four records, not because of my interest in what he had recorded as my trying to get in touch with my father after he had passed away by seeing his handwriting, with its characteristic semi-illegibility. In that regard, I have surpassed him with total illegibility!

My father had a single secretary, a succession of three, during those decades so almost all the notes were typed. He would add his own observations with a black pen.

These files came to roost in the cellar at home, where they remained until my mother went to a nursing facility.

I then had to get rid of my father's records, ten years beyond the legal time required for their preservation. I knew that I would be sad about doing this and consciously deferred the decision until it was necessary. I decided to have them burned not shredded since the former was easier and less costly. It was, however, like the cremation of thousands of people whose inner lives I never knew but constituted the professional life of my father. To our family, he was not only a wonderful husband and father but a dedicated physician, not just an extremely capable psychiatrist.

Consigning my father's records to fire was like placing him on a pyre, his funeral once again along with the records of the lives of his patients many of whom had preceded him in death. This process was leveling, the doctor and the records of his patients and their actual pasts finalized together.

Now, two decades later I have to dispose of the records of my patients, which number more in fewer years than did my father's. The reason is obvious: as a surgeon I was able to see and treat more people than could my father, a psychiatrist.

In keeping with the times and despite the cost, my office records will be shredded. Unlike a painter, there will be no retrospective exhibition of my works. All that I did for my patients will be eventually lost to posterity.

Balzac, whom I am fond of quoting, characterized surgeons as being 'actors of the moment.' Then photographs were uncommon and movie films non-existent. Balzac realized that no visible archive of the surgeon remains after he (always a male) passed from the scene. His exploits in the operating room whether heroic or stupid were forever lost after his patients completed their earthly stay. While it is true that a few painters

Robert M. Goldwyn

of the nineteenth century and even before, immortalized a few surgeons during an anatomy lesson, in an operating room or in a lecture, most surgeons of that era remain unrecorded.

Since I had been in practice almost four decades before I retired, I was able by law to get rid of many but not all records. Because they were stored, I gave the task to those who ran the depository. It was not only easier because I had less work to do but because I spared myself the anguish of participating in the act. However, when I was informed by letter that the records had been shredded, I experienced a kind of death – a part of myself and thousands of hours and thousands and thousands of patients in paper form had been reduced in a few minutes to shards. Even if I had chosen to retain the records for years beyond the requirement in order to reread my notes, I could never have been able to resurrect the moment or the patient or myself.

At Harvard College, those who ran the university said that if someone had been suspended, his name would be 'expunged from the record.' None of us really understood then and I do not know now what that means but it does have a stern finality. Not only was the person punished but was removed from a human memory or specifically the recall of a great institution. That is a frightening thought because it heralds what will happen to almost all of us even the most famous. Renard used the phrase 'escape from the pit of oblivion.' But very few do. Ask the most educated person you know to name as fast as he or she can the royalty of a European country, previous Nobel Prize winners, even governors of a state or mayors of a city familiar to that person and you will get a better understanding of what Renard meant by 'pit of oblivion.'

Those who have been memorialized through buildings or names of streets or lectureships are seldom remembered by those who enter those structures, travel those streets or attend the lecture. This disassociation, while not intended, is inevitable.

Samuel Johnson once wrote that if anyone wanted to get proof of the futility of human hopes, he should go to a library; one can also go to the foyer of a hospital or a museum to read names that rarely evoke a memory of the human being so little remembered except perhaps by immediate family and a few friends. Even worse is that only occasionally

Retired Not Dead

will someone take the time to read the name, usually on a dull brass plaque affixed to an unlighted wall.

During retirement one has more time to contemplate such matters, admittedly dismal. When one is very young, one thinks usually of the present; when one is older, one thinks of the present as well as the future, and when one is very old, one thinks more of the past, also of the present, but less of the future and, if so, not with joyful anticipation unless one is certain that he or she will have a glorious afterlife with every wish fulfilled.

Strange things happen to great historical figures. Consider that the great Napoleon now survives as a French pastry. But even when we consume it, we rarely think of him as a person and his life. This happened to me, in fact, on several occasions when I was eating a Napoleon in Paris, across from Les Invalides, his tomb.

I remember visiting the office of my college roommate and picking up a lovely Chinese vase on the fireplace mantle. When he told me that it was an urn containing the ashes of an Chinese grandfather. I quickly put it down. Fortunately it was not my roommate's grandfather. In those few seconds, however, I had held what was left of a human life, whose physical features, experiences, memories, pleasures, pains, skills and relationships were irretrievable, beyond my powers of fantasy.

If God were to read this, He (I'm not of the generation that thinks of God as a female), might say: 'So, Goldwyn, you have this fanciful idea of wanting to be immortal? Have I assessed you correctly?'

I would likely stammer and say 'Well, if it would please You, I would like at least not to be forgotten – too soon.'

I might receive the response: 'Consider yourself fortunate that I permitted you to live, to have had good parents, wonderful friends, a life meaningful and successful in the greatest sense of the word, to have had a good wife and, in fact, another good wife after your first wife died, to have had children who are are doing well and grandchildren. You have lived to an age not given to every human being and you have done so with enough to eat, with a comfortable home, in a wonderful, although not perfect, country – all this you have been given and now you still want more?'

I would probably mumble 'Forgive me. I did want more but now it seems less important.'

When the time comes, at least I will not have to shred my own medical records.

※

The Little King

The other day my wife Tanya was exasperated and accused me of often placing myself and my needs first without considering those of others, in this instance, herself. During the discussion, a euphemism for an argument which fortunately was subdued, she said I sometimes behaved 'like a little king.' It sounds better in French: Un Petit Roi. That designation is not to be confused with **The Little Prince** by St. Exupery.

In thinking about her accusation, I had to conclude that she was right. I do behave occasionally (really too often) like a little king probably because I was an only child and for more than four decades, a surgeon.

When I was growing up, I did not have siblings although I did have to heed the expectations and desires of my parents.

Surgery is a wonderful field for an only child, who finds comfort in accountability, responsibility, and authority. The operating surgeon is in charge for better or worse. I enjoyed that position. From an early age, I felt sorry for members of an orchestra who had to defer to the conductor. Maybe that sentiment arose from the status as an only child and my era, that of strong male personalities, beginning with the worst: Hitler, Stalin, and, for me, the best: Roosevelt, and Churchill.

I got the message early in life from my mother, who used to say: 'Why be a follower, if you can be a leader?' My father tempered this advice by emphasizing that one led by quiet accomplishment deserving of respect not by bombast and intimidation.

My wife's assessment that I was acting like 'a little king' (note no capitalization) was true in another respect: I was not behaving like a big king, not a Louis XIV but a much lesser Louis, more like Louis II, 846-879, called the Stammerer, the son of Charles the Bald, both largely forgotten but remembered by me because of their sobriquets.

This little king, in truth, could never sit on a real throne, except a daily type, and would not want to. My fantasies about being a conductor in contrast to a member of the orchestra have long passed. I was never interested in power. I did enjoy some attention but not too much.

Perhaps the reason is that as rare as my accomplishments might have been, they were puny compared to the truly great, the few whose story of their life has long survived their death. Furthermore being a king or a celebrity is not what it seems. A humorist defined a celebrity as 'someone who worked hard to be famous and then wears dark glasses not to be recognized.'

Sobering, however, was Shakespeare's comment: 'In sleep a king, but waking, no such matter.'

The Portrait

In August my wife, Tanya, and I spent a week of vacation in Santa Fe. As anyone knows who has been there, overload not boredom is the problem. One event among many, however, is worth recounting.

It happened in the historic Plaza, where we had just sat down. A man in his forties joined us. When questioned, he told us his home was New York City but was living outside Santa Fe. Soon we realized that he was sketching us. I did not want to be a curmudgeon and tell him to stop although I did feel uncomfortable because I knew I would have to pay for something I did not want. In the operating room, I would have taken control and told him to desist. Now retired, however, I have tried to adopt the attitude of letting some things happen and this was one of them.

Robert M. Goldwyn

My wife and I averted our eyes but after twenty minutes we could no longer resist and asked the artist to see what he had drawn. My portrait was emerging first causing me to tell him that 'I look like a dead Winston Churchill.'

He considered my remark bizarre and laughed uneasily. He told me he liked the idea of somehow having made me think that I resembled Churchill but he was upset that it was the dead version. Tanya was also discomfited as he recorded incipient jowls.

This phenomenon of someone sketching a portrait, un-requested, is common in the Plaza as I later observed. When I asked the artist what he expected in terms of payment, he answered 'A donation.' We gave him $25 for his efforts but then had the problem of what to do with our portraits that we did not like, perhaps because they showed us as we might look like to others but certainly not what we wanted to look like to ourselves.

Should we frame the double-portrait or hide it in a drawer, leaving the task of its disposal to our children? Or do we behave as did Oscar Wilde's Dorian Gray, who destroyed by knife what he considered a hideous portrait. Not being so dramatic we later folded it into a ball which we threw out. Will that act prevent us from aging? No. Why did we trash the portrait when we have kept, though not always shown, the numerous unflattering photographs that we and others have taken of us? I am not sure but perhaps we consider a portrait a more serious endeavor because it involves more than a simple click of a camera by most of us who are not professional photographers.

Another consideration is that generally when photographs are taken of ourselves, we know the photographer. In this situation, in the Plaza in Santa Fe, someone whom we did not know depicted us, confronted us with ourselves. Before I left Santa Fe, I had the fanciful idea of returning to the Plaza, sitting down and waiting for another artist to sketch me. Tanya had had enough of this and did not want to carry it further. My plan was to compare portraits but what would happen if the second portrait was like the first or even worse, at least to my eyes?

The British novelist, Anthony Powell, noted: 'Few persons who have ever sat for a portrait can have felt anything but inferior while the process is going on.' And, I would have added, 'More inferior when it is finished.'

Achieving The Impossible: Making Sex Boring

On one of my accidental forays into morning television, I happened upon a program that I admit held my attention but not for long; it was called 'Sexercise,' featuring three women, all plastic look-alikes with perfect faces, perfect skin, perfect figures, people without apparent individualities, whom I call the instant forgetables. The fact that they appear regularly or periodically on TV means that they are popular with millions, likely more women than men. I am in the powerless minority, by now a familiar position for me.

'Sexercise' turned out to be what women not only can do but should do to make coitus more pleasurable for themselves and their partners or, was it the other way around?. A woman who looked like the ideal aerobics instructor, emphasized Kegel's exercises, alternate contraction and relaxation of perineal muscles originally intended by Kegel for the treatment of urinary stress syndrome. A gynecologist, he published his findings in 1948 when the problem of relaxation of the perineal area because of multiple births was extremely common. With women having fewer children and marrying later and some fulfilling the roles of *Sex in the City*, Kegel's exercises are being used more frequently for a different reason: increasing pleasure rather than correcting prolapse and incontinence.

Kegel exercises should not be confused with kugel exercises, which Jewish women perform with their hands. Kugel is a pudding of noodles or potatoes traditionally found on the Jewish Sabbath table because it can be prepared before the holiday begins and kept in a warm oven. In his book The Joys of Yiddish, Leo Rosten repeats a saying: 'If a woman can't make a kugel – divorce her.' It is a wonder Jewish husbands survived as long as they did because of the high cholesterol content of this dish!

I am certainly no expert on sex (or Jewish cooking) – never was and at age 77 will likely never be. I lack also the primary credential of being a woman and the additional criterion of having postpartum urinary incontinence. As I was watching and hearing about the exercises – beyond Kegel's – that women were encouraged to do, I realized that perhaps for them and maybe for much of the audience sex had become a commodity if not sold then bartered. The 'expert' exhorted women to try yoga, in order to become more flexible, to liven up the sexual act with contortions known only to Vatsyayana and his colleagues and devoted followers of the **Kama Sutra**. So matter of fact was the discussion of 'sexercise' that it took sex out of the word and converted the whole process to physical exertion with advice that was presented so matter-of-factly that they could have been talking about grooming your dog, weeding your garden, or retiling your bathroom.

'Sexercise' was really about lower body mechanics. What was striking was that it never mentioned love as part of the journey together of two human beings who hopefully would be devoted to each other beyond mere lust. The participants in this television program and those behind the scenes should be complemented, however, to have adhered to the narrow role of 'sexercise,' making intercourse into a body act, like urination or defecation, but performed by two people.

With some modifications, what I saw on television could be shown to hormone-raging adolescents or to those interested in planned parenthood because it would certainly dampen the sex drive and eliminate the wonder of its consummation.

All this reminded me of what someone said about Henry Stanley's account of his search and his finding Dr. Livingstone in Africa: 'The worst possible book on the best possible subject.'

'Sexercise' is another example of the **How-to** mania in our country. We have so much of this in our culture that it is almost as if the average American over the age of 25 is incapable of getting up in the morning and to going to bed without the advice and intercession of nanosecond experts who have something to say, generally not profound, on every aspect of life, with suggestions that are as tedious as they are obvious: if you are over the age of 100, do not shovel your driveway; if you are told by authorities that a Grade Five hurricane will hit your community in two days, leave town; check your fuel indicator periodically so that you do not run out of gas at night or in a tunnel; do not let your five-year-old child walk alone to and from school in busy traffic; if your spouse inexplicably does not come home at night, suspect infidelity – and many more of the 'elementary, my dear Watson.'

Obsessive seekers of perfection seldom find it but frequently lose their commonsense in the process.

Helping and Teaching Children and Residents

While waiting for my flight at Boston's Logan Airport, I witnessed an all too commonplace phenomenon: a middle class parent over-helping a teenager with homework. The son, about seventeen, would express a thought and his father typed it into his computer but with embellishments.

'That's a good idea, John,' his father said on more than one occasion. 'Let's see what we (meaning I) can do with it.'

I doubt that the essay that his son would submit to his teacher would contain a footnote acknowledging the contribution and its extent by that parent to what should have been his own work. He would likely get an 'A' or 'B' for this shady activity, which is so prevalent that it is not considered fraudulent – and it should be.

That parents, usually university graduates or postgraduates, want so desperately to have their children succeed, as defined by their criteria, does not justify or excuse this kind of behavior. There is a difference between parents helping their children with his or her assignment and co-opting it without properly informing the teacher.

What lesson was that son learning? Not so much information but that any means to any objective is acceptable.

In discussing this matter of the zealous, participating parent with some friends who are younger, their reaction generally was: 'It may not be right but if we do not help our kids when everyone else is doing it, they will be at a disadvantage and I don't want to leave their future to that chance.' That 'everyone else is doing it' argument must be as old as when man first walked upright (walking upright is not living upright).

Those who train surgical residents realize that we are responsible for their competence in being able to think, plan, and operate effectively when they have their own patients. The resident cannot claim to have done an operation unless he or she has actually done it. A senior surgeon who has not allowed a trainee to do more than to assist in any stage of his or her residency is decidedly remiss and most likely unpopular. The issue is obviously not the popularity of the attending surgeon but the preparedness of the resident for a surgical career.

It would be an interesting study, if not already done, to compare how those who teach residents relate to their trainees and how they related to their children. My hypothesis would be that the similarities would be greater than the differences. Is there a factor of gender? As with the parent in the airport who was helping his son with his homework, so it might be with a mentor who is helping a resident learn a profession. We might be surprised by what we have imparted. Information, even technique, lose their relevance with the passage of years as medicine and surgery advances. The character and the style as well as the mannerisms of our teachers remain hopefully to guide and inspire.

I doubt that any surgical teacher today would do what Jacques Joseph did when some surgeons came to watch him do a rhinoplasty without paying him for his instruction: he would cover the nose with his hands so that they could not learn his method, reminiscent of King Oliver, a coronet player, who inspired Louis Armstrong, playing with a handkerchief over his fingers so that other trumpeters would not be able to copy his technique.

My father used to say that 'a parent, like a mother bird, is responsible to teach the off-spring how to fly and be safe when they are nudged out of the nest.'

Hurricane Katrina: Some Lessons Learned, More Forgotten

What likely will be called in the years to come the New Orleans disaster of 2005 will be material for hundreds of books, thousands of sermons, and millions of accusations mostly directed to how we could have prevented or ameliorated what happened. In the United States, the most technologically advanced country and the most litigious in the world, finger-pointing is a national pastime. A believer in either Darwin or Lamarck would have thought that most Americans would by now have eight or more digits on each hand!

My intention is not to be facetious about this calamity and certainly not to trivialize the enormous social, economic, physical and emotional damage to those affected – not just the inhabitants of New Orleans but also their families and friends living at a distance. I would like to offer some observations I hope readers will consider, possibly accept, or reject but at least consider:

- Nature is always more powerful than man;
- Each of us dies but Nature continues;
- Some natural disasters are so massive that at this time in our history they are impossible to prevent and may be impossible to predict with precision and immediacy;
- Any disaster whether through Nature or man, such as wars, will destroy human life as well as the environment;
- Any calamity will engender explanations which many, if not most, will believe: an act of God, stupidity, indifference of municipal, state and

federal officials, global warming, and numerous other suppose causes ranging from the rational to the irrational, from the obvious to the arcane;

- No society can ever react optimally to any major disaster to prevent loss of life, structural damage, disruption to utilities, etc.

A natural disaster on the scale of a tsunami or hurricane Katrina becomes an allegory for the inability of each individual to prevent his or her death: the implicit lament is why can't I or we or our loved ones live forever without pain and suffering? While we know that death will occur to all that lives, we do not emotionally accept that reality. For most of us the will to live is so strong that we deny the inevitability of death.

The important corollary is that our acceptance of death should not preclude our trying to take means to prevent it as, for example, by taking care of our health, outlawing drunken driving, building levees sufficient to stop flooding, having well-functioning machinery in airplanes and capable pilots – but even with all that, life has no affliction-free or trouble-free zones.

Medical, fire, police, sanitation, transportation and communication facilities, and the like, will always respond less than optimally to to the needs resulting from a disaster.

Human beings and groups of human beings, namely society, do not always have proper priorities and accordingly efforts and resources are misdirected. Decisions are not made impartially or rationally. My observations, I admit, are neither cheerful nor popular but I believe they are true. I do recognize the truth of T.S. Eliot's observation:

> ...human kind
> Cannot bear very much reality.

Forgive my changing a line from 'As Time Goes By' (**Casablanca**) – 'It's still the same old story, the fight between nature and human nature.'

Retired Not Dead

Be Exclusive, Buy a Maybach

I confess I never knew what a Maybach was until I read this morning's paper. It is a car. My ignorance of the Maybach is due to my general disinterest in cars, my pseudo-proletarian sentiments, and relative penury compared to the 310 purchasers in the United States who have paid the starting retail price of $327,250.

'... most super high-end car buyers are athletes, entertainers, or self-made entrepreneurs – buyers of such cars are used to having things their way without having to haggle' [K. Reed, For $300,000, you're getting more than a car, **Boston Sunday Globe**, October 9, 2005]. This customized car is produced at Daimler-Chrysler in Germany. Among the features of the 20 foot long 2005 Maybach 62 are 'a refrig-erated wine cooler, a 21-speaker surround-sound system, a DVD player, TV monitors in the back of both front seats, and two cell phones, one of which doubles as a remote control for the entertainment center.' For just $50,000 more.

What the elite owners like is not just the car but the perks such as free trips to Europe or a weekend in New York at a deluxe hotel followed by a private art showing, all of which elicited from one New England owner this comment: 'It's good that they do things like that to make you feel nice, like you're part of something exclusive.'

I am perhaps less than candid or insufficiently introspective when I state that I have never wanted to be 'part of something exclusive' and particularly not something based on a possession. There is a difference between feeling exclusive and feeling special like most of us. I like feeling appreciated but I have no interest in keeping out – excluding – others. As I have mentioned elsewhere in this book, my being an only child with no siblings for competition is likely responsible for this attitude, for my caring less about what others are doing and more about what I can or should do. Each of us is exclusive unto ourselves since each of us is unique, the ultimate in exclusiveness. Nobody has my same genes, RNA, DNA and even if I had been an identical twin, he would not have had identical experiences, memories, features, eccentricities, foibles, strengths, loved ones – the list is infinite.

Would the person who is quoted saying that he wants to be part of something exclusive feel better if only he were the sole owner of a Maybach and not 309 others?

It comes down to feeling good about oneself. Some always are comfortable in their own skin, as the French say, and others never are, no matter what they might have. To feel good about oneself because of who one is and not what one has saves a lot of money. I have just increased my net worth by $370,000 by not purchasing a Maybach. The mathematical logic may be wrong but the idea is right.

'Besame Mucho' ('Kiss Me A Lot')

This is not a personal request but, as many of you probably recognize, it is a title of a song popular in the early '60s. At my age and now in the early decade of the 21st century, I have to clarify that it is not from the 1860s. All this is a preamble to the fact that when I attended a meeting of the Turkish Society of Plastic, Reconstructive and Aesthetic Surgeons in Konya in September 2005, my wife and I went to the banquet. When the orchestra played 'Besame Mucho,' we got up to dance.

We never know when our childhood will catch up with us. As we were doing the rhumba, I remembered being sixteen and feeling like an outcast because I did not know how to dance. I told my parents I thought it was time I learned. With alacrity because they previously suggested it to me and I had rejected it, they enthusiastically enrolled me in a class with a few other struggling adolescents, mostly boys, in an old building that no long exists. I thought if I could learn just the foxtrot and the waltz, it would be enough. The dancing instructor, a 30-year-old woman, whose name but not her figure I have forgotten, advised me to learn some South American steps, the rhumba and the samba that were becoming popular. She was a strict teacher and insisted that we practice between our weekly sessions.

'How do I do that without a girl?' I asked.

'First I will tell you what records to buy and you set up your record machine somewhere in the house. You don't need a partner to practice. You pretend that your sports jacket is a girl and you hold one sleeve in your left hand and put the other over your right shoulder.'

The instructions were clear but when I followed them I felt ridiculous imagining how I looked to myself (I found an old mirror and put it against the wall) and how I would seem to a passerby (fortunately there were no windows). I used the garage during the day when my father or mother had the car. I whirled, desperately trying to dance suavely. I knew I was making progress when I no longer found it necessary to count to myself.

At that time, we had a lovely person named Nellie working for us. To this sixteen-year-old she seemed much older but, in actuality, she was just ten years my senior. Taking pity on my peculiar attempt to mimic Fred Astaire or his South American equivalent, she offered herself as a replacement for my jacket. This was decidedly not in her job description but I was grateful for her willingness to teach me and she was also pleased for the opportunity to relieve boredom.

At least three times a week, when I got home from school, I would practice with her, moving against a backdrop of garden tools and various ancient boxes. In my fantasy, I renamed myself 'Bobby Brazil,' in deference to what I thought was the source of the rhumba and samba, which, when I first tried to do them, I thought of them as gyrations. The Yiddish proverb says it well: 'To the one who cannot dance the band is at fault.'

As my Year of the Dance went by, I was gratified that my ability to do the rhumba and samba made me more popular with my dates, who no longer were impressed by the foxtrot or waltz. That episode in my life made me realize that much of what young boys and old males do is to please women, at first, their mothers, then their girl friends, later their wives and then, for some, their daughters and granddaughters.

A month ago when I turned 77, I decided to try to reach Nellie and miraculously I found her name in the Worcester phone book. She had not worked for us in decades. Unfortunately her husband had died a couple of years before. We talked a long time and at one point she said: 'Of all the things that happened in your family, the one I remember so clearly was both of us dancing in the garage. You sure had two left feet.'

The best I could reply was 'Nellie, if you think that I was bad then, imagine what I am like now.'

Throughout my life, I have danced many times but none has generated as many memories as when I was a tenderfoot gamboling in my garage 60 years ago.

What Remains? Not Much

Today (October 13, 2005) I read two things that could not be more disparate: the first was an item concerning the death, at age 75, of Anagelo Argea, Jack Nicklaus's caddie. He recalled the last major golf championship that they won in 1980 at the U.S. Open at Baltusrol, when many thought that Nicklaus was a has-been: 'They just kept cheering, "Jack is back! Jack is back!" He was grinning all over, smiling, signing autographs. He was so happy. We all were. People will remember us that day 50, 60 years from now' [***Boston Globe***, October 13, 2005].

The second piece I read a few hours later was from M. Kundera's ***The Joke***: 'By now history is nothing more than the thin thread of what is remembered stretched out over the ocean of what has been forgotten; but time moves on, and new eras will arise, eras the limited memory of the individual will be unable to grasp; centuries, millennia, will therefore fall away, centuries of paintings and music, centuries of discoveries, battles, books, and the consequences will be dire: man will lose all insight into himself, and his history – unfathomable, inscrutable – will shrink into a handful of senseless schematic signs...'

Sitting in my corner of the garden restaurant over an empty plate with no consciousness of having taken a bite, I contemplated how I too (at this very moment) was caught up in that vast and inevitable forgetting...

Since I am not a golfer, I do not know whether in a half century or more from now, many will recall the event that Mr. Argea described with such relish. Nevertheless, I am sure that his believing that he would be remembered would give him pleasure until the day he dies. If one takes the long view of what will remain concerning what each of us did with his or her life, then we would be paralyzed by the futility of it all. It would be difficult or impossible to maintain hope and enthusiasm if we thought that whatever we did counted for nothing. A person who is connected to others, family and friends, realizes that he or she does not have the luxury not to try to make each day count and not let it slip away through cynicism and inattention. Those we love and who love us, hopefully not unrequited, merit our responsibility, our best efforts so that the actions of each meets the expectations of the other.

A man's fate besides being born and dying requires a purpose in life.

Why are we here on this earth and what do we do while we are here? The same questions that, in 1897, Paul Gauguin expressed so well in words but better in his painting: Where Do We Come From? What Are We? Where Are We Going? (D'où venons-nous? Que sommes-nous? Où allons-nous?).

My guess is that those who believe strongly in God or a Creative Force of any sort or in any religion would be less likely to ask himself or herself these questions. That Gauguin, who considered himself a Christ-like figure, ready to become a martyr for his art, would still ponder these issues. It is interesting and indicative of man's uncertainty about his role in the universe.

I always thought it was remarkable most people, including myself, get up in the morning, undertake tasks and finish them, assume responsibility and try not to disappoint others. Certainly for the middle-class this behavior pattern is so common that it seldom attracts comment. Yet, the fact that it is integral to the functioning of society makes it worthy of note if not of surprise. Freud wrote about **Civilization and Its Discontents**: if he had been more of a sociologist, he could have just as well have written about Society and Its Expectations. Since birth most of us have been inculcated with comportment proper to what is wanted within the family and in the larger context of our society. Certainly we have drop-outs: those who do not want to work and are willfully unemployed but they are not by any means a large segment of our society. If they were, we would have what Emile Durkheim (1858-1917) called anomie, the collapse of normal societal functioning.

But we go on in our relatively circumscribed small orbits, intersecting with one another but usually not enough to be disruptive.

A former teacher of mine, Professor Gordon Allport, a sociologist, wrote about functional autonomy which he defined as activity continuing beyond the original reason that it was established. In short, a behavioral pattern that takes on a life of its own. An example would be a plastic surgeon who when he was a student worked hard and saved every penny to get through school and now even though he is extremely successful financially behaves as a miser. Admittedly this is a negative illustration. That concept, however, explains a lot that we do and continue to do sometimes more from habit than from conviction.

Even if we are dutiful and long-lived, only a few of us will do something sufficiently extraordinary to catapult us out of historical nothingness. Lack of fame that lasts (all is relative) does not nullify what we have done with our lives. If, for example, we have children, at least we have served as a bridge. But no surgeon, no matter how famous, can have a retrospective view of his or her work as Gauguin has repeatedly had since he died in 1903 at age 55.

His work lives on and can be gathered together for us to view in the state that it was when he finished. The human canvas, however, seldom lasts beyond 90 years; the surgeon's work dies with it but the legacy of that individual whom the surgeon hopefully helped to live a better life, if not an extended span with consequences, more good than bad, on that patient's family and their families. George Santayana (1863-1952) the philosopher in **The Life of Reason** wrote:

'That life is worth living is the most necessary of assumptions, and, were it not assumed, the most impossible of conclusions.'

Santayana later expressed the corollary of that philosophy: 'Let a man once overcome his selfish terror at his own finitude, and his finitude is, in one sense, overcome [**The Ethics of Spinoza**].'

A not so famous quote (source unknown):
I come from the nowhere!

I go to the noplace!
And here I am!

※

Excellence Is Where You Find It

When my wife and I were in Turkey this summer, we went by bus at night from Ankara to Denzili. Half way we stopped long enough for me to enter a cafeteria more out of curiosity than hunger. A young man who worked there, however, seeing my hesitation kindly shepherded me through the line to 'Eat something. It will be good for you.' I chose the dolma which in Turkish means a 'stuffed something,' usually in a grape leaf or vegetable shell, in this instance, green pepper. It was more than good; it was delicious, the best I ever ate in a restaurant while I was in Turkey. Admittedly I am neither a connoisseur nor a gourmet of any type of cooking, certainly not Turkish. The point I am making is that in this out of the way place, I encountered (and consumed) excellence. I have forgotten the name of the town and of the restaurant and I never knew the name of the chef. Inspectors or tasters for the Michelin Guide will never travel there. Only the locals and those in transit, like my wife and I, will share this unexpected culinary pleasure.

That Turkish Delight became an allegory for me with respect to many aspects of life. People may meet their lifelong mates under unpredictable circumstances in surprising places. We may read a book that no critic has deigned to review but we find it exceptional. And even a mediocre work of fiction may contain a sentence or a phrase worth remembering.

This phenomenon of excellence being where you never thought it should be and not being where you expected it to be is true also in our specialty. A majority of plastic surgeons in this country and throughout the world have never presented a paper or written an article; they may not have a national or international reputation but the quality of their care of the patient is excellent. Those who are fortunate to find these surgeons and their local community appreciate their superior skills and dedication but may not realize its rarity.

My father used to say: 'Anyone who does his work extremely well is unusual and deserves respect.' We encounter them from time to time: that person may be a carpenter, a police officer, a teacher, a cab driver, a receptionist, a waitress, and, if we are fortunate, our own physicians. There are, however, many doctors, whose fame exceeds their ability. They talk a better game than they play. A common saying heard at meetings is that 'If you really want to know how he (or she) operates and what the results are, ask the residents.'

Within any academic community, there are doctors to whom we would not want to consign ourselves or our family because of their marginal competence or their lack of commitment, compassion and, too often, availability. The opposite stereotype, however, is not true: 'That the well-known doctor, in whatever field he or she may be, does not deserve that reputation.' Jealous colleagues find it easier to lower someone than to elevate themselves. While they may be the first to praise an outstanding athlete, they are the last to acknowledge the greatness of someone in their own field. One of my favorite Russian proverbs is: 'The dogs bark most at the horse-back rider traveling the fastest.'

Shena Alexander, the American writer/editor, said it simply: 'The sad truth is that excellence makes people envious.' We should all be able to offer a private ode to excellence: search it out, acknowledge it and celebrate it especially when we come across it unexpectedly.

'Sauve Qui Peut'

Nicolas Boileau-Despréaux (1636-1711), a French literary critic and poet, allegedly first used this phrase, 'Sauve Qui Peut' – Save Himself Who Can – or, more crassly, Every Man for Himself. These words or their equivalent have been exclaimed throughout recorded history in the midst of a disaster, one notable example being at Waterloo when Napoleon's previously invincible guard retreated.

I have been thinking of 'Sauve Qui Peut' during the past few weeks as fears of an outbreak of avian flu have intensified. My apocalyptic vision of doomsday has been reinforced also by the wars in Afghanistan and Iraq, the tragedy in Darfur, the earthquake in Pakistan, and the hurricanes along the Gulf coast.

Since I am not a virologist, what I know about avian flu is not much more than what anyone else has learned from the media and the Internet. The information is more speculative then factual. The only certainty is our uncertainty. The 'bird flu' may or may not come to the United States and if it does, what will be its incidence, severity, morbidity, and mortality?

While most human beings are slow to act in response to what they perceive as a distant threat to their well-being and survival, they are quick to act when they believe that the problem is imminent, especially when local, state and federal governments exhort us to prepare for not just a serious disease but one with 50 percent lethality.

Some of my friends have already begun to stock water, food, rubber gloves, masks, bactericidal soap, Tamiflu, even vaccines in the hope that something they have on hand might be effective against the H5N1 strain of avian flu. Acquaintances whom I thought were rational have ordered amulets on the Internet. Despite hundreds of years of progress in science, when we doubt that it has much to offer, we rapidly regress. We may recite an incantation or a series of them or wear a talisman, acts that cannot harm but possibly help.

Articles appear regularly in the paper about proper diet, rich in fruits and vegetables and poor in saturated fat, as a way of strengthening the immune system. It certainly can't hurt and most of us should have been on this kind of regimen years before.

One measure that experts endorse is washing our hands frequently. Shakespeare's Lady McBeth knew about the benefits of hand washing 400 years ago. Her compulsiveness based on guilt for blood on her hands might have given her added protection against the bubonic plague.

Robert M. Goldwyn

My maintaining a sense of humor is like my whistling in the dark in the hope that it will restore confidence, especially when there is little else to do against an overwhelming force we cannot see but whose effects are terrible.

The possibility of being the victim of an act of nature reminds us of our vulnerability, of our finitude. The reality is that nobody yet has survived life. Why should we be spared? The thought of my dying from a pigeon is absurd, further evidence, if anyone needed, of the tragi-comic nature of life.

These ruminations have led me to re-read Camus' *The Plague*, published in 1947. The first time I read it I was a college freshman more concerned by the literary aspects of this work, not anticipating that it might present a possible scene for my later life. For those who have not read *The Plague*, I recommend it especially now and for those who have read it, do so again.

Camus uses the plague as a symbol of modern war and its effects on the individual and the community. Camus and France had just experienced WWII. People behaved then as he describes them in his novel when the rats infest the city of Oran, Algeria, where Camus grew up. People reacted as individuals – 'Sauve Qui Peut.' Soon they realized that they had to cooperate to overcome the pestilence. They rebelled against death but not as isolated persons. With time Camus' city becomes 'happy': people once again enjoy the sunshine and resume their everyday activities – until the next visitation of the plague or its equivalent.

If Camus were alive, he would not be surprised by how the world is reacting to the prospect of a pandemic, or even an epidemic, of the avian flu. For Camus, the plague was an allegory of evil, death; for us it is not an allegory; it is not symbol; it is itself. Like a few characters in his book, there are some who have already interpreted the recent disasters and the possible flu contagion as justified punishment for the world's godlessness. Although some physicians might have similar thoughts, they cannot escape their duty of fighting for the lives of others and hopefully their own.

Retired Not Dead

Another Triumph for Trial Attorneys

The Massachusetts legislature is very generous in spending money – other people's. Their self interest not surprisingly determines their actions. A recent example – and I could cite many – is what happened to a proposed law to 'crack down on drunk drivers' (M. Levenson, Softer bill on drunken driving OK'd, **Boston Globe**, October 20, 2005).

'Among the provisions thrown out was one that would have strengthened the hand of prosecutors by giving them permission to present certified court records, instead of witness evidence, to prove an offender's past drunken driving convictions during the sentencing phase of a trial... Lawmakers removed a section from the bill that required a one-year mandatory license suspension for a driver who refuses a Breathalyzer test, opting instead for a six-month suspension that could be challenged in court. Some advocates said that section was removed to allow lawyers to continue the lucrative practice of defending drunken drivers in court... The House and Senate versions of the bill were reconciled by a six member conference committee. The **Globe** reported earlier this month that five of the six lawmakers on the conference committee were lawyers who have defended drunken driving clients.'

The Massachusetts legislature, like those of other states, have a distressingly significant proportion of trial attorneys who are more interested in enriching themselves than in preventing vehicular fatalities. While they explain their stance as a way of defending an individual's liberties, they never specify whose liberties: those of the killer driver? those of themselves?

Another aspect of this legislative farce was the injudicious speed with which the compromised measure passed.

'They wanted to get it done this afternoon because Gino – the principal conferee on the House side – is going on a plane at Logan that leaves at 5:30 and they have to get to customs by 3:30. The lead House negotiator was scheduled to depart last night as one of the half-dozen lawmakers vacationing in the Iberian peninsula.' Massachusetts is blessed with such statesmen.

Robert M. Goldwyn

The day after the trial attorneys sabotaged a stricter bill against drunk drivers, especially repeated offenders whose previous records they did not want to allow in court, a 19-year-old college student at 2 a.m. drove her car into a group of fellow students, one died and three were injured. The driver's 'blood alcohol level was 11 times the legal limit for someone her age' (***Boston Globe***, October 22, 2005).

Throughout my medical career, beginning with my being a student, extending through general surgical residency, plastic surgical training, and then in practice, I have treated hundreds of patients with injuries resulting from drunken driving: the drivers themselves, their passengers, pedestrians, other drivers and passengers who had the misfortune to come into contact with a soused driver. The mayhem such a person causes is not restricted to the road. I remember an elderly couple who were having a quiet supper when a car driven by a devotee of Bacchus crashed into the home and into their kitchen injuring them but fortunately they survived.

In my personal life also, my wife Tanya's son, then nine, was killed (not in Massachusetts) by a drunken driver who happened to be a judge. My first wife Roberta lost her life (not in Massachusetts) also because of a bad driver who, though careless, was sober.

That more than 50,000 people a year die and thousands more are injured as a result of auto accidents is an appalling statistic not just because of its number but because the majority of these needless deaths could be prevented if our society cared enough. It is estimated that 30 to 40 percent of these deaths and injuries involve drunken drivers. Worldwide more than a million people have been the victims of vehicular homicide.

I used to believe that the beer-wine-liquor industry was primarily responsible for defeating harsh penalties for drunken driving. While they are partly to blame, others, such as owners of bars and restaurants, are also obstructionists. For many years, however, the major group has been the trial attorneys.

In a television interview, a mother who had lost two daughters in their twenties when a drunken driver, whose license on six occasions had been suspended because of his having 'driven under the influence,' asked the question publicly that many of us have posed privately: 'What would be the attitude of that defense attorney if that same driver is allowed on the road again and kills that lawyer's wife or child or grandchild – or most of his family?'

We need another Sophocles to write a modern Greek tragedy with the trial attorney as the protagonist.

You Are As Old As You Are – Even To A Real Estate Agent

One would think that at my age, I would have accumulated enough good sense to resist calling an 800 number to enroll in a sweepstakes which I have as much chance of winning as becoming the next Pope. Not so this past week when I was notified that my previous (note previous) entry moved me into 'the final phase,' an ominous designation at this stage my life. The letter required my merely dialing a number and promised that my chance of winning did not depend upon my purchasing anything. I should have learned from my mother who used to say: 'Believe that and I'll sell you the Brooklyn Bridge.' That bridge was not for sale but other things were: 'A diamond dream watch for you or your wife or both of you,' which I refused, 'The choice of three magazines subscriptions – we have a list of 300...', I declined also.

With slight exasperation in her voice the woman who was shepherding me through this call remained remarkably polite, so much so that she could have given a course to physicians on how to deal with difficult patients.

Finally this Miss Manners of Marketing asked me whether my wife and I liked to travel. My enthusiastic reply was a natural lead into her telling me that she had 'something special' for me. Would I do her the favor of listening to a colleague? I could hardly refuse. She thanked me and transferred me to someone with an Indian accent. I had been outsourced. As he was talking with me, I heard in the background other voices with similar accents.

What he was proposing was 'a time-share in some of the most beautiful resorts in the world.' He addressed me. 'First I have to know something and I hope you do not think that I am invading your privacy. I would like to know your age. Is that satisfactory with you?'

'Yes,' I replied.

'Are you between 30 and 45?'

'No,'

'Are you younger?'

'No,' I said thinking of my grandchildren

'Are you 46 to 60?'

'No,' I answered.

'Are you older than 68,' he asked me incredulously.

'Yes,' I said.

'Again I do not wish to intrude, sir, but how old are you?'

I replied, '77,' pleased to be able to surprise him but not happy that it was true.

'Well, sir your voice is remarkably young but at your age time-sharing is not right for you' – meaning I would not live long enough to enjoy the benefits of that kind of investment. He exited the line quickly.

This incident proved what I have long believed: 'You are as old as your birth certificate states.'

Of course I am old, I said to myself. That seller of time-shares had to say something complimentary and so he accorded me a young voice. He never asked about my general health nor rationally should he have done so. Did he know that I successfully passed my STEP test, that I walk two miles every day, that I drive a car on the street not the sidewalk, that I remember almost everything I want to recall, that my family history is good but not immortal? – No, my age sufficed.

As a reaction, I thought of my youth when my age was against me: when I could not drive until I was sixteen, when I could not vote until I was 21... a few other thoughts came to mind but not many more. The reality is that it is better to be young than to be old. The fact that I never wanted to own a time-share was hardly the point. What mattered to my ego was that even I wanted and could have afforded it, the purchase would have been more of an illusion than an investment.

Milton Berle once remarked: 'All my life I wanted to eat steak. Now I can afford it but I don't have my own teeth.'

Three Cheers (silently of course) for the Library

One of my heroes, Samuel Johnson (1709-1784) observed that 'No place affords a more striking conviction of the vanity of human hopes than a public library.' Another hero, Ralph Waldo Emerson (1803-1882) thought that 'A man's library is a sort of harem.' For me, it is a haven, probably because of my growing up as an only child. In a library I can recreate the solitude that those who never had siblings crave from time to time.

Libraries are the last bastion of silence in the United States of Noise. Mercifully they prohibit cell-phones. If I had my way, these gadgets would be treated as were guns in the wild west – left at the door – of more than libraries – in whatever place two people gather.

Although one goes to the library to 'look something up,' one should never impose that restriction on oneself. Browsing or meandering through a library has the potential thrill of any serendipitous adventure. I admit, however, there are some who lack the gene for curiosity, who are able to look-up a single word in a dictionary without seeing or learning from another word(s) along the way.

Most libraries are free. Where else can one learn so much with so little expense?

Every house has room enough for at least one book. Most middle-class homes could accommodate a true library or a semblance of one. Prospero in **The Tempest** expressed my sentiments:

Robert M. Goldwyn

My library
was dukedom large enough.

Because public libraries generally do not charge and because those who go there want knowledge, they are democratic places, probably among the last in our economically stratified society. But what about subways or busses, one might ask? While democracy reigns there, in the library, in contrast, one can almost always find a seat which they can occupy for hours without being disturbed or asked to leave except at closing time.

I have previously talked about the virtue of solitude but I have not sufficiently emphasized that of quiet, this in addition to books is the sine qua non – of a library. People usually try to be polite in libraries. They are conscious of not disturbing others with noise; they know how to whisper 'hello' or 'goodbye' but rarely engage in long conversation. Words are uttered quietly, minimally, almost apologetically.

Today because of thievery and terrorism, most libraries require a pass or identification, usually obtained without difficulty and at no cost.

Libraries are patently useful to those who want information and wish to learn. They are more than useful to those who like to read. Their greatest advantage, however, is probably for those who like to take a mini-vacation – an hour or several, away from the outside. It is anodyne to what Wordsworth had in mind when he wrote 'The world is too much with us...'

Although Samuel Johnson, whom I quoted earlier, thought that a public library epitomized to 'the vanity of human hopes,' he was egregiously in error with regard to a medical or scientific library which contains abundant evidence of hopes fulfilled by those who have made important discoveries benefiting human beings. Whether they undertook their work because of vanity is for me a moot consideration.

More important is the fact they exerted themselves and succeeded in improving all our lives. A library, therefore, is just not information but affirmation. It has an aura that no PC or Internet at home can duplicate.

An Ode to Jell-o®

Most readers would recognize that I have lied from the outset; this is no ode. Gertrude Stein might have written but did not: 'An ode to be an ode must be written as an ode' – namely a lengthy lyrical poem. I chose the title because the first letter of 'ode' is the same as the last letter of 'Jell-o'. That aside, I am writing in praise of something simple. Who among my generation – the 70-plusers – still eats Jell-o as a favorite dessert and not as a harmless common nutrient filler reserved for someone sick? I am sure that Kraftfoods knows the demography of its product.

Almost anyone my age recalls that Jell-o was the sponsor of the Jack Benny show that I used to listen to in the '40s from 7:00-7:30 p.m. on Sundays (EST). As much as I remember the humor, I recall the product and its announcer, Don Wilson.

In those days, even through the '70s, the menus of most restaurants had Jell-o listed as a dessert for those who wanted something 'light' as my parents and their friends would say. My mother used to advise me that 'you can't go wrong with Jell-o or, if you are in a restaurant that you do not know, with a toasted cheese sandwich.' I can still get the toasted cheese but I can't get Jell-o unless I buy it in a store.

After a heavy meal, my parent's generation would eat Jell-o to lessen the guilt for what they had earlier consumed. It was always there for them. But now if you order it, everyone at the table will think that you have diabetes or something worse or both (it is rarely on the menu).

I am not a diabetic but I am a Jell-o-phile. I admit to adding a bit of whipped cream to spruce it up. My Jell-o-philia led me to do some research via the Internet (www.kraftfoods.com/jello). I always knew Jell-o was born before I was but I had not known that the date was 1845 when the New York industrialist, inventor and philanthropist Peter Cooper, who also built the first American locomotive, obtained a patent for a 'gelatin dessert.' He did very little with this product and in 1887, sold it to Pearle B. Wait, a carpenter and cough medicine manufacture from LeRoy, New York. He and his wife produced a fruit-flavored version of Cooper gelatin which they (his wife's idea) renamed Jell-o, with the first flavors being strawberry, raspberry, orange and lemon. In 1899, Wait sold the business for $450 to his neighbor. The lesson is to be wary of neighbors smarter than you.

I enjoy Jell-o not just for its taste but for what it symbolizes and evokes: simplicity, childhood – that it is lower in calories than many alternatives I might have chosen is also a benefit.

My mother had to make Jell-o by adding water and sometimes fruit. I suppose I eat Jell-o for the same reason and with the same relish that most of us continue to enjoy the tasty things from the recipes of loved ones no longer here. This added ingredient of nostalgia not only improves the taste of Jell-o and that of our favorite childhood foods but also our life.

Seven Pins: Learning from a Shirt

Being older, retired, I have more time to learn from unexpected sources, in this instance, a shirt. It was a new one and, for me, an expensive one that I would not have bought if it had not been on sale.

The touch of a clean flannel shirt on the skin is a pleasure, a minor one but enough of them add up, something that Rupert Brooke, the English poet, who died too soon (1887-1915), understood well:

These I have loved:
White plates and cups, clean-gleaming,
Ringed with blue lines; and feathery, faery dust;
Wet roofs, beneath the lamp-light; the strong crust
Of friendly bread; and many-tasting food;
Rainbows; and the blue bitter smoke of wood;
And radiant raindrops couching in cool flowers;
And flowers themselves, that sway through sunny hours,
Dreaming of moths that drink them under the moon;
Then, the cool kindliness of sheets, that soon
Smooth away troubles... ['The Great Lover']

Not even Einstein discovered the law: the more expensive the shirt, the more pins one has to remove. It is not always true that the more one spends, the less inconvenience one confronts. In fact, the opposite is true – a phenomenon that Henry David Thoreau observed 150 years ago: 'A man is rich in proportion to the number of things which he can afford to let alone.'

The more our possessions, the more attention they demand. Is a couple with four homes, four times as happy and fulfilled as another with a just a rented apartment? Is the plastic surgeon who does 1,000 operations a year with a six figure income proportionately happier than the surgeon who operates less and earns less? My former Chief of Surgery (Peter Bent Brigham Hospital) Dr. Francis D. Moore, used to decry the 'notches on the belt' mentality – an allusion to how gunslingers of the old West used to notch up their kills. The point he was making is that quantity is not synonymous with quality and may even be an obstacle to excellence.

But returning to the theme of the seven pins, there is another lesson to learn: namely, one can get stuck more easily than if one had purchased a less expensive, pin free shirt. Most of us, and I am not exempt, wallow in surfeit. My friend and once co-resident, Garry Brody, used to say that we 'have an embarrassment of riches; our cups runneth too much over.' He also made the accurate observation that when we were residents, we would have been glad to have had the income of what we now pay in taxes.

Perhaps I am stretching the analogy precariously, even wrongly, about the shirt but life lived in retail is better than one lived in wholesale: item by item, singly enjoyed to the utmost is more satisfying and ultimately less expensive than life lived by the bulk.

The Ultimate Smart Car for Those Who Really Want to Own One

A couple of weeks ago when my wife and I visited our family in Chicago, we rented a Chrysler Pacifica large enough to seat us all. This 2006 model, which seemed a behemoth to me, was a distinct contrast to my 2000 Toyota Camry. Driving around Chicago, I felt like a haute-bourgeoisie truck driver, pretending to understand and master the far too many electronic features. I could not even find the radio button when our grandchildren, Madeline then twelve and Nathan seven, wanted their favorite station. My wife, Tanya, always comes through to solve these mechanical riddles.

That this $30,000 machine – the word 'car' demeans it, had more supposed benefits than almost anyone needs testifies both to Americans always wanting more of what they think they need and to my own distrust of technology which I find more challenging than helpful. It is no news that our economy would collapse if it were based on necessities rather than luxuries.

Having stated this, I do admit that the Pacifica did have something that had at least the benefit of prompting these thoughts. On its lighted dashboard words would appear from time to time to alert the driver e.g.
- Right Front Door Ajar
- Rear Lift Bar Up

And many more observations calling for action from me. I wish I had recorded all the observations that this Daimler-Chrysler creation made but managing to drive it was sufficient to occupy me without trying at the same time to write down everything that dashboard was telling me.

My Pacifica experience made me think of what the car of the future could be or could have. It will be interactive with any driver it gets to know. The car will have heard or over-heard phone conversations, family arguments, perhaps even activities usually reserved for the boudoir. Think about the possible messages that could appear on the dashboard of this automobile which will know at any time and will remember always the identity of its occupants.
- 'Change your internist. You never can reach him and when you do, he never gives you enough time.'
- 'Your financial advisor sounds like a phony used car dealer (and I should know). Check your quarterly statements more carefully.'

To your seventeen-year-old daughter alone in the car: 'Your date a couple of nights ago was interested in only one thing and it isn't your opinion of that crazy rock concert I brought you to.'

- 'Mike's gas station has just ripped you off. You paid for eighteen gallons of gas but I got only fifteen and a half. Mike has a tricky thumb.'
- 'Doc, I was disappointed in you for what you said to that fundraiser from the American Heart Association. You refused her. Here you're driving my $30,000 worth of spec and you can't spare 100 bucks!'
- 'Doc, your son Art drives too fast. He is going to shorten his life and mine. Why a cop hasn't flagged him down is a mystery. And last week he had two beers too many for him and me.'
- 'Doc, you're a good plastic surgeon. I assume you are because you're busy and you have enough money to buy me. But that lady you did a face-lift on two years ago who is still complaining and calls you while we're driving home is *driving* me crazy. How do you stand it? I know the money is good. I can help you if you let me take her for a long trip. Ha! Ha!'
- 'Doc, the tape you played this morning – with a surgeon talking about breast reduction without scars and his five year follow-up of 1,000 patients all with perfect results and no complaints, I have heard a lot in my day (and night) and even though I am not a plastic surgeon, I know a 150 dollar bill when I see one. Go to his office to see his patients and speak to his residents.'
- 'Doc, I see your face in my mirror. You look tired. Get more rest. I don't like being driven by someone who is exhausted and grumpy. You could get me into an accident.'
- To your wife: 'Mrs. Doc, you shop too much and I can barely carry all the bundles you've come home with. Get a new interest. Look beyond your closet. Volunteer at your husband's hospital. You will save money and have a better life. And, by the way, your two 'friends', Lisa and Jane, whom you left in me yesterday when you brought something to the cleaners – from what I heard, get new friends. They are jealous back-stabbers. Incidentally, go back to your former hair stylist. The one you have now couldn't make it even if he was the only one in Bulgaria.'
- 'For Christmas, the best gift for me would be a shower – gentle sudsing and don't forget to rust proof my bottom. And please on New Year's Eve, I don't want anyone getting sick in me. It's been a good year for us all. Thanks for the opportunity to be frank. That's what one should expect from people who know each other for a long time.'

Robert M. Goldwyn

With this truth speaking feature, the Pacifica, which comes from the word 'pacific': 'Tending to diminish or put an end to conflict: appeasing, calming –' (*The American Heritage Dictionary*) would certainly need a change of name. A logical one would be 'Truthmobile,' but that would likely frighten away buyers. The obvious solution is to make this interactive capability optional for only the hardiest among us.

Das Kar-pital

That the large and widening gap between the haves and have-nots in the United States has not led to a Communist Party or even a strong Socialist movement has long baffled me. The most offered explanation is the supposed prevailing belief among those at the bottom that they too can make it to the fiscal stratosphere where the have-it-alls reside. Indeed money mobility does happen – frequently, more than frequently, though not generally.

I am not an activist for either the Socialists or the outlawed Communists but if I were, I would promulgate by any means possible a recent article in the **Wall Street Journal** [G. Chon, A Rolls to Match Your Lipstick, **Wall Street Journal**, December 1, 2005], which would be unread by the poorest. For a proletariat ready to be aroused, with this article, no one needs to read Karl Marx's **Das Kapital**: 'As the market for ultra-luxury cars grows more competitive, auto makers are taking the customization arms race to a new level. They will fly in customers to watch their car being built; paint a car to match a customer's lipstick, or outfit a car with anything from a sink to a karaoke machine.'

I know that the number of potential customers is increasing throughout the world with two-thirds of the 1.5 million people with assets of more than $5,000,000 living in the United States.

That some customers have interior designers to help them decide on what the car should look like inside as well as outside adds to the absurdity and what I would term 'the obscenity of this extreme self-indulgence.'

As if that were not enough, we now have in the United States luxury garages to accommodate these mobile palaces and private driving clubs with 'lots of hair-razing turns' to allow members to be as wild as they want without encountering traffic or a ready-to-pounce policeman. One member, who owns more than one car, raced his Ferrari 360, commenting that 'what I find exciting is going into a turn at 120, then tapping the brakes and taking the turn at 90.' That he is a 41-year-old retired commodities trader when most doctors are only seven years out of their residency is by itself a commentary on what is possible and surreal in America [R. E. Silverman, The coddled car, **Wall Street Journal**, December 1, 2005].

While the masses watch and attend speed car races, some of the ultra-affluent have their own. At least they have the good sense to live out their fantasies away from the resentful eyes of the neo-Lenins among us.

Be Careful Whom You Call Fat

A patient was so incensed because her family doctor allegedly called her 'fat' that she reported him last summer to the New Hampshire Board of Registration in Medicine. He is now defending himself, hoping that he can maintain his license.

That hapless physician was guilty of telling the truth in a society that hates to hear it. His CME credits should have included one or more courses in political correctness, a term reminiscent of the 'political re-education' meted out to those who did not slavishly conform to the party line in the former Soviet Union and in the China of Mao Tse-tung and even in the China of today.

What is particularly ironic about the incident with the New Hampshire doctor is that it occurs in the state whose motto is 'Live Free or Die.' I hope the doctor will settle for living less free and not decide to do away with himself. My guess is that he will continue to practice after having been officially censured. My fantasy is that he will be required to attend sessions in incorrectness management. I hear the instructor, most likely a female psychologist, saying:

'Doctor, in analyzing what you told your patient, that unfortunate middle aged woman, I believe there are important lessons to be learned – not only by you but by all of us (including herself to show the universality of bad judgment).

'Instead of labeling her as fat, which nobody wants to be called by anybody else, you could have chosen different words. For example, you could have called her plump or heavyset. You might even have postulated that because of her genetic inheritance, through no fault of her own, her height was insufficient for her body mass. That she might be a devotee (three to five times a day) of large meals is not something to call to her attention. It could damage her psyche and have terrible repercussions for her husband, her four children, her three aunts, four uncles, eight cousins, and innumerable nephews and nieces. Even if you know for example, that she is a habitué of McDonald's, do not traumatize her by mentioning it. It is cruel and, furthermore, does not take into consideration the fact that she is victim of our culture, a defenseless target of advertising for these fattening foods – you note that I apply the adjective containing the word "fat" to an inanimate noun – never to a personal noun. In essence, that kind of patient has no choice even if you and I think that she might have.

'Doctor, I am frankly surprised that someone with your education – six years of elementary school, two years of middle school, four years of high school, four years of college, four years of medical school, and five years of postgraduate training should have to resort to the word "fat" when you could have thought of other words or phrases with less damaging psychological consequences. What comes to my mind are:

'"Strongly built."

'"A tad surfeit."

'"Generously proportioned."

'"Not anorectic."

'And for a man:
'"Portly," which implies also he is successful in business.

'Since that patient has lived her entire life in New Hampshire, you could have suggested that she was fortunate to be well insulated against the ferocious cold – you get what I am trying to say. Be imaginative, be inventive, be kind.

'I need not tell you that you never use the word "obese" to describe any patient. Even the word "overweight" can be an ego-bruising designation. How much better to say to such a patient, "For reasons that science cannot yet understand, you and millions like you have a bit of a tendency to accumulate a few extra pounds – a perfectly understandable situation in this society where walking is dangerous because of wild drivers and uncontrolled muggers. And even if you lived in a rural area, you could get struck by a moose or even by a bear."

'You see, doctor, how rich the English language is if you are willing to spend some time to take advantage of it.

'Doctor, do you have any questions?'

'Yes, Miss Dodge. In medicine, we are trained and I am used to being straight forward with people. I am not certain that at my age of 60, I can learn or retrain myself to be devious.'

'Oh, doctor, I am sorry you think it is being devious. It is simply being realistic and imaginative enough to take a slightly longer road to get to the same destination – the proper care of the patient. You don't drive from your home to your office without turning a corner. In the 18th century, it was more likely that one could go in a direct line from one place to another but this is the 21st century. We are an age of indirectness. You have to be willing to recognize this feature of our society. That is why the Board of Registration in Medicine suggested (really ordered) you to have a couple of sessions with me. By the time you have fulfilled your requirements, you will realize that direct honesty is the cruelest form of human behavior. Doctor, do you understand what I mean?'

'Miss Dodge, I do understand but I do not believe it.'

'Well, we do not have enough time to enter into a Talmudic discussion or Jesuitical disputation. Did you ever see the picture **The Manchurian Candidate**?'

'Yes. I did.'

'Then you can understand this final part of your relearning. You will be seeing Doctor Trancesky. He is our hypnotist and after a few sessions with him, he will help you eliminate the word "fat" from your mind's dictionary.'

'Is this really possible Miss Dodge?'

'Believe me, we have had more recalcitrant people than you. They are now models of public correctness.'

'What do these people do for a living?'

'You astonish me. It should be obvious. They are almost all politicians.'

Benign and Malignant Uninvited Guests Within Us

The chief executive of eminently successful commodities trading group recently underwent removal of a benign brain tumor and has apparently recovered well, if not fully. He remarked: 'I didn't want my career to be ended by this bloody inanimate object (**Wall Street Journal**, November 26, 2005).' That he is back at the helm after three months is gratifying but is not as surprising to me as his calling his tumor 'an inanimate object.' I doubt that when he made this statement he was thinking of his pathological specimen residing disembodied in a jar. Rather he was demonstrating his ability to depersonalize what was once growing inside him, converting a live tumor into a non-living object, without the capacity to grow and recur. Maybe this kind of thinking is what enables business titans to create their own reality to their own advantage.

I am in a different category with my prostate cancer, different because it is in the perineal area and not in my brain, different also because it is malignant. Twelve years ago it was supposedly 'totally removed with all margins normal and it will never bother you again,' as the pathologist told me. Despite that optimistic prognosis, I never considered my tumor 'inanimate,' without the possibility of regrowth. Unfortunately I was right. My cancer has survived, as have I, radical prostatecomy, radiation, and hormonal therapy. While the cancer may be controlled, it has never been totally vanquished. My fluctuating PSA values demonstrate its persistence. It is a crafty opponent, which or who lives off me. Whereas the man with the brain tumor thought of it as an object, I have endowed my malignant tumor with living qualities. It is a mouse (or rat) in my basement, in the nether region of my body. Sigmund Freud considered the cancer of his mouth and palate to be an 'unwelcome intruder.' I understand that attitude because I regard my cancer as neither something nor someone I wanted. It has intruded into my life, officially diagnosed two weeks after the death of my first wife in an auto accident. Referring to this unfortunate confluence of misery, a resident from India told me that in his town there was an expression: 'All the buses arrive at the same time.' His concern and that expression comforted me.

My cancer is the enemy within, a potentially lethal parasite maximizing every opportunity that it or he or she can to propagate itself, himself, or herself. I suppose a cancer does have equal rights in the evolutionary processes and the survival of species. In many ways, our body is a microcosm of the planet, with its competitive forces struggling not just to survive but to dominate.

I admit to teleological thinking. I have the quasi-belief that natural processes are not determined by mechanism alone but perhaps by their utility in an overall natural design, not the result of divine intelligence. That is why I ask myself as well as others with more knowledge about biology and evolution why cancer exists. What good does it do? I continue to fool myself by thinking that it must have a purpose because of its wide prevalence. Is its purpose to get rid of people no longer able to reproduce? Then why does it trim the ranks of those in infancy, childhood or young adulthood?

The peculiar irony is that the person who has the cancer is nurturing his or her own agent of destruction. It is worse than a fifth column, a term first applied during the Spanish Civil War to the supporters of Franco in

Madrid. That group worked secondarily to further the invading army's military and political aims; one's cancer is the primary enemy. Why I am using these military analogies I do not know but I suspect that it relates to my having grown up during World War II.

This anthropomorphizing of my prostate cancer as 'My enemy within' gives me the comforting delusion that I still have a fighting chance.

Going Public

As Yogi Berra, the legendary catcher and Mr. Malaprop of the New York Yankees said, 'You can observe a lot by watching.' And so it was yesterday when I was driving and saw a sticker on an SUV's rear bumper: 'I Love Someone with Autism.'

The driver was a woman, whose face I could not see. I assume that she was making a statement about a family member, most likely her child or grandchild. Aside from her personal reasons for proclaiming her devotion to someone autistic, the message was intended to make society more aware of this disease and more empathic toward those who have it.

By coincidence the day before I read an article about a United States billionaire, whose daughter has autism, a fact that has prompted her parents to donate millions of dollars to find its cause and hopefully if not a preventative or a cure, then ways of improving life for the autistic.

The bumper sticker and the efforts of those working in the area of autism deserve our admiration and support. But thinking that someone would put such a message on the back of the car for all to see, made me wonder what would happen if thousands or maybe millions of drivers declared their affection for those with characteristics not usually considered assets by most of society. The weirdness center of my brain generated the following:

'I Love Someone Who is a Thieving Dwarf.'

'I Love Someone Who Is Deaf (and/or Blind; and/or Mute) and Hostile.'
'I Love Someone Who is an Uncontrite Alcoholic.'
'I Love Someone Who is Homeless.'

Anyone seeing that would probably think: 'If you love him or her that much, he or she should not be homeless.'

'I Love a Red Sox Player Who is Presently in a Slump.'
'I Love Someone Who Spends a Lot On Clothes.'
'I Love Someone Who Has Extramarital Affairs.'
'I Love Someone Who Cheats On His Income Tax.'
'I Love Someone Who is in Jail.'
'I Love Someone Who is an Illegal Immigrant.'
'I Love Someone Who is a Voyeur.'
'I Love Someone Who is Massively Obese.'
'I Love Someone Who is Anorectic.'
'I Love Someone Who is a Druid.'

The list is endless. Fortunately bumpers are limited in space. The other problem is that the car might have multiple drivers and no one knows to whom the 'I' in the sticker refers.

Languages

I speak and write English fluently, not surprisingly since my parents and I spoke it from birth. I know French well but not idiomatically. I can get along in Italian and survive in German. I cannot converse in Hebrew but I can read it without understanding it. At 77, I doubt I will improve my linguistic ability. In that realm my personal score card will not qualify me for the Polyglot Hall of Fame but it would be considered good for most Americans at my age and background.

Robert M. Goldwyn

All this is prelude to what I recently learned and found interesting.

It is estimated that 6,900 languages exist with Mandarin the most widely spoken, followed by Spanish, English, Arabic, Bengali, Hindi, Portuguese, Russian, Japanese and German. I am surprised that French was not on the list (Dr. Knowledge, **Boston Globe**, December 19, 2005].

Fewer than 100 people are competent in 550 languages. A macabre statistic is the last fluent speaker of a language dies every ten days. By the end of this century, about half of the world's languages will have become extinct – still a challenge for anyone zany enough to learn the remaining 3,450.

Languages have evolved to answer human needs, with the brain, according to Chomsky, structured so that grammar is innate rather than learned. This is neither the place nor am I equal to the task of listing all the primary needs and conditions that form language. Some basics we all know, especially procreation and the need for human relationships.

Someone commented that language was given to human beings in order to hide the truth. In that regard and as happy contrast, some of the Native American languages require the speaker to say how he or she knows that the statement is true:

'You say things a little differently depending on whether you're talking about something you saw yourself or are relating a story from someone else. In fact, there are as many as eighteen fine gradations in expressing why one believes a statement to be true when one makes it… (ibid).'

If that were the standard, imagine how salutary it would be on those who report the news and analyze it, on those who appear in court as defendants, plaintiffs, attorneys, or even judges. So many languages, so much talk, and so little truth.

Relevant is the story of the Tower of Babel, which, as described in Genesis 11:1-9, tells about the Babylonians, who in an effort to affirm their own importance, tried to build a structure that would reach the heavens. God ended their pretentiousness by so confusing the languages of the workers that they could no longer understand each other; they abandoned the project and were dispersed throughout the Earth. And, if I might borrow the style of the Bible, so it has come to pass that we still cannot understand each other, even if we speak the same language. We may comprehend the words but not understand their meaning and, more difficult, not know whether we are hearing or reading the truth.

Each of us has languages within our language: the way we speak to each other at work, at home, at the mall, in restaurants, at cocktail parties – and the language we speak to ourselves, a language that reflects our experiences, our secret thoughts, our recollections, conscious and unconscious, bizarre or normal – a language so private and idiosyncratic, so disturbing that it overwhelms us and we repress it not because we do not know its meaning but because we do.

The novelist, Italo Calvino (1923-85) understood this:

'Everything can change, but not the language that we carry inside us, like a world more exclusive and final than the womb of one's mother.'

Death of a Flap

For a plastic surgeon, the death of a flap is a tragedy and for the patient, a greater one. Though never as a patient have I experienced its demise, I certainly did as a surgeon. When it happens, it makes one forget all previous successes. It never becomes a routine event but one that initiates many features of a classical grief reaction.

Although I retired from practice seven years ago, I can still recall thinking 'Why did this have to happen to me (and my patient)?' The circumstances usually do not justify blaming the patient unless he or she has not followed advice such as not smoking or somehow twisting the flap or ambulating too soon. One cannot get angry, therefore, at the patient. Each of us becomes the target of our own hostility and despair. The agony is familiar: What if I had never done the operation? What if I had done it differently, using another flap? How could I have been so careless to cut accidentally that small perforator? Why didn't I delay the flap when I saw that it was in trouble in the operating room? Why didn't I listen to the resident who suggested leeches? Why am I still trying to do these flaps? Am I too old for this young person's game? What am I going to tell the patient and her family who trusted me? What will be the next plan and will the patient and the family still have confidence in me? When do I let the referring doctor know? Will I have to go through another agony – a malpractice suit?

A dead flap is useless. It has no redeeming quality. It is a blatant botch for all to see. Usually there are no mitigating circumstances. Sometimes one cannot even learn from what happened because one is not certain what went wrong. To make things worse, one may have to operate the next day or the next week on the same kind of patient for whom one has planned the same flap.

Since I like baseball, I used to take comfort in remembering that even the best could have bad day, even a slump. They went on – why not I?

Like most after a significant loss, we survive (unlike the flap) and carry on, pushed ahead almost in spite of ourselves by non-stoppable time and by hour by hour, day by day duties. Our schedules to which we are tethered become our life-line. We feel as did Adlai Stevenson after losing to Eisenhower, 'I am too sad to laugh and too old to cry.'

We may vent our distress to our spouse, our best friend, or our colleagues young and old but we know we have to set an example not just for them but more importantly for ourselves. We have been trained not to let a defeat paralyze us. We are fortunate that waiting for us is another human being who needs us as another patient's flap is dying.

The plastic surgical world could do with another Arthur Miller to write the equivalent of **Death of a Salesman**.

Jack Armstrong, Where Are You Now That We Need You?

It has been years, actually six decades, since I was an avid listener of the radio program *Jack Armstrong – The All American Boy*. I remember that it was before supper when Jack and his friends, Betty and Billy Fairfield and their Uncle Jim went on adventures throughout the world. One of the lines from the theme song, 'Wave the Flag for Hudson High, Boys,' gives an idea of the qualities this program sought to strengthen: 'tall and strong we stand.'

What made this series real for me was that I lived in Worcester and Hudson was a neighboring town although I do not believe that it was the setting for this thriller. I do recall, however, that Wheaties was the sponsor and I insisted that my mother feed me this healthy slush every morning because I hoped that I would become like Jack Armstrong (tall with strong arms) and have wonderful, noble escapades.

What prompted these recollections was an incident this Christmas Eve in a community close to us. Teenagers somehow had rented a large room at a Radisson Hotel and partied with an abundance of alcohol and drugs. One mother tracked down her son and had the courage to call the police and inform other parents about the event and her part in stopping it.

Almost too obvious to state is that this could never have happened when I was young and certainly not at Jack Armstrong's Hudson High. He would have been doing something better, something less stupid, less self-destructive. What is certain is that he would have been with his family on the night before Christmas. The presence of booze and pot at the Radisson bash was almost less disturbing than the absence of family life that enabled, perhaps encouraged, the young to celebrate in their own way apart from their parents who might have been enjoying a similar evening elsewhere, beyond the pale of parental responsibility. There is more to being a mother and father than procreation.

In my ideology, I stand neither to the right or left but in the dull center. I can understand the concern of those whom some chastise as being 'too religious' about the collapse of proper values at home and in society. Why this is so and what can be done about it require more than a new Jack (or Jane) Armstrong TV series. I believe that life should be more than having fun, certainly more than that of the illegal kind. How a culture or society transmits what it considers proper values, those that enhance the quality of life and not just its prolongation varies throughout the world. The home is the earliest and most obvious place for transmitting worthwhile values; a church also but why not in school?

Robert M. Goldwyn

When I was Doctor Albert Schweitzer's surgeon for a couple of months in Lambaréné, Gabon in 1960, he discussed the fact that with the separation of church and state, schools were reluctant to teach moral values. He thought, and I believe correctly, that methods could be introduced to help students learn moral, ethical behavior. A distant example on a minor scale were the **McGuffey Readers**, first published in 1836, which became standard school books in 37 states after the civil war. They were popular not just for teaching reading but for their stories that had a moral, nonsectarian lesson. In business schools now some of their case studies emphasize the desirability of behaving ethically if not for a better society then for better business, an irresistible coupling.

It is unfortunate that those teenagers and their parents missed the opportunity of celebrating together if not in their individual homes then perhaps at a charitable event even in the same room at the same Radisson Hotel with a modern Jack or Jane Armstrong as their emcee.

Self-Destruction as a Sport

While all sports are potentially hazardous, a couple seem designed to be harmful to the player. The first concerns 'Ballists', those who wish to play baseball according to the rules from the 1800s – without mitts (J. Pereira, Old, Old Ball Game: Three Hits, a Run, Two Broken Fingers, **Wall Street Journal**, October 22-23, 2005). Not surprisingly the incidence of shattered fingers and deformed hands is high. While today's baseball can result in an injury to the hand, older versions almost guarantee it.

Catchers are particularly prone: 'In one game this summer, a foul ball broke the finger of Peter Duda, the Granite catcher. His replacement, Mike Connor, proceeded to break his finger the next inning. Unable to find a second replacement, Mr. Duda returned as catcher and played the rest of the game. He has since broken two other fingers at the old ball game. One will have to be fused back together after the season ends later this month, he says.

Despite the pain, Mr. Duda says, playing the game, '[F]eels as if you're in a dream world, away from all the craziness of daily life.' I wish I had the training and the opportunity to be Mr. Duda's analyst.

That there are in the United States more than 100 teams who play 'vintage baseball' is astounding and attests to the mysterious, perverse nature of the human species. I used to care for hand trauma almost always in those who had accidentally hurt themselves. There were others who purposely slit their wrists and an infrequent patient who purposely had put his finger in a saw at work to receive compensation. The 'ballists' of today, unlike the ballplayers of yore who had no mitts, are macho to the point of being wacko.

The other so-called sport whose existence perplexes me is sponsored by The International Federation of Competitive Eating. The winner is the one who downs the most Buffalo Wings in ten minutes. The prize in a recent competition in Boston was $6500 (J.P. Kahn, Indigestion for all, **The Boston Globe**, November 11, 2005). I doubt that this year's winner went to a restaurant to celebrate.

Interviewed before the match was 'Rich "The Locust" LeFevre, a retired accountant who holds records for birthday cake, chili, corn dog, pizza, smoked pork, Spam, and TexMex Rolls.' Surprisingly for a champion 'gurgitator' he is 61 and weighs only 132 lds. His wife is also what is known as a 'competitive eater.'

Q: 'When did you start eating competitively?'
A: 'Five years ago we got on "Ripley's Believe It or Not" for eating twin 72-ounce steaks in an hour. Things took off from there.'
Q: 'How did you feel afterwards?'
A: 'Full.'

Mr. LeFevre was wonderfully honest. He said that his least favorite food at competition was Spam 'right out of the can.' His favorite: a 5ld birthday cake which he consumed in less than twelve minutes, beating William 'The Fridge' Perry, the ex-Chicago Bears defensive lineman. One would think the 385ld 'Fridge' would have had a lot more gurgitator capacity than 'The Locust' LeFevre. Yet LeFevre is clearly a serious, even dedicated, eater. He told the interviewer that when he is not in an eating contest, he is very 'health-conscious,' restricting himself to skinless chicken breast, fish, fresh fruit, and vegetables, with wheat germ and flaxseed oil every day.

Through evolution our bodies have developed a hardiness and strength that permits us to fend-off and recover from the stresses of living, even living stupidly. Like the situation of the ball players mimicking early games, the competitive food-bingers may be recapitulating prehistory when our forebearers might have eaten as much as they could as quickly as they could before others stole their food, all realizing that the next kill could be days or weeks away. If we had not evolved these survival traits that in different circumstances can turn self-destructive, we doctors would have much less to do.

'Brush Like A Dentist'

It used to be said of the eminent Sir William Osler (1849-1919), who epitomized to generations of doctors and patients the wise, knowledgeable and compassionate physician, that he could conduct unforgettable teaching Rounds on a patient with only a common cold. Although not an Osler but as a mini-essayist, I am always on the alert for something meaningful, at least to me, that I can transmit to others. It may be an article I read, a person I met, or a brief phrase – 'brush like a dentist.' Some will recognize this as a TV ad for an electric toothbrush.

What is remarkable in this age of the overblown, this ad was admirably specific: 'Brush like a dentist,' not think like a dentist or be a dentist. Implied, however, was something more: the user's expectation that he or she will have the proficiency of a dentist at least during the tooth brushing session.

The power of the pen may be less than that of the endorser or endorsement. Every boy or girl who plays a sport will likely have or wear or both an item carrying the name or approval of a revered athlete. I had a Joe Dimaggio bat with his factory generated signature. It somehow had a reverse effect: the opposing pitcher did better than I wielding it.

Would the purchase of a Tiger Woods endorsed car improve my golf game? Would that it were so easy!

Here are a few possibilities:
- Buy the kind of writing pad Hemingway used. (Although I would like to write as successfully as he, I would not want his life's ending).
- Use the kind of pencil that was Einstein's favorite! Who knows what could happen? (nothing)
- Take a vacation where the rich and famous go (and you will become a lot poorer).
- Wear this latest by the designer Gotcha-Money (and you will become more alluring, more desirable to yourself).

In that regard, I remember attending a fashion show in Paris where my daughter, Laura, was working. I could not and still cannot believe the kind of dresses purchased by the over-weight, over-rich and decidedly plain women yearning for a miraculous transformation. Only rebirth with different parents could help but, as we physicians know, never underestimate the power of hope. And we plastic surgeons are not immune from such fantasies. At almost every meeting of the American Society of Plastic Surgeons I bought an instrument that some famous plastic surgeon had found useful and usually had designed. Only occasionally did it improve my performance and the patient's result.

I am writing this just before the income tax deadline. If I had an H & R Block type computer, I could think like an accountant. That I might be jailed for inadvertent fraudulence is another matter. But if it came to a trial and if I wore the same kind of suit that I have seen on TV trial attorneys, I am certain I would be acquitted.

Inconsistency

Most of us know and a few of us – myself included – have used Ralph Waldo Emerson's rationalisation to justify their behavior: 'A foolish consistency is the hobgoblin of little minds, adored by little statesmen and

Robert M. Goldwyn

philosophers and divines.' For those too embarrassed to ask, hobgoblin is an evil or mischievous or ugly elf, who might have more than one of these features.

Consistency is frequently synonymous with inflexibility unless one is consistent in his or her inflexibility. Semantics aside, consistency implies acting in a predictable pattern, which, depending upon the circumstances, can be either reassuring or exasperating or both. For example, 'Consistency is a virtue for trains,' once said by Stephen Vizinczey, a contemporary Hungarian novelist and critic.

The opposite of consistency, of course, is inconsistency and my Inconsistency Case of the Month (which I present as if I were at Rounds) is Mr. Clarence Ray Allen, 76, who was executed at San Quentin, where he was residing because he had killed his son's girlfriend, and from where he had ordered the murder of three witnesses who had testified against him. He has the dubious record of being the second oldest inmate put to death since capital punishment was resumed about 30 years ago. Four months previously, he had had a heart attack (he was a diabetic) that ultimately confined him to a wheelchair. Allen requested the prison authorities to let him die if he went into cardiac arrest before his execution (D. Thompson, 'Calif. execute 76-year-old inmate', **Boston Globe**, January 18, 2006).

The spokesmen at the prison stated: 'At no point are we not going to value the sanctity of life. We would resuscitate him' – and then execute him, as, indeed, happened. Whether or not that official recognized the irony in his statement I do not know. We doctors are trained to value life and frequently we resuscitate and keep alive patients whom everyone, including the family, and secretly even ourselves believe would have fared better without such zealous, terminal attention.

The general question of when to resuscitate or when to 'let nature take its course' is difficult enough but more so as it relates to Mr. Allen, who would have been revived so that he could be killed, perhaps by the same people. He was given intravenous injections of potassium chloride but who administered it was not specified in the article.

When the San Quentin official used the phrase 'sanctity of life,' he raised, if not for himself, then for us and certainly for Mr. Allen, the larger consideration of whose life is to have sanctity and/or to be granted sanctity. The easy answer is everyone, honored only in the abstract but not, for example, a policeman killing in self-defense an actual murderer or soldiers dying in a war.

Oscar Wilde wrote that 'Consistency is the last refuge of the unimaginative,' he likely was referring to himself but Aldous Huxley recognized the larger dimension: 'Consistency is contrary to nature, contrary to life. The only completely consistent people are the dead.'

We should be glad we are alive and inconsistent although at the same time condemned to be searching for consistency.

Operating Room Talk

It would be illegal but certainly interesting to record secretly the conversation in the operating room among doctors, nurses, anesthesiologists, and other personnel. Thoughts expressed there are not be voiced anywhere else, including other parts of the hospital. Every operating team and especially one that works together often has a strong esprit de corps, at least during the time of the surgical procedure. A surgeon usually known to be discreet outside the operating room, may reveal opinions and intimacies that in retrospect he or she would find embarrassing. Marriages that appear solid expose their soft center. Personal habits, preferences, likes and dislikes tumble forth. Implicit in the setting of an operating room is that what happens here, stays here. The reality, however, can be much different if someone peddles the remark beyond the operating room. Again, Oscar Wilde: 'If you see no evil, hear no evil, and speak no evil, you will never be invited to a party.'

For residents and medical students, who place those older, especially mentors, much higher where the air is purer, to witness what goes on at the top is an unforgettable awakening experience. 'Doctor ____ is just like some of the people I know.' More serious, however, is the thought: 'When I get to be his (or her) age, will I be like that?' The idea that it could happen is dispiriting.

Robert M. Goldwyn

During World War II, there was the poster 'Loose Lips Sink Ships.' More relevant to medicine today and the threat of malpractice is that anything that might have a bearing on the care of the patient is discoverable – 'loose lips sink defendants.' Small talk can have large consequences and even if it is not recorded, it can be recollected, at least by prodding from a competent plaintiff attorney.

In our anxious era of political correctness gone wild, any comment that could possibly have racial or gender negative implication can have serious consequences. Calvin Coolidge, our 30th President, would have done well in these times. If remembered for nothing else, what he said should never be forgotten: 'You don't have to take back what you don't say.'

What we discuss in the operating room and outside relates to the times in which we live: current happenings, books, movies, media presentations, politics, celebrities, hospital intrigue – all this with a background perhaps of either modern or classical music playing. The untold history of surgery and surgical life, particularly relating to the operating room, has yet to be compiled. We do have scattered jottings of what was said during some operations. A spectacular example concerns the Danish-born Christian Fenger (1840-1902) who emigrated to Chicago, an eminent surgeon although he had only average manual ability. Dr. William Mayo was present when 'Fenger made a brilliant diagnosis of a fibroid tumor of the brain and operated to remove it. Although as he was closing the wound the patient died. 'Dr. Fenger, the patient is dead,' said the anesthetist quietly. There was no answer. Again, more clearly, 'Dr. Fenger, the patient is dead.' Still not a word.

Carefully, the surgeon sewed up the incision and as carefully wound the bandages around it. Then he said softly, 'You damned fool, to die just as you were cured.' [J.L. Stone, G. Meglio, E.R. Laws, **Development of Pituitary Surgery: The Chicago Contributions**, J. Am. College of Surgeons, 201:784, 2005].

Maybe it is just as well that operating room talk is not documented, only occasionally written down to be recounted and transmitted through the oral lore of surgery.

Recently reported [**Surgery News**, January 2006] was a study of the social dynamics in the operating room. A major finding was that surgeons rated the quality of their colleagues' collaboration and communication skills during surgery much higher than their colleagues rated those of the surgeons. On a 100 point scale, surgeons gave fellow surgeons a grade of 85, anesthesiologists an 84, and nurses 87; whereas nurses graded surgeons at 48 and anesthesiologists graded them at 70. Knowing the temperament of most surgeons, I was not surprised that in this survey surgeons generally thought all was well, 'while other team members disagreed.' The conclusion was that a serious disconnect exists among those who work together and supposedly should communicate better. A discussant of that paper thought that the first step in improving the situation was for 'surgeons to realize how others feel.'

Operating room talk is not the same as communication.

'Now for Some Questions'

In the past few weeks I attended readings by two authors of their own works: P.D. James from **The Lighthouse**, and J. Houston from **New Boy**. I subsequently enjoyed each of these books with the added pleasure of having heard them read selected passages.

At each of these events the time came for the moderator calling for questions, looking at the audience expectantly. He did not have to wait long. Most asked relevant questions and did so with humility, but there were a few who used the occasion not to obtain information but to advertise themselves and what they considered their cleverness, knowledge and importance.

In my father's dictionary they were 'blow-hards,' who, contrary to the effect they wanted to produce in others, made fools of themselves. Each was a middle-aged male dripping with affectation whose wife I pitied for having had to endure him and, worse, share her bed. How could they, seemingly well-educated, have so little awareness of the negativity they radiated? Maybe it was due to their education – the wrong sort – a pursuit of knowledge without the cultivation of social awareness. They were what we kids used to call 'show-offs.' Unfortunately for the audience, they were displaying their pomposity.

I have a few colleagues who never resist the opportunity of presenting their wisdom and hostility in a carefully crafted question, usually directed toward someone younger who recognize that the objective is less to illicit information from them than to impale them. It is an act of mean spiritedness toward the most vulnerable in the medical arena, someone young, usually a student or resident. That someone older chooses to behave in such a puerile, harmful way is remarkable yet understandable since we know that aging is no guaranty of maturity and predictor of social awareness.

It is surprising, nevertheless, that someone at the pinnacle of his career has the need to display his power and knowledge in this fashion. The lesson imparted by such an individual is distinctly different from that intended. Their narcissism prevents them from taking an inventory of themselves as they prepare another question for another author at a public reading.

The Folly of Extreme Behavior

In his excellent biography of the great Rabbi, philosopher and physician Moses Maimonides (1135-1204), Sherwin Nuland, a professor of surgery at Yale, writes about a self-appointed young prophet who claimed that he was the herald for the coming Messiah. Maimonides rejected him and his prophesy. Later this man was arrested, brought in chains before the Shiite ruler of Yemen, who wanted proof that he had been sent by God. The prisoner, presumably deranged, asked that his head be cut off because he was certain that God would immediately replant it. Not surprisingly he died headless and remained so [S.B. Nuland, **Maimonides**, New York:Schocken, 2005, p.89].

I have witnessed similar events in the academic and medical community of some people who have thought they are so important that when they do something outrageous or make extravagant demands, they offer to resign if they fail to get their way and are surprised when the institution decides it can get along well without them. These self-styled 'indispensables' carry brinkmanship to the point of self-destruction.

Throughout my career I have had friends and colleagues, young and old, throw down the academic gauntlet and then have to pick it up and sheepishly leave the scene. Those who run an institution, such as a hospital or a medical school, will ultimately not let any single individual dominate for as long as that person thinks he or she can or should. Only a conceited fool gives an unacceptable ultimatum.

When I grew up, I thought that Franklin Delano Roosevelt was indispensable but when he died, Harry S. Truman and the United States fared well. Roosevelt, in fact, predicted this in a campaign speech in 1932: 'There is no indispensable man.' As in the French proverb: 'Il n'y a point d'homme necessaire'.

There is a considerable and crucial difference that exists between fighting for the truth and battling for entitlement. This distinction becomes more obvious to others as it becomes less obvious to the 'indispensable man (woman).' That individual would do well to remember the English proverb: 'Every dog is entitled to one bite' – and no more.

Vivid is my memory of an irate Khrushchev decades ago banging his shoe on the lectern at the United Nations and storming out to the surprise and bemusement of the audience – all to no avail as far as what he had demanded. If he had had an English nanny, an unlikely possibility because of Khrushchev's poor beginnings, he might have been taught that proverb and spared himself and the world much turmoil.

Long Talks, Long Walks

More than 60 years have passed since my close friend Sam and I, both fifteen, used to sit on a stone wall on Sunday afternoons while we discussed the meaning of life, the inevitability of death, events of World War II, which was coming to an end, the Holocaust, its fact and significance: if that could happen, how could God exist?

As normal adolescents , our talks veered toward the carnal, which at that time in our life we could only barely contemplate. We were both too shy to ask a girl in person to go to a movie so we would make the telephone call together, each of us infusing the other with sufficient courage. Remember that no cell-phones existed and we generally had to get through a parent, usually the mother, to have the daughter come to the phone.

Sam and I would occasionally go to the art museum to sneak a look at books on nudes. Since my father was a doctor, I had the advantage of his library and geographically easy, albeit secretive, access to his anatomy texts. Back then we could not understand why we were becoming increasingly attracted to the opposite sex and to certain areas of the body that I had never seen. Sam did have a sister but I was an only child and both sets of parents were by no means swingers.

Our philosophers' wall was equidistant from each of our homes. I had not realized then but I do now that we walked a great deal, many miles every day and we never thought much about it. There were no school buses although there were some that stopped near our school. We usually walked home after classes had ended. In those days there were open fields and hills near my home. We enjoyed crossing them, feeling the wind on our faces, and seeing birds, butterflies and some small animals. We knew that nature was good for us and we had the fantasy that if we could work for a summer on a farm, we would return in the fall bronzed, muscular and fit. It never happened.

Sam was considerably taller than I so I lengthened my stride to keep up with him. People sometimes comment now that I take longer steps than my height would seem to entitle me. I would accompany Sam on his newspaper route. Papers and the mail were delivered twice a day, a luxury that we never appreciated and now seems incredible.

In those days most families like ours owned only one car which, the father, as the head of the house, used. That left us children and even our mothers the choice of meager public transportation, walking, or staying at home until our fathers returned. While the last was acceptable to our mothers, it was not to us – and so we walked.

When I look back at Sam and myself, we had our life's directions well mapped: I, to become a doctor and he, a lawyer. And as the Bible says, 'So it came to pass.' Society then did not allow us time to 'get our heads together.' Maybe it was the war that lessened self-indulgence and spurred us to get on with life.

Contemplating the world and discussing it were our ways of learning, of combining our experience and insights, of improving our verbal ability, none of which we realized was happening. In those days the world came to us either from what we saw or what we heard of from the radio or the movies; there was no television. When my father decided to purchase a 'television set,' it was a momentous event in our home, made more so by the enormous antenna that had to be mounted on our roof. It looked like a remnant from the Battle of Britain.

As long our memories persist, Sam and I can resurrect the past. Then we never talked about it because there was too little of it and there was much more of the future. For us the telescope of life has reversed.

Those walks, those talks and that time of life I knew even then were good. I treasure those memories and the years that spawned them.

'Doctor, Can You Give Me an Idea of What I Will Look Like After My Facelift?'

Dr. I. Haddit, a practicing plastic surgeon for 20 years, congratulated himself on what he would reply to the next patient who asked him to describe his or her expected result after facial rejuvenation. The question, he realized, was appropriate but he was weary of the lengthy explanations, photos, and more recently, electronic depictions that he had long-sufferingly displayed with tedious explanations, all of which did not seem to satisfy the patient but would soon kill or retire him.

Robert M. Goldwyn

Miraculously he had just found a solution to his problem in a most unlikely place, one of the exhibition catalogs that usually filled his wife's mail. This one was about an artist who specialized in landscapes which to Haddit were uninspired and uninspiring. But what did he know about art? What he did know, however, was overblown writing:

'It was obvious that Jeffrey was not painting portraits of the landscape, but that he was painting the living world from the inside out. His landscapes were about the upward and downward rush of phloem (he knew the meaning of phlegm but had to look this one up: 'the food-conducting tissue of vascular plants, consisting of sieve tubes and other cellular material') and xylem ('the supporting and water-conducting tissue of vascular plants...woody tissue') that created the turgidity of trees, the dauntlessness of erect plants dancing boldly in the sunlight, the coalescence of trees full of leaves turning into anthropomorphic and zoological-looking entities. The paintings were about energy that catalyzes biology, the cosmic wind which in Cabalistic terminology would be called ruach (a Hebrew word that means both wind and spirit).' (***A Sparkling Life Force, New Paintings by Jeffrey Hessing***, G.Y.Hirch, Pucker Gallery, Boston, 2005)

'What the hell does that mean?', he asked himself. First he was exasperated but then elated, remembering Pasteur's words: 'Chance favors the prepared mind.' With the thrill of a discoverer and the cry of 'Eureka,' Haddit did a little dance. His agility surprised himself. Fortunately his wife, Clara, was not home to witness it. She would likely call the next door neighbor, Herb Schultz (a serious psychiatrist). Maybe, Haddit fantasized, I can get both of them to dance with him. 'Now,' he thought, 'I am really going crazy.'

Haddit realized that no longer would he have to give detailed specific responses to the generic question of 'How will I look afterwards.' Those efforts often left the patient perplexed and himself always exhausted. The situation was shortening his life and ruining its quality.

'Haddit got it,' he murmured, feeling himself happy and invincible.

When he heard Clara at the front door, he rushed to it, swung it open, and embraced her with a fervor that she had not experienced since their honeymoon three decades ago. She was startled, even delighted, but then suspicious: perhaps he had been searching the Internet and chanced upon a pornographic website. She comforted herself by remembering that he was as adept on the computer as a koala.

In due course, he explained his brilliant breakthrough. Like most wives, she gave him an understanding look devoid of understanding.

He rushed through dinner, barely recognizing what he had eaten. He was distracted until he went to bed and then restless all night, anticipating the next day's patients. 'Please, dear Lord, may there be a facelift patient in the bunch,' he prayed. And indeed, there was.

Mrs. Simpson, 55 years old, had a sagging face and a bulging wallet, a wonderful combination for Haddit. She would also be what he and the trade called a 'good patient.' More than that, she was predictable in her behavior and did ask 'Doctor, can you give me an idea of what I will look like after my facelift?'

Haddit was ready. He had practiced what he would say during the 45 minutes drive to his office. 'Well, of course, Mrs. Simpson, nobody, certainly not I, even someone as experienced as I am, I must say, cannot give you a precise idea of what you will look like following the procedure. I can tell you, however, what I think you will look like, what the result will likely be. I wish I could guarantee it but I am not God – only doing His work,' lowering his head, feigning a humility he never possessed.

'My guess is that the operation will restore your face to yourself. It will liberate the Jane Simpson in you. It will re-establish the balance between you, middle age, and the fast approaching old age, (Jane Simpson shudders) reverting you to who you are, were, and can be. The change will be subtle but significant, in a sense of investing your now tired face (Jane Simpson shudders again) with an élan, a vitality, a youthfulness, a hopefulness, and an optimism – that's the real word, optimism that you undoubtedly have (she likely never had it) but has left you, as it would anyone going through the number of years that you have had to endure (she thinks about all the work that she did in high school, college, law school, her marriage which has never been easy to another lawyer in the firm, their long hours of work, their too few hours of vacation and play – yes, he understood her, he knew that she had 'endured' – what a genius this man is, a seer).

Robert M. Goldwyn

'Your face will be lifted and uplifting, bringing your body along with you, enabling you to revel in all of life's choices, to explore all its byways, not just in your home or in the garden or the fields nearby or the beaches in the summer but everywhere – and, please do not get too much sun – no, no, no!', he says with a mischievous smile, acting like a principal of a high school, an analogy that Mrs. Simpson also has conjured.

'You see, Mrs. Simpson, an anatomic result anyone can produce but I pride myself in doing more – in creating what your genes, those of your parents and grandparents and others long before have imparted to you but also what you have done with your life. Of course, the appearance of the individual features that make up a face are important but taken together, they are trivial compared to the overall effect, the result that transcends mere body parts: the neck, the cheeks, the eyelids, the forehead – they are but fractions of a majestic whole and that, my dear Jane, if I may call you that, (her heart beats wildly hearing him say her first name combined with the prospect of this transformation – whatever it is). She nods a vigorous assent because she feels that it is a privilege to have this kind of man, this kind of physician, this kind of surgeon, a skilled magician working on her behalf.

'I could go on but I frankly believe that I have talked too much already. The excitement of what I think I can do not to you but with you and for you is thrilling, even exhausting but in the operating room, it will stimulate me to render you to yourself, to restore your face to your face, to enhance your body, which, after all, carries your face,' Haddit realizes that perhaps the last was stretching it (making an unconscious pun to himself when he thinks of a facelift).

'Mrs. Simpson, now favor me (he adores that expression) with any question or questions that you might have,' leaning forward with a look of deep concern and interest.

'Doctor, my only question is simple: how soon can you schedule me?'

'As soon as possible. I am sorry that so many are on the waiting list already. It could be a long time (he has nobody scheduled beyond next week) but let's see what my secretary and chance can do for you, for us.'

He escorts her to the door and tells his secretary: 'Please help Mrs.

Simpson as soon you can. She is really a special person' (anyone who writes him a check or has a credit card is special).

After he closes the door, he thinks to himself 'Haddit did it. Haddit's still got it.' He pirouettes, so great is his joy.

⁂

Irrationality: The Inexhaustible Fuel

Spain today (January 17, 2006) banned smoking in public places. Since Spaniards are second only to the Greeks in consuming more cigarettes than any other country in Europe, reaction to the new law was brisk, to say the least. Radio interviews presented the expected [approximate quotations]:

'It's about time.'
- 'I'm going to smoke no matter what. Going outside where you work isn't going to hold me back.'
- 'The government should stick to more important things.'

One man, however, rewarded me with the unexpected, a remarkable example of irrationality:

'Our country should set its own rules and not be influenced by America. Because America doesn't allow smoking in public, why should we go along with it? The next thing that will happen is that we will be having the death penalty, just like in America.'

The fact that this man consumes cigarettes and imposes a death penalty on himself seems not to have entered his thinking. He is against the death penalty for others but not for himself, especially when it is self-inflicted.

I realize that anti-Americanism is partially responsible for his warped thinking. I know also that not all smokers or second-hand smokers will die from the affects of nicotine. What astonishes me, however, is that someone in Spain would rail against the penal system in United States, three thousand miles away, and not hold tobacco companies responsible for far more deaths in his own country.

In my mind is an image of that interviewee with a lighted cigarette venting his anger to the reporter about the role of government in causing death, capital punishment, but not in saving life, banning smoking in public places or for minors.

In my state of Massachusetts the legislature is considering a law that will enforce the wearing of seat-belts in cars. A popular argument against it is that failure to buckle-up can harm only that person. While that may be true, it does not take into account the socio-economic consequences to society of caring for injured drivers and passengers, not to mention the physiological trauma to families having to contend with the loss or injury of the individual who refused to use a seat-belt. The larger issue and one that seems infinitely debatable is how far should the government go to protect the health of its citizens. The more practical consideration is how far a government can go before its citizens protest or rebel. The sentiment is 'I would rather die sooner in freedom than live longer in constraint – according to the dictates of others, namely government officials.'

The older I become I realize that a good education is not synonymous with a rational mind. In fact, the better educated have more ability to mask their irrationality and obstinacy, as the minutes of faculty meetings can attest.

Enjoying the Tidbits

I am guilty of what Benjamin Disraeli (1804-1881), one-time Prime Minister of Great Britain, described: 'Little things affect little minds.' Since there are many more 'little things' than great things in life, why not enjoy what is easily accessible? It does require, however, alertness. Little things can be just words or phrases, brief but cogent, small but powerful, whose meaning and ramifications far transcend the several letters composing them. They need not concern earth erupting events. Disraeli, for example, was once asked to define the difference between a calamity and a misfortune. Invoking his political enemy Gladstone, he responded, 'If, for instance, Mr. Gladstone were to fall into the river, that would be a misfortune. But if anyone were to pull him out, that would be a calamity.'

Admittedly I look for these 'little things'. For example, yesterday, I read about Sister Bridget, who is in charge of a residence for people with multiple sclerosis and other neurological diseases. She is battling her own affliction, breast cancer, an experience that is testing '... her conviction that illness is a comma in life, pausing the flow of living but not ending it' (R. Barlow, Faith helped nun through the shadows, **Boston Globe**, January 28, 2006).

In the January 2006 issue of **Art in America**, I found a reference to Mierle Laderman Ukeles, whom the writer, N. Princenthal, identified as 'artist-in-residence of New York City's sanitation department since 1978.' What does he do all day or perhaps at night, I asked myself, much the way my daughters would question me when they were very young: 'Daddy, what do you do when you leave home?' Since my reading about Mr. Ukeles, I have had wonderful fantasies about what it would be like to lead Mr. Ukeles's life. I am sure that he has had none with regard to mine.

From Man, The Unknown by Alexis Carrel, whose early work with vascular suture and organ transplantation gained him the Nobel Prize for physiology or medicine in 1912: 'Longevity is only desirable if it increases the duration of youth, and not that of old age. The lengthening of the senescent period would be a calamity. The aging individual, when not capable of providing for himself, is an encumbrance to his family and to the community. If all men lived to be one hundred years old, the younger members of the population could not support such a heavy burden. Before attempting to prolong life, we must discover methods for conserving organic and mental activities to the eve of death... The number of centenarians must not be augmented until we can prevent intellectual and moral decay, and also the lingering diseases of old age.'

Maybe true but too harsh for my thinking and my age.

Oscar Levant (1906-1972), pianist and composer, in his memoirs quoted a fellow mental patient: 'There's no cause I wouldn't die for.'

– Confirming the truth of Oscar Wilde's observation: 'Because a man is willing to die for a principle does not make it right.'

And this:
> From my boyhood I remember
> A crystal moment of September.

R.P.T. Coffin (1892-1955) an American Poet.

That couplet, I suppose, has stayed with me because I was born in September. The sculptor, George Segal (1924-2000), had the same idea: 'I think a minute of existence is miraculous and extraordinary.' His work, indeed, captures people in that minute and gives them life.

In **Black Dog of Fate**, the novelist Peter Balakin had this line which few would dispute: 'Everyone is still alive for the time being.'

And one of mine about a colleague: 'He is who he isn't.'

Another morsel worthy of our attention was what Ernest Hemingway wrote to F. Scott Fitzgerald:

'Ah Fitz, but we are profound chaps – we word lads.'

Look for the tidbits; enjoy life in a minor key.

William T. Bovie and his Theory of Social Behavior

In preparing for a recent talk, I read again an article I wrote (Bovie: The Man and the Machine. Ann Plast Surg 2: 135, 1979). It was about William T. Bovie (1882-1958), a pioneer in the field of electosurgery, responsible for the still used 'Bovie', which he developed in collaboration with the famed neurosurgeon, Harvey Cushing (1869-1939) at the then Peter Bent Brigham Hospital in Boston. During my research into the life of this eccentric physicist, I found a passage from a talk he had given at the Mayo Clinic:

> I have noted a phenomenon which may be raised to the height of a fundamental law which I have called the 'momentum of

organization.' I may illustrate this in the following manner. Suppose I have a large box filled with objects of a simple geometric form as, for example, a set of cubes, and that along the bottom of the box I packed the cubes in a different arrangement. Let us say that I packed them as close as may be with each cube standing on one of its corners and then suppose that the other cubes are dumped into the box in a perfectly irregular manner. I shake the box and thus agitate the cubes until they have assumed the most stable position possible. It will be found that the most stable position, that is, the one having the least free energy, will be the one in which all of the cubes are standing on their corners so that they fit with those which form the bottom layer. This law of 'momentum of organization' may be applied to all kinds of organizations. For example, when the band marches down the street all the boys begin to fall in and mark time; the men and women on the pavement move with a rhythmic tread. Or we may carry the law into that realm of psychic organization which we call personality and we will find that the condition of least free energy, that is the condition when we feel the most comfortable about things, is when the new ideas have been fitted in with the old ones which we call our personality or our way of looking at things. Understanding is merely the turning over of the new idea until it fits our particular thought pattern. Sometimes it is impossible to fit our new ideas into our old thought patterns. Then we discard the new idea, or the old thought patterns must be rearranged. Some people unwisely lay down false thought patterns in their children's minds. Psychologic storms during adolescence are the result. [Bovie WT: Concerning the stuff we are made of {the Mayo Foundation Lecture}. Rep Staff Meet Mayo Clin 1:45, 1926]

As I was re-learning about Bovie and thinking about his theory of social behavior, I read an article in **Science**: 'Recent models from theoretical physics have predicted that mass-migrating animal groups may share group-level properties, irrespective of the type of animals in the group.

Robert M. Goldwyn

One key prediction is that as the density of animals in the group increases, a rapid transition occurs from disordered movement of individuals within the group to highly aligned collective motion.

'Understanding such a transition is crucial to the control of mobile swarming insect pests such as the desert locust. We confirmed the prediction of a rapid transition from disordered to ordered movement and identified a critical density for the onset of coordinated marching in locust nymphs. We also demonstrated a dynamic instability in motion at densities typical of locusts in the field, in which groups can switch direction without external perturbation, potentially facilitating the rapid transfer of directional information' (Buhl, J. Sumpter D.J.T., Couzin, I.D., et al from From Disorder to Order in Marching Locusts, **Science** 312: 2006).

The authors 'confirmed the prediction of a rapid transition from disordered to ordered movement and identified a critical density for the onset of coordinated marching in locust nymphs,' thereby matching postulates from models of phase transitions from order to disorder in statistical physics, a field undeveloped in Bovie's era.

I am not a physicist. In fact, my knowledge is less than rudimentary, embarrassingly so. When I was at Harvard College, obtaining a respectable grade in physics was a major impediment to my getting into medical school. That I was successful was due in great measure to the help I received from one of my roommates, David Lee, who later won the Nobel Prize in physics. When I heard this wonderful news, I got in touch with David telling him that if it were not for me, he would never have been going to Stockholm for that special recognition.

In discussing Bovie's theory with other physicists and social scientists, I have concluded that while his theory is provocative, it may be simplistic since human behavior is more complex. I have observed, however, that the more intellectual a person considers himself or herself, the more reluctant he or she is to admit that any phenomenon is simple. Even Einstein was initially criticized by some for discovering a theory they considered too simple in its concluding equation.

I majored in sociology and psychology in college and despite my studies then and my subsequent medical career, I still cannot explain satisfactorily to myself and certainly not to others why individuals or groups behave as they do. In my naive view, there seems to be an ongoing struggle between wresting order from disorder and when that state is achieved, creating more disorder. In problems they attempt to solve, psychologists, sociologists, and physicists have more in common than they recognize.

Compromises Along the Way

In Trevanian's novel *The Main* (1976) the protagonist is an aging, burned-out detective, a widower, 'A man who has come to prefer peace to happiness; silence to music.' The sameness of his life inside his Spartan apartment and outside, in the routine of his job, gives him comfort but no exhilaration, no aggravation but no ups, perhaps an occasional down. His universe is contracted more by choice than circumstances. His social orbit is small but without large problems. He is alone more than lonely. I know people like him, men who have lost their wives through death or divorce and seek no replacement, those for whom, as the saying goes, 'Time hangs heavy.' Most I never knew when they were young but in a twist from what was said of Al Gore being 'an old man's idea of what a young man should be,' they are a young man's idea of what an old man should be.

Sometimes I walk with them around the local reservoir. They appreciate company and the chance to reminisce. They have the aura of sadness, perhaps depression, of being passive, letting life take its course without their exertion or protest. One man, in his late seventies, a widower with two children living nearby, said: 'What is, is; what will be, will be' – an attitude different from how he described his early and middle years as an entrepreneur. Once part of the scene he like others are now observers. Their life makes me glad that mine is not like that. A few told me that they wished they could find someone to marry, as did I after the death of my first wife. The way they say it, however, is wistful, detached. They seem as incapable of doing it as climbing Everest.

'I can't go through all that dating again,' a retired lawyer confided. He is content or thinks he should be with what others would regard as too little. His married friends, mainly the wives, want to introduce him to someone they think will make his life better. 'But why take the risk?', he said adding that when one is young, one is expected to seek a mate but 'why now?', not saying but likely thinking 'when life is almost over.' Without realizing it, he and others like him have given the last rites to themselves. Farthest from their mind now is an 'extreme make-over.' They are what they have become. Fewer variables in their life, less to go wrong and less to go right. They and their compromises are compatible.

From Pediatrician to Gerontologist

I made a mistake the other day: I called a classmate from my college and medical school days. His wife answered and told me that she and her husband had just been to a new doctor, a gerontologist. 'After all,' she said, 'we are at the age when we have too many problems for just our regular internist.'

Whether or not she was wrong in her assessment, I do not know but I can say that the news unsettled me.

I responded with diehard defiance, hoping to convince myself at age 77 that I can still see an internist. I proclaimed this a bit strongly and my friends (he was listening on another phone) who have known me for years recognized my denial and the reasons for it and gently called it to my attention.

In our society some of us may progress from pediatrician to internist or family doctor and gerontologist along with other '-ists', a couple of the worst being oncologists or radiation therapists. In my day there were no adolescent doctors, specifically no doctors for adolescents. My daughters, however, did have such a specialist, but when they entered college, they relinquished quite happily that feature of being 'underage.'

For reasons that are perfectly clear, uncomfortably so, I hope I can avoid seeing a gerontologist because I do not like the label and what it connotes. The measures I use include a better, not necessarily a proper diet (well sort of), exercise (not enough), continuing abstinence from nicotine (I never smoked) and from harmful drugs (I never took them) – only possibly hazardous prescribed medications.

When I go to see my doctor, an excellent one, I hope that he will not retire from his practice until I do from this earth. It is reassuring to see in his waiting room people even older than myself.

In Michael Connelly's **The Closers** is this relevant passage (relevant to me at least):

> She pointed to a photo of a young Gordon Stoddard, who had much longer hair back then and didn't wear glasses. He was leaner and looked stronger as well.
>
> 'Look at him,' she said. 'Nobody should grow old. And everybody should get the chance.'

So that is where I am, having been given the chance and trying to maximize it. The reason that I and my plastic surgical patients do not like to see ourselves grow older was not just a matter of vanity but of survival. The process of aging and its perception are reminders of decline and death. One can perhaps forestall its progression but one can never stop it and certainly never reverse it. After a facelift, for example, the patient looks younger and may feel younger but is not younger – a reality that reminds me of the title of Eudora Welty's book, **Losing Battles**.

So many, perhaps too many people, myself included, are little Ponce de Leon's spending an inordinate time in life thinking about aging and/or attempting to prolong it. When I was young I used to hear my grandfather, who came from Austria, say in German:

'If money could buy everything, the rich would live forever and the poor would die young.' As a leveler, death has no equal.

The irony that mocks us is what 'ends this strange eventful history' is a 'second childishness' [*As You Like It*]. Note the great Bard, (whoever he really was), did not term this 'childhood,' since it is not – no second chance to do it right or even wrong.

Planning For the Future: Some Cool Thoughts

For millennia, even before recorded history, humans, but not all, have believed in an afterlife. The ancient Egyptians spending a large part their earthly existence in building pyramids is prime evidence. Regarding the question of whether there is life after death, Samuel Johnson remarked: 'All argument is against it; but all belief is for it.' Has there been a life before this life? Millions of believers in some Eastern religions have that credo.

While many I know are convinced of an afterlife, I have heard of only a few who place their faith in suspended animation. These individuals literally think outside the box. Called cryonauts, they have plans and paid money to be frozen with liquid nitrogen with the expectation of future revival by being thawed back into life when medicine has advanced sufficiently.

'Some 142 human bodies or heads, including that of baseball legend Ted Williams, are now held in cold-storage at one of two U.S. Cryonics facilities' in Scottsdale Arizona and in the Clinton Township, Michigan. (A. Regalado, A Cold Calculus Leads Cryonauts To Put Assets on Ice, **Wall Street Journal**, January 20, 2006).

What Ted Williams did not do, as far as I know, but what some have already arranged is to design a special will and trust that leaves their assets to themselves, to be restored to them at considerable appreciation when they return to claim their own inheritance. One financial adviser confirmed that his client 'does not want to pass away,' a monumental understatement.

In another category, that of monumental hubris or madness, a hedge-fund industry pioneer, now 73, is arranging a trust of several million dollars that he has directed to be invested in 'no-load index-tracking mutual funds to avoid managing and trading fees.' This is a peculiar reversal in which the owner is frozen while his assets are not, in the hope that they will grow.

I have not seen a psychological profile of people who do this but I expect that most are male, all are rich, confident to the point of arrogance, and sufficiently self-centered to believe that they are entitled and able to be exempt from what happens to everybody else.

All this confirms that the power of hope is much greater than the power of reason. Jean Kerr, the twentieth-century author and playwright, put it nicely: 'Hope is the feeling you have that the feeling you have isn't permanent.'

Shortly before Henry David Thoreau died, a friend asked him whether he believed in an afterlife. He cleverly dodged the issue: 'Oh, one world at a time!'

If I had known more about cryogenic suspended animation, I might have fantasized about seeking it immediately when trying to deal with a dissatisfied patient in my office. Maybe I could have escaped into my cold room, pushed a button, and by previous arrangement consigned myself to an arctic slumber until the statute of limitations expired – while I did not. But, and it is too horrible for me to think, she might also have chosen to become a cryonaut and we might thaw out at the same time, even in the same room!

Seeing Without Feeling

A few weeks ago the residents presented a patient at Rounds. Like most Rounds today in most American hospitals, going to the bedside has become obsolete. We sit in a room and Powerpoint brings the patient to us. We see the patient on a screen but we cannot interact except with his or her image.

The patient whom we discussed was a 35-year-old woman, single, with severe lupus affecting her kidneys, causing extreme weakness and an inability to care for herself; as a result she developed many decubitus ulcers. When questioned, the residents obviously knew nothing about her personal life although they knew much about her medical problems and their management. More than what I considered inadequate in a few matters in their care of that patient was their disinterest in what it must be like to be that person – what would they experience if they were in her place and predicament? The enormous pressure on residents to treat patients can cause occupational blindness: the inability to view and experience the patient as an individual who we could be if circumstances or destiny were different. We physicians should have greater awareness of the fact that little separates us from our patients. Our patients become a distant 'they' and behind this mental barrier, we remain 'we.'

Not to be forgotten is the inscription on the gate of a cemetery in Northern Italy: 'Noi Oggi; Voi Domani' – We today, You tomorrow. And quite possibly 'we' can become 'they' today. 'We are well until we are ill,' as one of my colleagues, Clinton Koufman, a general surgeon, frequently remarks. While we physicians cannot become obsessively preoccupied with our vulnerability, we certainly should not forget it. This would be helpful not just to our patients but to ourselves. It might make us appreciate more what we have that is good instead of focusing on what is bad which, in perspective, may not be that bad.

Presenting a patient in absentia has emerged because the old teaching Rounds, with the professor in the lead, was cumbersome, perhaps time inefficient, and potentially embarrassing for the patient. It did have the benefit, however, of immediacy and of not rendering the patient, as does the computer, a photograph, a human being without body or soul, a depiction.

What I witnessed that morning was the out-sourcing of the patient, even within the hospital, to a point distant from the bed. A patient, a human being, is much more than the information he or she may generate. As more patients seek treatment, as health costs mount, and the number of available physicians decrease, our society will become increasingly dependent on the computer and its capabilities. Already, for example, X-rays taken in this country are read abroad, instantaneously and presumably accurately. The patient and the doctor can transmit facts to each other with efficiency but little warmth. George Orwell's vision has already come to medicine. No wonder that so many patients, despite what medicine can do for them, are dissatisfied with their care.

Memory: the Miraculous Attic or Basement

What, how and why my memory retrieves from storage is strange and inexplicable. Today, for example, I remembered what Sammy, a stable owner in the Barbados, said to me more than 20 years ago: 'I am closer to dying than I am to living.' He was about 70 and I know better now than at the time what likely prompted his thought. That recollection dredged up another – from F. Scott Fitzgerald's **The Great Gatsby**: 'So we beat on, boats against the current, borne back ceaselessly into the past.' From there somehow my mind got in touch with the author Djuana Barnes: 'In youth one may have been a peacock, in old age one is a sparrow.' Congratulations to the person who could at least have been a peacock!

Whatever else a peacock has, it cannot sing and that leads me into this passage from the prayer book on Yom Kippur, the Day of Atonement, the holiest Jewish holiday: 'Alas for those who cannot sing but die with their music in them.'

Fortunately for me, my memories are not restricted to the spoken or written word. Several months ago I was driving behind an orange truck, its lights flashing. The jacket, orange also of the man riding in the back provided its identity: Brookline (my town) Sewer Department. He was about 30, good looking. How would the family of some of my upper-middle-class friends react to him if he were in that jacket when he came to call on their daughter compared to what their response would be if he were wearing a Harvard College sweatshirt because he was a student there or an alumnus? The fact is that nobody treats everybody the same and not only because of social class or money. Other determinants are gender, age, race, group identity, friendship, or the circumstances of the situation. These not need be instances of mistaken identity as in books or on TV but situations arising from false stereotyping.

When I was writing this, I had another memory – that of myself when I was ten. It was occasioned by the doorbell's ringing. Standing there were two boys about ten who offered to shovel the snow from our steps. I told them that I was sorry because we had someone contracted to do this (and our large driveway). I wanted to give those boys money, possibly as a way of bridging in reverse the time gap of 65 years. I was sufficiently rational to realize that if I tried to shovel the snow now, I would never return to my childhood and my old home but more likely it would be the Intensive Care Unit.

How to be More Than You Are

I had been in practice about ten years when one summer my wife and I with our two daughters went to Paris for a couple of weeks. As I was waiting to check into our hotel, a man in front of me introduced himself to the clerk as a doctor and signed the necessary forms. Before leaving, however, he handed the young woman a copy of the **New York Times** saying: 'I told everyone at the hospital that I was going to Paris to deliver a paper. Here it is.' Though her English was good, she could not grasp the significance of what she was witnessing. Even if she had been fluent in English, she would have found, as did I, his behavior bizarre, almost reprehensible if it had not been so comical – and pitiful. To have to plump one's ego by resorting to this kind of trickery shows a peculiar kind desperation, not 'quiet' in Thoreau's sense of the word but a sad, gnawing discomfort with oneself. I never found out more about that doctor than he looked in fifties and was from America. I should have liked more information to explain why he felt the need to engage in these shenanigans.

I was reminded of that incident when I just visited relatives in Florida. The woman in her mid-eighties tried without success to get an early appointment with an orthopedic surgeon whose secretary informed her that 'He is so busy. He talks all over the world.' How does one not speak or 'talk' whenever and wherever one travels. As far as I could determine, this doctor was competent and likely was invited to discuss his work. The emphasis, however, his office placed upon his being in constant demand throughout our planet seemed an exaggeration, at least to me. If his talking was not on a professional basis, then he was doing what a few of my friends also do when we go to a restaurant: specifically talk for a few minutes about business as a pretext for making the meal a tax deduction, something I had never done. The Internal Revenue Service at least insists on some evidence to determine whether the deduction is valid. The individual who 'delivers a paper' or 'talks all over the world' without being a legitimate invited speaker engages in that behavior less for reasons of income tax than of ego.

What about me? Can I pass my own scrutiny? No, since I recall that when I first opened my office, I assigned the number 125 to the first patient because I realized that every folder was visibly numbered. I thought at the time that my stratagem was clever but now I realize it was a dishonest and pathetic – even stupid. I should have made the number 1,125!

Not only are there tricksters among us but many of us have that potential, hopefully not to be actualized often. The danger is not that we fool others but eventually ourselves beyond the point of recognition, recovery, or redemption.

Robert M. Goldwyn

How Scientific Am I?
Not as much as I should be.

I am not talking about my scientific knowledge whose gaps unfortunately widen with each year. I am referring to superstitions, of which I have more than I like to admit. Although I may not act on them, I am aware of them.

Like most things, it started in my childhood, namely with my mother. My father had no superstitions but my mother had enough for both of them. In fairness to her, I should emphasize that she did not invent them but passed them on:

- **Never** open an umbrella inside the house.
- **Never** put a hat on a bed.
- **Never** refuse to give money to a Gypsy who may ask for it at your door (they might wish bad fortune on you).
- **Never** knowingly cross the path of a black cat or have it cross yours (my mother likely never heard that in Yorkshire, England, sailors' wives kept black cats in order it insure the safety of their husbands at sea. At the other extreme, in Northumberland is the belief that if a cat passes over a coffin, disaster is prevented only by killing it!).
- **Never** walk under a ladder (especially with a painter overhead).
- **Never** buy anything with an image of a bird.
- **Never** give a knife as a gift, or an empty purse or bag without putting a penny in it.
- **Never** set the table for 13 (as in the Last Supper) or stay in a room numbered 13 or compound the hazard by being on the 13th floor in a room having the number 13.
- **Never** 'tempt fate' by combining these don'ts: entering your room 1313 on the 13th floor with a wet umbrella that you open while you are throwing your hat on the bed!
- **Never** boast about your good fortune; it could be unlucky but it is certainly ill mannered.

My mother probably had other magical beliefs that I have either forgotten or repressed.

As I mentioned, I do not contort my life to accommodate to those superstitions although when I transgress one (or two), I am keenly aware of it. Maybe my mother knew more about what might befall me negatively than I did or do.

When I became older (note that I avoid the phrase 'grew up'), I knew that my mother was reluctant to have her fortune told and avoided clairvoyance. She occasionally played cards but never tarot. Of all of my mother's superstitions, there is the only one I have maintained assiduously: not having my fortune told. I confess I fear that I might about a future misfortune. That news, I confess would make me anxious – to use the younger generation's term 'would freak me out.' Tending to the obsessive, I might let an ill-omened prediction lessen my joy of each day.

In my travels I have frequently been tempted to have my fortune told, the more exotic the setting, the greater my desire, as, for example, when I was in Marrakech's Jemaa el Fna, 'Execution Square,' where I almost succumbed – not to an execution but to having my destiny divined. I must give some credence to fortune telling, to magical thinking, or I would not avoid it. Marlene Dietrich (1904-1992) might have had me in mind (talk about magical thinking) when she said: 'Superstitions are habits rather than beliefs.'

I think I understand what 'The Kraut,' the name that Ernest Hemmingway gave Dietrich, meant but I have never been able to understand exactly the English proverb: 'He that would have good luck in horses, must kiss the parson's wife.' I suppose it depends upon the pedigree of the horse but more perhaps on the looks of the parson's wife.

Finally in my defense, I pose this question: 'Who among us would feel comfortable in going for an important job interview when a black cat crosses the path while you are entering the building under a ladder to the 13th floor to room 1313 on Friday, the 13th?

Robert M. Goldwyn

Life Smarts

Some people have high IQs but not if we judge them by their actions. Their intrinsic intelligence succumbs to their apparent inability to make the right decisions about important matters of their life. They posses all the senses except the common variety.

People who are smart, which is not the same as a clever, know what they want, and at least attempt to get it. Among the capital crimes against ourselves are selecting the wrong mate, the wrong job, the wrong place to live, wrong financial planing, wrong habits, i.e. smoking, alcohol, poor diet, drugs, dangerous sex, never exercising as well as other acts of self-destruction.

It takes a very smart person to recover from a dumb act. It takes a much smarter person not to do something dumb. Since we all err, our mistakes should be on a minor scale but any mistake, if not admitted and corrected, can lead to a monumental problem. If one doubts that truth, carefully read your next morning's newspaper.

William Booth (1829-1912), the English evangelist and founder of the Salvation Army, clearly understood the problem: 'It is against Stupidity in every shape and form that we have to wage our eternal battle. But how can we wonder at the want of sense on the part of those who have had no advantages, when we see such plentiful absence of that commodity on the part of those who have had all the advantages?'

One may have had few advantages or none in his or her road to becoming a doctor but now being there is itself an advantage and too good a one to lose because of lack of life's smarts.

The English poet and composer, Henry Carey (c.1687-1743), who is credited with writing 'God Save the King,' authored this doggerel that I remember from my childhood:

> Of all the girls that are so smart
> There's none like pretty Sally.
> She is the darling of my heart
> and she lives in our alley.

I wondered what happened to Sally. Did she stay smart all her life? And if so, was it because she rhymed with alley?

※

Ratio

I comfort myself by thinking that an indispensable quality of an essayist is the ability to write about something he or she knows relatively little. In this instance I have chosen a title that might indicate I have a knowledge of mathematics. I do not. While I can add and subtract faster than most, especially the younger generation at the supermarket checkouts, I can do little more than that. I am glad I do not have to help my grandchildren with their math.

Most plastic surgeons today have had to pass courses in calculus. I was fortunate that when I applied to medical schools, no such requirement existed. There is, however, much in the plastic surgical literature about ratios, mostly relating to the optimal proportions that constitute beauty: the length or width of one body part compared to another, considerations that have preoccupied luminaries long before our specialty of plastic surgery began: Plato, Leonardo Da Vinci, Michaelangelo, Durer, as well as a myriad of others obsessively searching for predictable proportions and ratios that could explain and guarantee beauty of the human form.

My quest for a ratio is related only indirectly to the physical form; it is ostensibly simpler but may be intrinsically harder, namely: how many plastic surgeons must be trained to produce one dedicated almost exclusively to reconstructive surgery? This is a serious variant of the prototype joke that unfailingly offends more than it amuses e.g. How many (insert any ethnic or occupational group or gender you wish to insult) do you need to change a light bulb?

The question of who and how many we train in our specialty to do reconstructive and/or aesthetic surgery is discussed by program directors in plastic surgery mostly among themselves, much less so in meetings or in print or on-line.

I recently heard a lecture by a well-known plastic surgeon in his fifties who began his career in reconstruction and now is almost exclusively in cosmesis. The trainees in the audience later debated whether it would not be better and more honest to make one's debut as a cosmetic surgeon and not become one later when older. Their reasons were:

- Remuneration for reconstructive procedures is usually fixed and generally decreasing when that for cosmetic operations is unregulated and rising. One can make more money more quickly and possibly for more years since cosmetic surgery and non-operative procedures are not as physically demanding.
- Patients for aesthetic surgery are elective and emergencies are rare.
- Scheduling in the office and outside, particularly if one has his or her own surgicenter, is simpler and if it is in the office, simplest.
- Bureaucratic hassle is less since one does not have to contend with a third party payer and insurance forms – only informed consents.
- If one has his or her own office – surgical facility, conditions are more efficient and their use will cost the patients less and will increase the income of those who own the facility.
- The person doing cosmetic medical care of any type is usually not under the control of a chief of a department or division and is not restricted to academia, where the practice of aesthetic surgery is generally looked down upon as it is now by most chiefs of surgery who are likely to be general surgeons.

The residents, however, raised other points:

- Does one really have to train so long in general surgery and in plastic surgery, at least six years, if one wishes to do only cosmetic surgery?
- If I am an aesthetic surgeon exclusively or primarily, will I feel like a real doctor?
- Am I betraying the reasons I went into medicine as a career if I deal only with improving appearance and not restoring it?
- Will non-M.D.s be doing cosmetic adjunctive procedures, such as injecting botox or fillers?
- Does one even have to become a plastic surgeon or a dermatologist

to do what a properly trained cosmetologist could do and is doing already in many offices of many doctors?

Since we human beings, certainly those who consider themselves medical commissars, have shown a remarkable inability to predict the future and the manpower needed for medical care, it would seem at this time not to fix the ratio, not to finalize the numerator and denominator. Just as water seeks its own level, the needs, desires and values of our society will determine what jobs will exist and how many people will be needed and should be available. Remember just a few years ago when almost anyone who had basic skills could become a secretary. The once indispensable secretary that we knew when we began our practice is on its way to become an extinct species like the village blacksmith of Longfellow's time.

Who knows what is next? If a simple external procedure or means to tighten the skin were available, those doing invasive facial rejuvenation would find less need for these procedures. While understandably this might be a disquieting thought for some plastic surgeons who resist innovation and would fear loss of income, it is an exciting prospect for patients who could achieve their goals with less risk, minimal or no pain, faster recovery and greater predictability.

Since all medicine is moving in the direction of non-invasive and non-M.D. participation, it is reasonable to postulate that much of what we call cosmetic surgery will increasingly become cosmetic medicine, not requiring prolonged surgical training or even a medical degree. As so many past predictions of the number of doctors or nurses or technicians the healthcare system of our society requires have been egregiously wrong, I would be a fool to attempt even a guess. What I do know, however, is it is becoming increasingly difficult for a new patient to find a doctor or any patient to get an early appointment.

Robert M. Goldwyn

Are You Happy?

A recent poll from the Pew Research Center found that 84% of the 3,000 Americans surveyed described themselves as being 'very' or 'pretty' happy (C. Crossen, Whether People Define Themselves as Happy Depends on the Era, **Wall Street Journal**, March 6, 2006). 15% stated they were not happy but the most intriguing statistic was that 1% could not decide.

A conclusion based on interviewing 3,000 people in a nation of nearly 300 million may not be valid. The observation, nevertheless, that a small proportion of people did not know whether they are happy or unhappy deserves more attention than it received in this article. Maybe they have a different world view from most of us. Knowingly or not they may be adherence of the Stoic philosophy, a movement which began in Athens by Zeno of Citium (Cyprus) around 300 BC and had its greatest influence during the next 500 years. Zeno argued that the good for man is not 'health, wealth, or any set of values that identify happiness with worldly success...only virtue and vice are good and bad, respectively; virtue alone, a wholesome state of mind (is always beneficial) and vice alone (an unwholesome state of mind) is always harmful. Everything else is "indifferent" for happiness... A virtuous man has all that he needs for happiness...' (**New Encyclopedia Britannica**, Volume 11, 15th Edition, 1986).

Maybe those few, whether they are Stoics or not, are happier or less happy than they think they are because they do not spend as much time as others who pursue happiness at an enervating pace but are condemned never to find it. Yet, because of the enormous effort that they have made, they console themselves by saying they are happy. If they did not, they would have to suffer from the realization that much of their time and effort have been futile.

In America, people are under pressure to say that they are happy although they protest the shortcomings of society. Liberals who seem to find unhappiness everywhere may be just as happy personally as conservatives who seem to ignore unhappiness anywhere.

Most studies suggest that people who consider themselves happy live longer, a sufficient reason not just to be happy but to think one is happy or at least to state it.

I take issue with philosopher Bertrand Russell (1872-1970) statement: 'Men who are unhappy, like men who sleep badly, are always proud of the fact.' Telling people when I am unhappy gives me little solace and them, boredom. Unhappiness is negative energy. It is more efficient as well as healthy to be happy or at least to consider oneself so. How unfortunate if one would have as an epitaph: 'Born with the chance and capacity to be happy or unhappy, he (she) chose the latter.'

I admit to the value judgment of preferring happiness to unhappiness. I never was nor could I become a Stoic. The only friends whom Stoics could have are other Stoics. And there are not many in 21st century America.

Notwithstanding all this, I propose a toast to the lucky or unlucky few among us who do not know whether or not they are happy. I raise my glass but I cannot think of appropriate words to accompany this gesture.

'Nuanced Decision'

Let us start with the definition of 'nuance': 'A subtle or slight variation, as in meaning, color or quality: a gradation.' (**The American Heritage Dictionary of the English Language**, 1976. I suppose it's time to buy a new dictionary).

The term 'nuanced decision' is one I have heard frequently in reference to the remarkable ability of politicians to ignore a question or straddle a decision, especially in public. It takes someone clever and slippery to decide not to decide but to be able to give the impression that he or she has decided. How to pretend to commit oneself is an art mastered by many people at all levels below the top of an organization. For some this capability is an asset but not usually for surgeons and their patients. Surgeons are seldom reluctant to make a decision even if it is the wrong one.

Robert M. Goldwyn

Imagine the following scene in the office of Dr. E. Vasive, a 55-year-old plastic surgeon, who likes to do head and neck surgery but is terrified of possibly damaging the facial nerve, particularly so on this occasion because the patient he is seeing is Ms. Sue Yoo, Esq., a trial attorney, referred because of a tumor of the left parotid gland. The examination and the consultation are coming to an end.

'Well, Doctor, what do you think I should do?', Ms. Yoo asks.

'As you know, Ms. Yoo, you have a growth in your left parotid. It is most likely benign, about an 80 percent probability. Yet, one will never know until it is removed.'

'Do you think that it should be removed and, if so, will you do it?'

'Theoretically, of course, and possibly actually, it should be removed but in addition to the risks of surgery – from bleeding afterwards to a possible infection or even, I dislike saying this, death, we have the additional hazard of possibly damaging your facial nerve, leading to a temporary partial paralysis or to a total permanent paralysis so that your face on one side is like a mask.'

The patient, who has a reputation of being fierce and dauntless in her work, gasps, her face whitens, and overwhelmed she slouches in a chair as if to escape the reality of that possibility.

'What would you do, Dr. Vasive, if this were you or your wife?'

He is prepared for this and replies: 'It depends upon how I feel about myself or my wife,' with a chuckle – that has no effect on the dispirited Ms. Yoo.

'Seriously,' he says, 'if this happened to myself or one of my family, I would recommend removal because of the possibility that it could be cancer now or might become malignant later. However, and this is a big **however**, I would want to be sure that my wife understood the terribly adverse and unfortunate consequences should a major complication occur, such as a facial nerve injury or, heaven forbid, death. With regard to my wife, our life together would be over if she should die – a horrible devastation for me and her and our family. If the facial nerve were permanently violated (he has learned to use that phrase in certain situations with women), then the rest of her life would certainly not be what it could be and would likely be sad, hour-by-hour, day-by-day, week-by-week, month-by-month, and year-by-year.'

Dr. Vasive knows just how far he can go and tries in a measured way to rally the patient's sagging feelings.

'Look, I know we have spent time, perhaps too much time, emphasizing the bad that could occur. Usually – but not always – things go well, splendidly. I wish I could say that it would definitely be so with you but I cannot and I will not guarantee an outcome, particularly with regard to this tricky procedure.'

Ms. Yoo has not realized that the procedure is less tricky than her prospective surgeon.

'There has been a lot for you to digest today, Ms. Yoo,' Dr. Vasive says. 'Think about what we discussed today. Talk it over with your husband, your children, your family, any close friends, even a neighbor you know well (he calculates correctly that if she discusses her problem with forty people, at least ten will advise her not to have the procedure).

Now Vasive becomes magnanimous, a true Oslerian physician, and says, 'I would not be unhappy at all, in fact I would be pleased (that is an understatement), if you had a consultation with somebody else, maybe two or three others. I would be happy to facilitate that.' (He is thinking of a colleague whom he detests and considers mean spirited, 'Let him deal with a facial nerve injury in this young trial attorney.')

Ms. Yoo gets up, sighs, walks with her shoulders bent, far different from how she entered the office, and heads for the door which, Dr. Vasive opens for her as would any true gentleman.

'I wish I were the type that could blindly encourage patients to undertake any operation. I like to be thorough about what I do and I want the patient to have almost as much knowledge of his or her problem as I have. While I can advise, I certainly do not feel that it is my right to impose my judgment on another human being, particularly someone as intelligent as you. If there is anything I can't stand is a surgeon who rushes someone into the operating room. I pride myself in not doing that. In any event, please let me know within a couple of weeks what you are thinking. In the meantime, I will write to your internist, Dr. Gifthorse, and tell him about our consultation' (note 'our').

Ms. Yoo in a weak voice asks the secretary, Ms. Akterr, to call her a taxi. Although she parked her car in the garage below, she fears that she lacks the stamina to drive home.

Conclusion: surgeons should not be politicians in their treatment of patients. I am not sure, however, whether our country would be better if politicians behaved more like surgeons.

The Olympics and Plastic Surgery

This title sounds like a nightmare subject our high school English teacher would have assigned us. The directions would have included finding similarities and differences, if any. And there are many.

The most obvious quality both share is a standard of excellence, based on achievement as a result of native and acquired aptitude(s), persistence, and hard work. Not everyone can become a plastic surgeon, and even fewer, an Olympian. There is an exclusivity but not because of gender, race, ethnicity, or money – but of the highest performance.

Becoming a plastic surgeon or participating in the Olympics share the mandatory long training with competent mentors (coaches). Achieving set standards is mandatory to entering the Olympics and to becoming a qualified or certified plastic surgeon.

A major difference between the two is that the age at which most athletes end their Olympic career is when most plastic surgeons have finished their training. Another significant dissimilarity is that the plastic surgeon or any physician has a chance to earn a medal over a 30 to 40 year period, not in a few minutes or several hours of competition. The medical-surgical profession is the longest marathon of all.

Professional athletes, of which the Olympians are a rarified example, are entertainers in addition to whatever else they may be. Doctors, even those who participate in shows like **Extreme Makeover** are not, even though some may try to be. Even the most Hollywood obsessed plastic surgeons have to perform well for his or her patient or suffer consequences more severe than not winning a medal – a lawsuit. Lindsey Jacobellis, the snow-border, despite her monumental screw-up, will not become a defendant. While she may have disappointed millions, she did not violate an informed consent since none existed.

Those who participate in the Olympics add to the quality of life of their viewers and themselves, family, and friends. They do not save or prolong the lives of others even if they risk their own.

What about the plastic surgeon who does only aesthetic surgery? He or she does not usually save or prolong life although admittedly may improve its quality. Some, including doctors, surgeons or even plastic surgeons, might legitimately question whether the long years of training are necessary for someone who wishes only to engage in improving appearance. Should society devote so much of its resources and energy to providing facilities for aesthetic surgeons and their procedures?

Likewise one might question the spending or wasting of inordinate time, effort, and society's assets both in personnel and in facilities, on fielding a champion team in, for example, curling or the luge. Aside from a particular sport, does it make sense for young people and their parents to become absorbed to the point of irrationality in trying to execute a feat lasting less than three minutes, having practiced for endless hours daily, for weeks, months and years just for that fleeting moment of truth, to borrow from the lingo of bullfighters.

A young Turkish figure skater expressed her doubts in an interview about whether what she was doing was really 'worth' her family moving from her home to Canada, spending their fiscal resources, more than $25,000 the first year to $75,000 in later years, to allow her to be in the Olympics. Her perspective and wisdom did not receive the attention they deserved, eclipsed by the superficial hype surrounding the media's coverage of these events. The reason was most likely do to the fact that this talented young athlete expressed doubts about what she was doing not only with regard to herself and her family but in essence, she was questioning the intrinsic value of some aspects of the Olympics.

The outcome, even the existence of the Olympics contribute little to the advance of civilization – heretical thought to be sure. Not so medicine and those who practice it and seek to advance it. I am talking about optimal care of patients by those who act according to the highest standards of their profession.

As charming and obviously masterful and 'cute' (an adjective given by a female TV anchor) as the 'flying tomato' might be, does his mastery of snow-boarding warrant that much attention? Probably yes but so should the activities of those his age who help others in need and strive to become scientist, physicians, or anything that benefits society.

I am not against physical activity or sports or even the Olympics per se but I do object to the excess surrounding it. Competitive spirit in human beings seems ingrained but its expression could theoretically be better modulated or directed.

Readers might accuse me of championing a dour society valuing only attainments of the mind not of the body. I plead guilty perhaps only to restore balance. It seems a distortion of what is good for youth and the human body to extoll an athlete when he or she continues to compete after numerous injuries and multiple operations. That person becomes an inspiration to many others and a salvation to orthopedic surgeons repeatedly caring for him or her. Please excuse my hyperbole.

The reason that the ancient Greeks valued the 'Golden Mean' was that it was and is so rare. Nothing much has changed in the years between their Olympics and ours. While records of individual performances were recorded, nothing like the *Guinness Book of Records* existed. For anyone doubting the human capacity for ambition, stamina, excellence or stupidity, the *Guinness Book* furnishes copious evidence. How we spend our time between birth and death has an infinite range of possibilities. Unfortunately the years we have are finite.

Pes Anserinus

Several weeks ago I injured a part of my body that I never knew existed: my pes anserinus bursa, which, I found out, lies below the tendinous expansions of the sartorius, gracilis and semitendinosus muscles at the medial border of the tuberosity of the tibia (Stedman's *Medical*

Dictionary, 24th Edition). Despite my having taken three years of Latin, I did not know that 'anserinus' comes from anser, goose. I did know, however, that the pain was sudden and severe, so much so that I could never have attempted the goose-step, reminiscent and redolent of the Nazi era, even if for some perverse reason I wanted to. How many of Hitler's troops developed the same problem (as if I cared?)?

I had been feeling some stiffness in my left knee for a couple of days and then abruptly I could not walk because of the severity of the pain. I went to the emergency room with my wife, Tanya, pushing me in a wheelchair. My consolation was that I knew that what had befallen me was not life threatening. To buoy my spirits I reminded myself that great athletes do injure their hamstrings. Maybe I did when I was watching the Olympics the past few days – coincidence or fantasy?

After an ultrasound to rule out phlebitis and X-rays to exclude a fracture or arthritis, the doctors told me that I had a spasm of the quadratus and the hamstring muscles. A few weeks later my orthopedic surgeon recognized that it was bursitis of the 'pes.' For me it was a 'pest,' which responded well to an injection of cortisone.

Like some of my patients who have tried my patience, I have gone into more detail than I perhaps should to make the point that we, even doctors, can get suddenly ill and need help to deal with a part of the body that comes into our consciousness only when it is malfunctioning. The larger lesson, as we who treat patients and may already have been sick should know, is that the universe shrinks down to the part of the anatomy whose wellbeing we previously took for granted.

Pain constricts ones universe so that our view of it is microscopic. Pain also, as I have learned, rapidly dulls without medication our ability to think normally, globally, and creatively. In short, I could do no writing, only reading, during the first two weeks. My admiration increased tremendously for those friends and patients I remembered who have been able to perform adequately despite discomfort. Even more remarkable are the few who can produce monumental works in the arts though having to contend with unremitting physical and mental pain. And what about a mother who maintains a household and cares for her children and mate even when chronically ill.

Robert M. Goldwyn

I had it easy. My pain was not that of a mortal disease. I had the comfort of knowing that it would improve and even if it did not, it would not shorten my life. Not so for so many others whom all of us have known. There is nothing worse than pain without hope.

In the past, although I enjoyed my walks around a nearby reservoir, the idea of doing it at an early hour on a cold morning was less than tempting. Now just to be able to resume that routine seems a privilege.

༄

The Curse of Alzheimer's in Reverse

The March 24, 2006 issue of *Science* reminds us one can suffer from too much memory, a problem most of us do not have and, as we age, are less likely to experience:

'A woman known as 'AJ' remembers every day of her life since she was fourteen. So unusual is she that neuroscientists have coined a new term – 'hyperthymestic syndrome' – for someone in whom 'remembering dominates her life.' AJ, now in her early forties, caught the attention of neuroscientist James McGaugh of the University of California, Irvine, in 2000, when she sent him an e-mail saying 'since I was eleven, I have had this unbelievable ability to recall my past.' The memories, she wrote, are 'nonstop, uncontrollable, and totally exhausting.'

I can believe it. The incessant recollection of something I wanted to forget is maddening and enervating. I am thinking of those occasions when I had a patient with a complication because of an error I made, a decision I took – the wrong one, after having carefully considered alternatives. Is there a surgeon or a physician who has never said to herself or himself 'If I had just done what I had thought of doing'? Maybe it was a wrong incision, a poorly designed flap, the facelift pulled too tightly, cauterizing too near a branch of the facial nerve when one should have known better, accepting a patient for a cosmetic procedure when you recognized but ignored clear signs of an unstable personality, someone with unrealistic expectations, – and the list goes on, goes on, goes on, like poor AJ's memory, cycling the bad memory but never recycling it into something useful and certainly not healthful.

Most plastic surgeons are obsessive, at least those who do careful work but, as in other areas of life, a virtue can become a vice. What AJ has is not the photographic memory or stupendous recall that we wish had been ours as medical students. No, she is caught in a Kafkaesque – Proustian nightmare(s). If too much of a good thing can be bad then too much of a bad thing is worse. Psychologists talk about selective memory; the opposite, selective forgetting may be more important. Arthur Conan Doyle observed or perhaps it was his detective, Sherlock Holmes, that the mind was like an attic; one can store only so much without making room for another item. But no attic has infinitely capacity and it is a rare human mind that does. Most of us are more worried about becoming a sufferer of Alzheimer's, as was my mother, than of developing unfailing recall and the inability to shut down the system. The news about AJ was not all bad. When scientists asked her to recall her previous 24 Easters, 'in ten minutes, she came up with the dates as well as details of her activities. Every date but one was accurate....' That single lapse offers hope for her.

The Worst Battle to Lose

In Natsuo Krinio's novel *Out* (New York: Vintage, 2003) appears this sentence: '[H]e was simply a man who had lost his battle with himself.'

Is there anything more devastating one can say about someone or, worse, about oneself?

Many, too many, lose their battle against cancer, an enemy in war or die fighting for an unsuccessful cause; millions more end their life unrealized, without even battling for whom they want to be.

Plato, in his ***Apology***, quotes Socrates' credo: 'The unexamined life is not worth living.' The choice to lead an unexamined life avoids the battleground of inner strife. No risk, no gain – maybe no pain but definitely more superficiality and calmness, and less self recognition of failure.

My former Chief of Plastic Surgery at the University of Pittsburgh Medical Center, Dr. William L. White, observed: 'You're young only as long as you are stretching yourself.' And he was not referring to yoga. Being challenged or more accurately allowing oneself to be challenged, confers a feeling those older need more than the young for whom confrontation and obstacles seem built into their lives. They have the energy and the desire to overcome but they must also have the ability to accept defeat. That kind of youthfulness not every youth possess and many who are older would not want to find it again if they had every had it. Internal commotion is not for everyone.

Although the Old Testament urges that we be content with our lot in life, Horace (65–8 BC) saw it differently: '[N]o man living is content with the lot that either his choice has given him, or chance has thrown in his way, but each has praise for those who follow other paths...' Because of this striving, we have battles with ourselves: some we lose, some we win, hopefully more of the latter. Even if we are successful in what we set for ourselves to accomplish we cannot guaranty ourselves happiness which is the most elusive entity next to immortality. Are we the only species that can lose the battle with ourselves and recognize it?

Perspective for Self-Preservation

A few days ago I gave a talk at the Sixth Breast Cancer Conference in Düsseldorf, Germany. Aside from the individual presentations, of major interest was the fact that, in Germany, gynecologists, not general surgeons, treat breast cancer; they do the reconstruction after they have done the mastectomy. Rarely is a plastic surgeon involved.

What caught my attention also was something not in the lecture hall but on a sign outside: 'Ich habe Krebs, aber der Krebs hat nicht mich.' (I have cancer but the cancer does not have me). It was fortunate

I read that wisdom because when I returned from my trip I found that my PSA had increased. I should be accustomed to these periodic increases that fortunately have thus far responded to hormones. Even though my oncologist says that he is 'not worried,' I am. My intervals of despondency, though intermittent, are thankfully brief, a few days, the last even less so because of my remembering that quote. For an obsessive, as I am, who likes to have the comfort of being in control, of having everything in order, this is an impossibility in the long term. The obsessive, especially if he or she is a physician, wants health to be perfect or, minimally imperfect. As we age, we lower our standard for perfection in matters of health and, if we are wise, in other areas. Since we cannot return to being pristine and perfection is beyond our grasp, all we can hope is to contend with manageable problems. When most of us were young, we had illnesses against which we railed but would now welcome in exchange for our present difficulties. 'How much can I expect from a 77-year-old carcass,' I ask myself.

Parts of our body are waging guerrilla warfare, sometimes silent, against us while we knowingly or unknowingly attempt to quell these inner rebellions. We have enemies within but allies also: Our immune system and hopefully competent medical care. Strategic also is a buoyant emotional outlook which cannot be purchased or prescribed. It has to be homegrown.

Fenway Park: 60 Years Later

April 11, 2006: Opening Day, Fenway Park, Red Sox Vs Toronto Blue Jays. Among the expected fanfare (literally) was the appearance or reappearance of about seven surviving members of the 1946 Red Sox team. They appeared in two vintage autos entering through the center field gate to the delight of a sell-out crowd of more than 35,000, all standing, cheering and those my age, remembering. Most of that bygone team were in their eighties and had to be helped from the car. A few leaned on their canes but all were smiling, delighting in being able to return to the same park they had graced six decades ago. After they had been placed in formation, each threw an opening ball to a member of the 2006 team, tall, strong, young, just as they had once been. The scene left few eyes dry among those who recalled the way we and they were.

Dick, my friend from childhood, said, 'And they are the lucky ones.'

'But so are we,' I replied.

'Play ball' sounded through the speakers, in a high pitched cry from the legendary pitcher, Charley Wagner, now 93 and appearing fitter than the rest of his teammates. The '46-ers made it back into their cars which slowly left the park as everyone again rose and applauded in homage.

A young man about 30 sitting in front of us, turned to Dick and me, 'You guys must have seen a lot of games here.'

'We sure did,' we replied in unison, our faces and voices reflecting our nostalgia. Dick related that, in 1935, when he was five he had even shaken hands in this same park with the mighty Hank Greenberg, then a rookie with the Detroit Tigers. Our new acquaintance shook his head incredulously. It was as if someone had told me when I was his age that he had met Babe Ruth. The only things lost are those that have not been recorded, remembered, or experienced again.

That day in Fenway Park I was seeing the game as the boy I used to be and with the father I used to have. It was a special afternoon when the past and the present fused deliciously. And the Red Sox won.

'He Is At That Time In His Life'

This was what I used to hear my mother and her friends whisper when, as a child, I happened to walk into the living room. They were not referring to me but to some man they knew who had done something they considered wrong. Most usually, as I found out, it was a middle-aged man, never a women, having an extramarital affair. For my mother and her sisterhood, a word never used by them, the phrase 'middle-age crisis' did not exist although what it described certainly did. Men had their 'flings' but then it rarely led to divorce. In our Jewish community, I knew only one man who had left his wife and they divorced. He, but not she, was considered a pariah.

My mother and father used to say: 'You don't break up a family. If you have to stay together for the good of the children, why is that so bad?'

Since my father worked at a Catholic hospital (St. Vincent's) many of his colleagues and friends were Catholic, to whom divorce, even separation, was abhorrent.

'He is at that time in his life' never referred to anything good, never to circumstances that condoned the behavior being described. Only when I was older did I realize that everyone is at that time in his or her life. How could one be at a different time. The present tense, after all, means the present.

To this day I find myself muttering 'after all, I am at this time of life,' when I have to see the doctor, when I add more pills to the little container (not so little now) that I carry with me, when I no longer have the energy or strength I had, when another friend dies and I attend the funeral, and, horror of horrors, when attractive young women on the subway give me their seats.

I console myself by remembering, more candidly – forcing myself to remember, that whatever time it is in my life it is still life. Recently when I was interviewing applicants for residency in plastic surgery, one of them said in surprise, 'I never thought that I would be able to meet you,' referring likely to having read something I may have written but more likely, to the possibility that I no longer existed. My mother doubtlessly would have said, 'Well, you are at that time of your life.'

Looking at Your Looks

'Linda had seen how she started looking more and more like her father, even a little like her grandfather. Our ancestors survive somewhere in our faces, she thought. If you look like your mother as a child, you end up

Robert M. Goldwyn

as your father when you age. When you no longer recognize your face and notice how unrecognized, it's because an unknown ancestor has taken up residence for awhile...' [H. Mankell, **Before the Frost**, Vintage Books, New York: 2004].

In our society the people, more so women, spend an enormous amount of time considering their appearance. My view as a plastic surgeon is admittedly biased but, nevertheless, the observation is valid. Do those blind from birth behave differently? They cannot look at themselves but they may ponder relentlessly what they would look like to themselves and to others if they had visions. We know only what we look like because of a reflection, principally from a mirror, maybe from a photograph, but in the most primitive societies, from a reflection in the water.

Since our earliest beginnings, recognition was critical to survival: knowing friend from foe, family from outsider. Our culture's preoccupation with looks has less to do with preservation than with our values. Please understand that I am not free of inordinate self-gazing. Our involvement with our appearance extends beyond ourselves to our homes, offices, cars, pets, and all those most significant in our lives. How one looks has become more important than who one is.

The fashion industry is a pathetic commentary on our disordered priorities. Woman have always had to bear the burden of looking younger. Oscar Wilde, in **The Picture of Dorian Gray**, had this line: 'As long as a woman can look ten years younger than her own daughter, she is perfectly satisfied.' And, as we plastic surgeons know well, when a patient thinks she is getting to look more like her mother, that is the stimulus for her making an appointment for facial rejuvenation. Just as one should not 'bite the hand that feeds you,' I suppose I should not criticize the sentiment that has given me financial independence. Some patients did want to look 'beautiful' but they were the minority. Most desired to look younger, to remain as much the same as possible, even though they realized it was a hopeless fight. Yet the exertion energized them. That exertion by itself made them feel younger even if they did not appear so in the office. Although some were flagellating themselves for being vain, I, like most plastic surgeons who want to maintain a practice, did not agree with them. Honesty is sometimes a luxury few can afford.

'No, you are not vain; you are simply trying to maximize your potential,' I recall myself saying or a variation of that theme. One would not need to be a genius in marketing to realize that consumers spend more money if they feel less guilty; rather they are more eager to buy the wares if they feel that they deserve or are entitled to them. Everyone plays the game generally to the mutual satisfaction of all parties.

Oscar Wilde again from ***The Picture of Dorian Gray***: 'It is only shallow people who do not judge by appearances. The true mystery of the world is the visible, not the invisible.' Why the visible preoccupies us much more than the invisible is that it is obvious, and instantly accessible.

Blackberries in Winter

That I can go to a nearby supermarket and buy blackberries in the middle of a New England winter amazes me. That I have to pay more than I would like for them – a luxury – does not lessen the delight of this modern wonder, at least as far as I am concerned. Most Americans today live better and longer than did most people over the past 70 centuries, including kings and royalty. The exception – and it is a big one – are the homeless and those below the poverty level in this country, about 50 million – a sixth of our population. The rest of us have more access to better housing and health care, better hygiene and sanitation, and more varied foods than Sir Thomas Moore could even dream of when he wrote ***Utopia*** in 1516. His was not the first, Plato's Republic being the model. Plato could never predicted what we have today but he did understand the inevitability and the persistence of human dissatisfaction. He likely would have had a 'I told you so' reaction to hearing somebody complain now at facing a drive of 180 miles in three hours, just as he might have heard some grumble at having to go eight miles in three hours on a donkey. Perhaps built into the human species through evolution are the drives to explore, to modify, to improve, to be discontent. We have a low threshold to routine and boredom. We are restless creatures who continually seek activity and more. While the Old Testament preaches the value of being content with one's lot, most of the characters in that great book were not. Even God is not totally happy with man's behavior. And why should He be?

Yet, even with world population overflowing and the persistence of poverty, our species now lives in a relative cornucopia. It means that most of us have a considerable time between birth and death to decide what we shall do? The options are theoretically endless but life is not.

We are of our time, however. We conform to our society's current expectations. It serves no purpose telling someone that he is better off than his counterpart hundred years ago in terms of income, security, housing, education for his children, medical care and longevity. Everything is relative. Albert Einstein not surprisingly understood it well: 'When you are courting a nice girl an hour seems like a second. When you sit on a red-hot cinder a second seems like an hour. That's relativity.'

What is relative is not necessarily pertinent. Imagine saying to a patient who has a weakness of the mandibular branch after a facelift that she is lucky not to have metastatic breast disease. She might well reply, 'Doctor, you should feel fortunate that I am only going to sue you and not shoot you because of your botch-up.'

My father used to say: 'While our family could have more, most people have far less. We should be grateful for what we have and for good health particularly.' I am grateful for blackberries in the winter, or in any season, as I can afford them and eat them with pleasure since – and for this I am especially grateful – I am blessed so far with a competent gastrointestinal system.

There's Agony and There's Agony

S. Pfeiffer, Ritz concierges can ease trauma of adjusting to student life, the *Boston Globe*, April 26, 2006: 'For many college freshman and boarding school students, the adjustment to living away from mom and dad can be difficult. Now students accustomed to a certain lifestyle can turn to The Ritz to make it easier: "To ease the transition between home and campus life, the Ritz-Carlton Hotels of Boston have launched a service that will help families book chauffeured sedans, deliver fresh-baked cookies prepared by hotel chefs to dorm rooms, and do students' laundry." With roughly a quarter-million college students in the Boston area, hotel officials believe the new service has plenty of potential customers. "Every parent wants to pamper their child when they're going through the daily agony of college," said Ritz spokeswoman Caron Le Brun, "and this makes for a little softer transition."'

When I went to Harvard College, my parents and I considered it a privilege without any 'agony.' For the first few months many freshman experienced the effects of separation; we had our periods of loneliness but these did not last long as we had courses to attend and homework to do. A few of us did send our laundry home to be done by our mothers, then to be returned in that once familiar but now obsolete aluminium mailing container. In retrospect I suppose a reason for doing this was not just to save money but to keep our attachment to home. After a couple of months, however, we found laundries that were within our budget.

I have never met Ms. Le Brun, the spokeswoman for the Ritz, I expect she is very competent, but because of her job truly believes that any inconvenience is an 'agony.' The culture of deluxe hotels fosters this attitude in their guests and in their staff. If it were not present, why go to the Ritz in either capacity.

Imagine what it would be like if you received via a delivery van from the Ritz-Carlton a box of just baked cookies as your roommate, perhaps on scholarship, witnesses this event. Doubtless your relationship would not be improved.

My wife and I like to go to modest neighborhood restaurants (but not exclusively). The waiters and waitresses are mostly college students whom we admire for their overcoming economic obstacles to secure a worthwhile education. They do their work very well, usually with a smile and humor. I doubt that many of them who are confronting the true agony of financial survival consider that they are enduring 'the daily agony of college.' Our nation has more than its proper share of the pampered and the spoiled, many of whom condemn the economically stricken for receiving welfare checks while they never perceive their own outrageous entitlement.

I pity those young people of means whose parents truly believe that their children are 'going through the daily agony of college.' Their mothers and fathers are teaching them a lesson that they would do well to forget while the college is trying to instruct them in knowledge and values that they would be wise to remember. More realistic perhaps is the French saying: 'Once spoiled, always spoiled' (Une fois gâté, toujours gâté).

Aesthetic Surgery and Beyond, Inc.

This year's recipient of the World Aesthetic Society's Gold Medal for excellence was Sylvester S. Sharpee, M.D. (known as 'triple S' to his friends). His acceptance speech follows:

> Thank you for this remarkable honor from this distinguished Society whose standards and achievements I, as well as thousands of others internationally, have long admired. I realize that in recognizing me you have also honored Aesthetic Surgery and Beyond – ASAB – with which my name has long been associated. Your president, Dr. I. M. Fedrimmeled, specifically requested that I take as my subject how ASAB began, its present status and its future direction.
>
> Twelve years ago, when I was 45, I had already established a successful practice in aesthetic surgery. I was doing non-surgical procedures also: botox and filler injections, laser treatments,

microbrasions – the whole works including selling my own brand of cosmetics which a commercial firm in India was supplying to me. But I was still a retail operator doing one patient at a time even though I employed eighteen assistants; they also were treating one patient at a time. The next logical step was to start a spa. I did and even though it was doing well I realized that I was still limiting myself to the aesthetics of a patient's body.

One night my wife, Glenda, and I were sitting on the balcony of one of our getaway places – this one happened to be overlooking Lake Como. Glenda said, 'This is an aesthetic experience without having to go through cosmetic surgery. This is an emotional lift.'

Her remark was really responsible for my seeking a new direction in my professional life. Why, I asked myself should I deal only with the aesthetic confines of the patient – the body – and ignore other aesthetic aspects of his or her life? Appearance, after all, does not end with one's body. That is when I started Aesthetic Surgery and Beyond, Inc. – ASAB.

Everything is a matter of education and my staff and I spent hours, months and a couple of years reminding, really indoctrinating, our patients that beauty was more than skin deep, was more than just their body but beauty included their environment.

We had brochures printed to reinforce our message, which was essentially: 'Why beautify your body and live in plain or ugly surroundings?' To our fiscal advantage the immediate connection for most of our patients was to their spouse or important other. 'Why should I look better when he (she) looks so bad?' We saw our practice grow with tandem surgery, not necessarily scheduled at the same time. Let us say that Jennifer had a facelift; soon after her husband, John, would have his eyes done or a chin implant. I knew that our new direction would be a boon to our practice but I had not anticipated that in one year I would be hiring four younger plastic surgeons, two dermatologists – and, in keeping with Aesthetic Surgery and Beyond, a landscaping team – exterior decorators – and finally, interior decorators. At first dubious, patients began to throng to benefit from this expanded concept of aesthetics.

Because a patient and his or her surgeon or aesthetic medicine

Robert M. Goldwyn

professional has developed a bond, there is trust and that patient is more likely to deal with us rather than a randomly selected group of gardeners or painters or interior decorators. At the same time that this was happening, we did not ignore the obvious: we established our own group of hair stylists for men and women, and fashion consultants are now part of our team. We are in the process of beginning our own line of clothing – the complete range of apparel including shoes.

Although we encourage all of our patients to have periodic examinations by their physicians, we restrict ourselves to appearance. Whatever else happens to the human body, it is always better to have it look good. I realize that this is a departure, and some of you may consider it a sacrilege from the usual role of a doctor but I and my kind of plastic surgeon is more than a simple doctor or physician. Let other doctors be restricted to the patient's body or psyche. In a way, I suppose, we do deal with their psyche and emotions but in the broadest possible way.

I hope this audience will forgive my missionary zeal, quite unexpected, I am sure, from what one is likely to hear from the usual plastic surgeon or the usual doctor, for that matter. Lest you think that we are purely selfish at ASAB, we are not. Since beauty extends beyond the body to the immediate environment, so it also must reach the larger environment. We are the most environmentally conscious group in America; I say this modestly. Not only do we wage a campaign against obesity – one massively overweight individual pollutes and destroys the environment, not to mention millions of them – but we advocate cleaning up neighborhoods, replanting trees, eliminating trash, especially the visible type, and planting millions and millions of flowers.

You might have heard this week about our launching a new service – BOP (Beautification of Pets) – better grooming, better attire.

A commonly voiced objection to our efforts is that they seem to be wasted in a world that faces nuclear annihilation. But that's just the point. As a doctor, I cannot stop nuclear madness; I cannot stop wars in Africa; I cannot settle the problems of the Middle-East. In the meantime, however, I can improve the appearance of people in the world and the appearance of the world while its fate may be in the balance. As a missionary I must be able to accept failure along with success, that is my lot in life.

I hope you will join me in this grand adventure by introducing each person who comes to you for aesthetic improvement to the infinite opportunities of beautification of the self and the planet on which we reside.

The Photograph

I was recently a guest lecturer at a surgical symposium dedicated to plastic surgery (Maine Medical Center, Portland, May 11, 2006). I had not been there before and enjoyed meeting the staff and the residents. Dr. Jeffrey Donaldson, the Chief Resident in General Surgery, ready to begin his plastic surgical training at the University of North Carolina in Chapel Hill, had arranged an interesting program. At the end of the day he and a couple of senior plastic surgeons wanted their pictures taken with me. While flattering, this event which has really become a ritual among plastic surgeons initiated a cascade of memories and thoughts, not all of which were all pleasurable. On the plus side was the obvious: a few thought that I was of sufficient importance to them to have their photo taken with me. That brought back memories of what I used to do when well known members of our specialty came to lecture or visit. In those years these men – and they were almost all males – seemed old, very old, and I was conscious that I would have a visual memory of them after they had died. In disbelief I now realize that I am older than most of them were.

As we stood in a line for the photo, I realized also that I was shorter than anybody else. Maybe it would have been so when I was younger but undoubtedly whatever stature I have achieved in my specialty I have not maintained in my physique. To dispel my discomfort, I turned to humor, as I usually do, and commented: 'I like being photographed among Japanese who usually are smaller than me.'

Robert M. Goldwyn

I am beyond the stage of wishing that my photo showed a younger, better looking me. That Goldwyn is no longer, having been succeeded by another edition, definitely of greater age without necessarily the compensation of more wisdom. Since I am retired, I have less knowledge of current operative plastic surgery.

The photograph will show in inescapable concreteness the juxtaposition of youth and age and what each connotes. Pertinent is the French proverb, which I cited elsewhere in this book: 'If youth knew; if old age could.'

Many years ago I read about a couple probably my age who had just sold their home to a young family. The woman, now a grandmother, commented: 'I have just found my replacement.' That consideration, as I stood with the residents and junior staff, consoled me although the experience made me wistful. The greater consolation which bestirred myself to remember was that I was there in sufficiently good health to participate in the occasion and even to have the luxury of becoming wistful!

Spas for Kids: Just What Our Society Needs

'While her pedicurist massaged her feet and then trimmed her cuticles, Lexi Blickman perused the pages of **Cosmo**, checked out the latest hair styles, and chatted about her upcoming trip to Egypt. She peered into a bucket of nail polish bottles and plucked a bright blue named Azure for Sure to be decorated with stripes of Magenta Metallic. If the colors seem giddy, chalk it up to Blickman's age: 8...' [D. Belkin, Girl-geared spas enjoy boom, **Boston Globe**, May 17, 2006].

In our society which has extremes of everything but common sense we should not be surprised that upscale salon services for girls under ten exist. What is astonishing, however, is that it is the fastest growing segment of an $11 billion industry. The United States has remarkable energy for the non-essential even when it is fighting terrorism, warring in Iraq and Afghanistan, coping with the threat of nuclear weaponry in North Korea and Iran, and confronting the problem of poverty and inadequate health care of its citizens.

This newspaper account concerns a spa in Concord, Massachusetts; others exist not only here but throughout the country. This community is known for its wealth and liberalism, a not unfamiliar pairing. This does not preclude those concerned with the problems of victims and the economically disadvantaged indulging themselves more so than even the Medici could have imagined. We plastic surgeons can rightfully ask whether cosmetic surgery is part of this phenomenon; the honest answer is yes. A consoling thought is that it is a continuum or, if one is musically inclined, a variation on a basic theme. Pure aesthetic surgery is generally for teenagers and older, e.g.: rhinoplasty, chin implant, breast augmentation, eyelidplasty, facelift, mastopexy, to mention a few. But one can go 'straight from Pampers to pampered,' as expressed by a letter to the editor from an irate reader [I. Sonnenschein, **Boston Globe**, May 19, 2006]. She questions: 'When did the norm become so ostentatious? Since when has our society developed such a myopic perception of reality that whatever a child wants, a child gets?' While I agree with her reaction, I differ in the interpretation. The problem seems to me not what the child wants but what the parents want for their child. Perhaps the mothers described in that article, with the fathers complicit, think that they were wrongly deprived of spa lounging early in their life and wish to spare their offspring such hardship.

The line is fine between spa-ing and spoiling. **The American Heritage Dictionary of the English Language** (1976) has among its several definitions of 'spoil' the following: 'To impair the value of quality of; to damage... To over indulge or over praise so as to do harm to the character'; both apply.

In the article I cited, an owner of one of the spas said that she is very busy with prepubescent customers. 'The time is right. People are looking for something like this.'

Everything has its risks and on the downside a stylist who gives 4-year-olds a pedicure says that it takes a lot of concentration. 'Their feet are so tiny you have to be really careful... Since the little ones have been walking only for a few years, there isn't much in the way of calluses to rub off, or even dead skin.'

There is even a special name for a child pedicure, a 'mini-peddi.' One of the mothers 'scoffed at the idea that a day at the spa' is harmful, 'You can be good at sports and smart and still like to look good or have your head rubbed or your feet taken care of. A little pampering isn't going to make you any less of a well-rounded person.' – That remains to be seen. I am glad, however, that I am not the one (and I hope my grandson would not be also) taking her daughter to her first prom. She is likely to become jaded by age ten.

Spas for the very, very young reflect other aspects of our country, which wallows in the quicksand of avid consumerism while about one of six cannot afford minimal health care. Plastic surgeons will likely see younger and still younger patients for cosmetic procedures. I emphasize that I am not talking about operations to restore children to normal if they have congenital, developmental or acquired deformities. Will our specialty create the surgical equivalent of child spas?

PSA 6

More than once – perhaps too often – in this collection, I have mentioned the fact that I have had prostate cancer for the past fourteen years. My treatment has been generous: surgery, local irradiation, hormonal and other medications, including my own contributions of such scientifically unrecognized preparations found in nature food stores, where I thought I would never venture but fear and hope are effective in changing attitudes and habits.

As anyone with this problem knows, regular PSA (Prostate-Specific Antigen) assays are routine, unfortunately in my instance too much so. I can well identify with women who have periodic mammograms and their anxiety about the results, particularly waiting to be told.

At the time I am writing this, my PSA rose to six, not ominous by itself but the trend is not reassuring, despite the optimism of my doctor. Putting these thoughts on paper helps me reduce my anxiety without, I hope, not transplanting it to readers.

A repeat of a James Bond movie and another spy thriller gave me the idea of calling myself PSA 6 – not MI6 and not Agent 007, whose exploits and looks I could never match.

I am sure that a psychotherapist would recognize this defensive mechanism. But I am not sure what he or she would call it: namely, changing reality into absurdity. A touch of added humor costs nothing and does much, at least for me. Secretly, however, I want to be more than a comical figure, perhaps even one with heroic possibilities, just as I would imagine agent PSA 6 to be if I did not know that he were I.

As PSA 6, I have given myself a new identity, even freed myself from myself in this transmutation. Being PSA 6 is different from having a PSA of six. Freud, where are you now that I need you to confirm my interpretation?

If I were in the secret service, or in any branch of the intelligence network, I would retain my cover of PSA 6 unless some malicious individual or group exposed me, thereby ending my usefulness as well as my code name. The fact that it is related to the level of my PSA allows me the possibility of changing the number, hopefully in a downward direction. I might become PSA 007 or even better, PSA 000.

Humpty Dumpty told Alice in her Adventures in Wonderland that 'when I use a word, it means just what I choose it to mean – neither more nor less.' So also with my code name.

How to Make Relaxation Into Work

While walking around the reservoir today, I saw a man in his sixties bait fishing with three poles. He did not see me because he was too busy running from pole to pole to pole, re-baiting and re-casting. I am not sure what he wanted from this activity but it certainly was not relaxation. His motions, really antics, made him look like a character from a silent movie with everyone and everything speeded up. I have no statistics but this kind of person doing this kind of activity, really hyperactivity, is more likely to happen in America than elsewhere. Whatever he had in life, he lacked sitz-fleisch, the ability to sit.

My father taught me how to fish, how to cast with bait and flies, and, most importantly, how to enjoy it. He used to say: 'Fishing is really wonderful. You can delight in the scenery, the sound of the brook, even if you might be disturbed by a fish.' He introduced me also to Izaak Walton (1593-1683), the English biographer and author of the classic: **The Compleat Angler**, which also had in its title: **The Contemplative Man's Recreation**, published in 1653. I doubt that Walton had in mind the revved fisherman I saw.

Walton wrote: 'He will find angling to be like the virtue of humility, which has a calmness of spirit and a world of other blessings attending upon it.'

As we know, for better or worse, by our thinking we can transform almost anything we do or have done into what we would like it to be. It is possible that this angler might have told his wife that he had had a 'wonderful, relaxing day.' Compared to his other days, he could have been right!

The author, W.G. Carleton understood the problem: 'Oh, Lord, teach me when to let go' – but not with a fish on the line!

Perhaps only the Italians are smart enough to know the value of ***fare niente*** in the leisurely pursuit of **la dolce vita**.

'Listening with the Third Ear' – Even One Will Do

Some readers will recognize that part of the title is from the book by Theodore Reik: *Listening with the Third Ear: The Inner Experience of a Psychoanalyst*, 1948.

Born in Vienna, Reik (1888–1969) was one of Freud's pupils. Reik's point was that an effective psychotherapist has to hear not only what the patient says but what prompted those thoughts. The success of the treatment depends considerably also upon the therapist's skills of self-observation and self-analysis. Basic to what a psychotherapist does and what a plastic surgeon does or should do is listening. Listening obviously involves the capacity to hear but more, the willingness to listen. Although listening to the patient is the basic first step in treating the patient – something we all learned early in medical school – it has become decreasingly present, even ominously absent, in the relationship between the patient and physician. If Oscar Wilde had been a doctor, he might have said, 'I would listen to the patient but it takes too much of my time.' The irony is that not listening to a patient ultimately consumes more time.

Several factors are responsible. A major reason is that doctors are under pressure to see many more patients than their schedule should allow. Since time is money, the economic push is to spend less time with more patients. Another cause of this phenomenon is that compared to decades ago, the doctor's office is more likely now to have secretaries, physician assistants, printed forms, even computers available to take a history, thereby 'sparing' the physician from what should be one of his or her primary duties to the patient.

Many doctors today believe that diagnosis is less dependent upon the history than physical examination, which is also becoming perilously abbreviated. Doctors rely increasingly on laboratory tests, radiography, and other technological aids. One physician told me that 'in the time it takes me to do a physical examination, I can order the right tests and get to the diagnosis and the treatment much sooner.' While that may be possible and under some circumstances, laudable, it should be more the exception than the rule but the opposite is becoming true.

Listening is caring. In that regard, Mueller stated: 'You will be judged more on how well you care than on how well you cure' (**Bull Am. College Surg**, May, 2006). While under some circumstances that may not be correct, it does emphasize that patients want physicians who are personal as well as competent. The fact that the diagnosis and treatment may be flawless does not obviate responding to the human need for warmth, a crucial ingredient, in any relationship, especially that of the patient with his or her doctor.

Robert M. Goldwyn

We have drifted so far from the prototype of the 'old family doctor,' that when patients today encounter a physician who is caring, the patient may be suspicious, believing with twisted reasoning that a doctor who is brusque must be more skilled. I remember a patient who, as I was taking her history, said to me: 'I want a plastic surgeon not an internist. I want somebody to do a surgical job.'

I replied, 'I may not be the suitable plastic surgeon for you because I am not just a body mechanic.' She replied that she did not have the time to 'waste' and I was happy to escort her to the door (no consultation fee charged – and gladly for both of us).

Throughout centuries despite the vicissitudes and advances in medical care, patients still want and expect more personal interaction with their physician than they would from a representative of the Internal Revenue Service or from someone at the checkout counter in a supermarket. But even then, most of us appreciate a warm 'hello' from most people with whom we interact. How barren it would be if people went about their tasks too absorbed even to articulate superficial niceties!

In questioning my friends, many of whom are physicians, and their spouses, I have found out that only rarely does even a family internist take the time to ask appropriate questions, appropriate at least by my standards, such as 'Tell me how things are going at home? Is your husband (wife) well and how are the children? Are you working too hard? What are the stresses now in your life? Are you eating properly and sleeping well?' In short, all the queries that would give a physician an idea of the patient's personal life, data beyond blood pressure, pulse, EKG, chest X-ray, etc. Perhaps it is my age but I still believe that by the end of a consultation, no patient and no physician should be strangers to each other. That does not mean that the physician should intrude in ways that are distinctly inappropriate, whose apparent purpose is not to obtain information in order to help and treat the patient optimally. I also do not think it is inappropriate for a patient to ask the doctor how he (she) and his (her) family are doing, perhaps whether a vacation is in prospect, etc.

The questioning of a patient should not be an interrogation. While the objective is to get information, the other purpose is to know the patient as a human being. This takes time; this requires listening. Hearing is not the same as listening and thinking while listening is another dimension in the patient-doctor relationship.

Aside from his notable skills, Theodore Reik as a psychoanalyst had the advantage of seeing patients frequently, maybe more than once or twice a week, perhaps an hour for each session. As plastic surgeons, our schedules are different but the fact that we may spend less time in the office with the patient is no excuse for us to spend the least time.

Listening to a patient offers the opportunity of enjoying the patient, not just 'getting through another patient' in an over-scheduled day. The plastic surgeon or any physician who sees too many patients in too little time almost certainly will enjoy work less and become his or her own agent of burnout.

Learning Along the Way

In Milwaukee I took a shuttle from the hotel to the airport. The driver in his late twenties had the unusual habit of when answering a question, adding 'And you know how that is.' This was true whether he was asked about the time, the weather, or a building or monument that we passed. After a series of 'And you know how that is,' which become irritating, I decided to break the cycle and inquire about himself, an invitation few people can resist. With appropriate modesty he told me that he was a graduate student in engineering and that his hobby was botany. He asked me whether I knew that the endive plant, whose leaves we use in salads, has as its root chicory, which can be used with coffee or as a substitute. I confessed my ignorance.

That incident proved again my father's wisdom in exhorting me to remember that I could learn something from almost everybody and not to limit myself to my experiences and knowledge. I can hear that driver nodding his head, saying 'And you know how that is.'

Robert M. Goldwyn

Advertising and Marketing in Plastic Surgery: Uncomfortable Realities

A resident now finishing his training in plastic surgery and planning a solo practice with no academic affiliation asked me with apprehension whether he had to 'advertise' to succeed. 'Possibly,' I replied reluctantly, 'but only if you wanted to do mostly aesthetic surgery.'

In the '60s when I began my practice – solo but with an academic affiliation – that question was never asked because advertising in medicine was considered unethical and illegal. A subsequent ruling by the Supreme Court validated it but only if the advertising was non-deceptive. Local and national medical and surgical societies could no longer penalize a member for 'indulging in advertising,' a phrase, commonly used. If an organized group attempted to prevent an individual from properly advertising, it would be successfully sued for restraint of trade.

The reality, uncomfortable for me, is that advertising and marketing are rife now in almost every phase of our society, not just by corporations and educational and religious institutions but by individuals – doctors. In plastic surgery reaching the public through the media has become commonplace in an astonishingly short period of time. Prospective patients are viewed as consumers who can be encouraged, cajoled, and cleverly coerced into seeking surgery for their appearance.

For some individual doctors, they need not market and advertise themselves because their hospital or local and national organization will happily perform the task. These activities are undertaken with the aim less of improving the wellbeing of patients but the fiscal wellbeing of physicians and the institutions with which they are affiliated.

The young doctor, whether internist or plastic surgeon, who joins a hospital, whether academic or not, is almost guaranteed a referral of patients because the majority of insurance companies direct patients where they must go for their medical care. It has become increasingly less common for any full-time, salaried doctor with any university hospital to scamper around to attract patients since most young physicians I know are soon overburdened with too many patients. And if that young doctor cannot keep more than his salary, there is less incentive for him or her to undertake the care of more patients.

The situation is strikingly different for the self-employed, solo practitioner who usually must struggle initially to acquire patients unless he or she is in a community or at a hospital where his or her services are much needed. The tyro plastic surgeon will soon realize that remuneration from reconstructive procedures, which take longer to perform than aesthetic operations, pay much less. The once highly motivated reconstructively oriented plastic surgeon will see his or her interests veer increasingly toward the cosmetic. This transition may be subtle or deliberate and while the increase in earnings will be gratifying, the young plastic surgeon may feel guilty that he or she is providing more luxuries than necessities in terms of the function and survival of patients. 'Ah, but I am improving the quality of life,' he or she may say with some truth but often with less conviction. As income rises and emergencies decline, and 'lifestyle' becomes better, the twinges of uncertainty or guilt may or may not disappear. The solution for some is to do only aesthetic surgery, replete with selling cosmetic products and running a spa, for most of the year and then serve for a few weeks in a third world country as part of a surgical team repairing clefts and performing other reconstructive procedures. That doctor may consider this a perfect compromise and he or she may be correct. Nobody has the right to be judgmental of others and of what they choose to do with their lives as long as it is not harmful to others.

For those interested in rising to the top in aesthetic surgery – cosmetic medical care – advice abounds. For example, in **Medesthetics**, July/August 2006, a dermatologist stated: 'Keeping your name out there is very important. For marketing to work, it must be consistent' (L.W. Lewis, Small Town, Huge Success). This can be done, the article notes, by hiring professional help, by providing WEB sites, by appearing on local cable channels, by sending newsletters to patients who often share them with their friends – prospective patients, hiring the right people in the office ('start by treating your staff…'), and you might consider yourself, as did that doctor, 'very happy with my profession and my business.'

In the same publication, C. Whitman, at Medspa Consultants, tells doctors to 'bring them [patients] in with seminars' and instructs how to attract attendees by offering the right program and 'converting guests to patients.' For those older and involved in the training of residents, not to discuss with them the issue of marketing and advertising among other decisions they must make after residency would be avoiding our responsibility. Yet words mean less to residents than does the behavior of their mentors with regard to how they conduct their practices and their personal lives.

We who teach are older than those we instruct and we must recognize that what we did in our time may not be the best for them in their time. One unquestionable reality that residents face is that reconstructive procedures are becoming less remunerative; whereas returns on cosmetic surgery and related procedures are ever greater. Nonetheless, the most important lessons for any young person in plastic surgery is to recognize that, first, one's career and personal life are inextricably entwined and, second, ultimately how we assess ourselves is much more important than how others do. We cannot wear another person's clothes: we must show those we teach that we are comfortable (hopefully) in our own. We must not ask them to wear ours.

Viagra®: a Symbol of Our Times

Except for some philosophers and all social scientists most of us are so much part of our culture, so immersed in it that we seldom step back to view it as it is. The problem is that we cannot see the trees for the forest that surrounds us, that imprisons us without our awareness.

What set these thoughts in motion was my attending a baseball game awhile ago at Fenway Park. As an aside, the Boston Red Sox won. Perhaps it is a sign of my age but I cannot recall the score or worse, their opponents. Perhaps also as a 'sign of my age,' I do recall the large advertisement on the wall in right-center field; it was for Viagra®. I thought back to my childhood when there would be public outrage if in the press or on radio or, later, TV the words 'erectile disfunction' were used. Indeed, as one of our residents, Eric Liao, remarked, 'Elvis wasn't even allowed to move his hips without being criticized.'

But back to Fenway, where 35,000 fans, of whom a significant percentage were women, entered the Park, watched the game, cheered, booed and left without, I am guessing, even a few commenting on the presence of the message and of this sexual hype.

Viagra® has become part of our culture and our history. Like the Ford and Kleenex, the trademark has become the product. So also Viagra®. It is not just of a medication but it has transformed itself into the problem it purports to treat, e.g. 'He has a Viagra® situation,' as one women said on a TV soap. That even a former United States Senator and Presidential hopeful, Robert J. Dole, was promoting it without being criticized (probably envied for the endorsement fee he was earning) and that audiences nationally and internationally could watch him with more bemusement than shock is proof of how ordinary the subject of sex has become.

While open discussion of sexual problems may be distasteful to some, it is a healthy indication that we are more at ease in bringing to the fore all medical problems. This has permitted patients to come for earlier diagnosis and treatment and hopefully better survival.

In this decade most Americans are far more comfortable discussing problems and requesting aid to solve them than were past generations. What used to be talked about in hushed voices is now openly described, analyzed, and debated to the point of boredom. While our openness can sometimes seems absurd, it is better than the even more absurd and hazardous secrecy that characterized the times of our parents and grandparents. Many of them suffered in silence and shame, unlike the Americans of today. Notwithstanding, as plastic surgeons, we know that some still do.

Personal health has become a public matter: support groups, media coverage, on-line chat rooms. Even when I was in practice, an occasional patient came to me because someone in the supermarket observed his or her deformity or that of her child and suggested treatment; sometimes the concerned individual happened to have been my patient. Nowadays

Robert M. Goldwyn

there seems to be no boundaries; whereas previously there were too many. This change has been fortunate particularly as it concerns sexually transmitted diseases and AIDS. This has been true also for alcoholism and drug addiction. Acknowledgment of a medical entity is not synonymous necessarily with approval. The power of political correctness has forced many not to voice their disapproval. Outside the medical field, those who consider themselves healthy are still more likely to be judgmental than those afflicted – until they themselves experience the same illness real or imagined. Very few of the 6.5 billion people on Earth will have perfect health, and enjoy it, from birth to death. Many, in fact, would be happy if they suffered only from what Viagra® could ameliorate.

Not Hearing a Complaint Doesn't Mean There Isn't One

When interviewed about Princeton [J. Hechinger, The Tiger Roars, *Wall Street Journal*, July 17, 2006], its President talked about many issues, including increasing the number of undergraduates, battling a law suit from displeased donors who wish to retract their gift of $750 million, eliminating restricted eating clubs and supporting working parents. Ms. Tilghman is an effective President and a well-known molecular biologist. She said: 'Congress is considering an "academic bill of rights," which supporters say is necessary because conservative viewpoints aren't always welcome on, as they see them, liberal campuses. The Princeton student body recently passed a similar measure. What do you think of this?'

Ms. Tilghman: 'I have never in five years had a student in my office complaining about this issue. The risk going forward is setting a precedent that could lead Congress to begin to think about other ways to regulate the kind of material that is taught in universities. And I think going down that path is dangerous and a mistake.'

Retired Not Dead

I agree with the President of Princeton about the inadvisability of Congress attempting to pass an 'academic bill of rights' even though I recognize that, according to recent studies, about 85 percent of the faculty of the Ivy League universities are implacably liberal. The point for discussion was Ms. Tilghman's comment, spoken with certitude, that 'I have never in five years had a student in my office complaining about this issue.' While that may be true, she certainly must have heard about these concerns because her student body recently passed a measure similar to what Congress will be considering – namely, guaranteeing that those with conservative views will not experience hostility and discrimination.

I can well understand why Ms. Tilghman has never had a student in her office complaining because I believe that the student(s) would be intimidated by her official position and her views. That she has not heard a complaint does not mean that it does not exist.

As to disclosure, my college was Harvard and I rooted for it when we played football against the Tigers of Nassau Hall. I admit also that as a physician I have on more occasions than I wish to recall found it comfortable to assume that a patient who did not voice a complaint about me or my treatment did not have one. Yet we doctor are authority figures who must, even if unwittingly, inhibit patients from complaining.

I remember many years ago when a member of the board of trustees at a Harvard hospital complained to the Chief of Surgery that Harvard Medical students who wanted to apply for internship and residency in surgery feared that they would not be accepted because they were Jewish. That Chief of Surgery either because he was naive or artful allegedly said that nobody ever complained to him about that problem. Indeed he might have told the truth because it would have been a rare fourth year medical student who would confront him and his hospital about their anti-Semitism, which was definitely a reality in those years.

It is discomforting also to consider how often we might discourage residents from telling us about what displeases them and hear what they want us to do. The cliché of 'sweeping it under the rug' is possible only if dust or a paperclip is the problem but most difficulties are bigger.

Robert M. Goldwyn

Fragments

On my desk is an expanding manila folder, once thin, then heavy, now obese, containing thoughts and writings of others, plus some of my own.

In England Now, *The Lancet*, 338:814, 1991: 'It seems that the wife of the early 19th century American lexicographer, Noah Webster, discovered her husband one day sitting in their kitchen with one of the servant girls on his knee. 'Noah,' she exclaimed, 'I'm surprised!' 'No, my dear', he is supposed to have replied. 'I am surprised, you are astonished.' Mercifully history is silent on what happened next.'

Arab proverb (A. Edwardson, *Sun and Shadow*, London: Penguin, 2005): 'You are not a man unless you have written a book, planted a tree, and fathered a child.'

Idem p.10: 'He wished he could put the clock back. The people strolling down the street didn't know, they knew nothing. Nothing. They didn't know they were living in paradise.'

This passage came to my mind recently when the wife of a dear friend became ill: 'A year before we all were walking down the same street and, indeed, "we knew nothing" and "were living in paradise".'

'That's the way it was, it is, and likely will always be.' (To myself after an incident involving an ungrateful patient)

Johann Schiller: 'Live with your century but do not be its creature.'

Mark Twain: 'When I was younger I could remember anything whether it happened or not.'

RMG: I shall leave this earth with more questions than answers.

RMG: Society tends to homogenize old people, blending old men and women into a subspecies making it easier for society to deal with them as if they were anonymous.

R.C. Fox, *In The Belgium Chateau*, Chicago:I.R. Dee, 1994: p.190: 'One loves others, one can only love others.'

'...Penny by penny a California gas station has raised $177,000 for research into a rare and devastating bone disease that afflicts two local teenagers. ...Clark Crandall, 54, owner of the Main Street Shell Station in Santa Maria, learned that six years of donating a penny for every gallon of gas sold had paid off: Researchers had identified the gene defect behind fibrodysplasia ossificans progressiva (FOB)' (***Science***, May 5, 2006, p.687). He had displayed pictures of the two girls and on a billboard daily tallied the money raised – an instructive example of how one can make a difference if one wishes.

RMG: Only in grammar can we find a past perfect.

RMG: With age we understand more and realize we can change less.

Tanya Goldwyn: 'A bright nebbish' (Yiddish for 'an innocuous, ineffectual, weak, helpless or hapless unfortunate').

RMG: In the Romany language, 'calico' can mean yesterday or tomorrow and 'merrapen' can mean life or death.

Tanya Goldwyn: 'You live forever as long as you are alive.'

M. Parrots, ***The New Republic***, February 13, 2006: 'Why shouldn't a bird review an ornithologist?'

RMG: He probably rides elevators to feel close to people (about a lonely looking man).

P. Balakian, ***Black Dog of Fate***, Broadway Books, 1997: 'Everyone is still alive for the time being.' [...] 'He is who he isn't.' [...] 'Your hearing loss is more obvious than your hearing aid.'

RMG: As thrilling as Jell-o.

RMG: A subterranean thinker.

Italian proverb: 'He who knows more, believes less.'

Said of Andre Malraux about his novel ***Les Noyers de L'Altenburg***: 'In full possession of all his shortcomings.'

RMG: He made everyone feel as if he or she were one step away from greatness.

RMG: A surgeon is a kind of person who goes to the bathroom in someone's home and does not run the water to muffle the sounds.

RMG: He was adept at creating a false echo.

RMG: God rewards disproportionately the authors of 'how-to' books.

RMG: Destination never to be reached.

W. Baldessarini, fashion designer: 'The well-dressed man thinks of every-thing: great shoes, great suit, great smell. Smell is an important part of the outfit for harmony. When you are looking great, but your fragrance is wrong, my suit feels pain.'

Unknown: 'That life is incomprehensible does not make it meaningless.'

Advertisement for Acura: 'Life and your car are connected.'

RMG: Perhaps man is meant to succeed occasionally and struggle eternally.

Yiddish proverb: 'If I try to be like him, who will be like me?'

J.B. Priestly: 'When I was young, there was no respect for the young, and now that I am old, there is no respect for the old. I missed out coming and going.'

E. Larson, New York: **Crown**, 2003, p.42: 'His Astigmatic Soul'

George Segal, sculptor: 'I think a minute of existence is miraculous and extraordinary.'

Oscar Levant quoting a fellow mental patient in **The Memoirs of Amnestic Hollywood**: S. Frisch, 1989, p.273: 'There is no cause I wouldn't die for.'

Idem, p.319: 'Underneath this flabby exterior is an enormous lack of character.'

Idem, p.13: 'I'll double-cross that bridge when I come to it.'

Advertisement in a local paper: 'Stressed? Depressed? Auli and Ken Batts, Psychotherapists Brookline'

Joseph Joubert (1754-1824): 'To teach is to learn twice.'

R. Dangerfield: 'I am at the age where food has taken the place of sex in my life. In fact, I just had a mirror put over my kitchen table.'

Announcement outside a Baptist church in Marble, Vancouver, May 16, 1992: 'It is better to construct the future than to varnish the past.'

RMG: Proximity without closeness (About a couple in a restaurant).

Advertisement for EarthLink Cable Internet: 'The average American spends: 1.2 years waiting on hold 5.6 years waiting in traffic and 7.8 years waiting in line.'

Advertisement for TEMPUR-PEDIC: 'You spend ⅓ of your life in bed. Isn't it worth investing in the perfect mattress?'

John Quinn, a well-known collector of American art. S. Watson, **Strange Bedfellows. The First American Avant-Garde**, New York, Abbevile Press, 1991, p.354: 'One looks at things out of hospital windows very differently from what one does out of other windows.'

M.C. Smith. **Wolves Eat Dogs**, New York, Simon & Schuster, 2004, p.70: 'The bloom of disease'

D. Fesperman, **The Warlord's Son**, New York, Knopf, 2004: 'Were others similarly afflicted with this coursing highway of banalities and clichés, he wondered – quotes and phrases dislodged from deep memory banks and careening aimlessly. Snatches of old ad jingles and glib voices from his childhood.'

Fesperman must have had me (RMG) in mind.

Epilogue

I thank readers for having accompanied me on this non-linear journey which, though personal, I hope has been more than that.

In the preface I referred to the novel by Jules Romains, **The Death of a Nobody**, whose antihero, a retired train engineer, when looking from his apartment window onto the city of Paris, said: 'I should like to know if one single person ever thinks of me.'

It would be worse than sad if that sentiment reflected our life. The best preventative is to find fulfillment in helping others or at least relating meaningfully to others – even in retirement.

Robert M. Goldwyn

Printed in the United Kingdom by
Lightning Source UK Ltd., Milton Keynes
139829UK00001BA/84/P